MASS MEDIA

· · · AND · · ·

POPULAR CULTURE

BARRY DUNCAN

Harcourt Brace Jovanovich, Canada

Toronto · Orlando · San Diego ·
London · Sydney

Canadian Cataloguing in Publication Data

Duncan, Barry
  Mass media and popular culture

Includes index.
ISBN: 0-7747-1262-7

1. Mass media. 2. Popular culture. I. Title

P91.D85 1988   302.2'34   C88-094554-0

The major inspiration in the development of this project came from my colleagues in the Association for Media Literacy, in our efforts to make media study an essential part of school curriculum and from the exciting teaching opportunities created by the School of Experiential Education in Etobicoke. I want to thank HBJ staff for their constant support and, above all, my wife Lynn for help and encouragement at all the right moments.

The author and publisher gratefully acknowledge the following educators for their evaluations and suggestions:

Neil Andersen, Assistant Head, English Department, Lester B. Pearson Collegiate Institute, Scarborough, Ontario
Penny Thacker, Head of English, Downsview Secondary School, North York, Ontario
Michael Thomas, English Consultant, The Protestant School Board of Greater Montreal, Montreal, Quebec

Editorial Director: Murray Lamb
Project Editor: Kathy Evans
Copy Editor: Jessica Pegis
Permissions Editor: Liz Kirk
Director of Art and Design: Mary Opper
Art Direction and Design: Gary Beelik
Designers: Katinka Oszter/Arnold Winterhoff/Julia Naimska
Assembly: Sandra Quigley
Photo Research: Sandra LaFortune
Cover Illustrator: François Chartier

Printed in Canada   3 4 5   92 91 90 89

TABLE OF CONTENTS

INTRODUCTION

By the time you finish high school, you will have spent an average of 11 000 hours in school and 15 000 hours watching television. And that's just television—add to that the time spent seeing films, reading magazines and newspapers, listening to music, looking at advertising, and the result is many, many hours of media involvement.

But because of the pervasiveness of the media and popular culture, we rarely step back to take a critical look at how they work, what they are actually saying to us, and how they affect us. This book asks you to do just that, by thinking about media or popular culture issues, reading about them, thinking about them some more, and responding to the readings. You will be asked to recognize, take apart or "deconstruct," and analyze the images and messages you are bombarded with daily.

The readings are from books, newspapers, magazines, television, and radio transcripts—a variety of sources. In your responses to them, you will have the chance to: write essays, scripts, plays, ads; keep a log; interview; discuss; design; use computers; role-play; film; videotape— and more. To help you, there is a Reference Section in the book with instructions and guidance for some of these activities. See pages 206– 219.

The following section, "Key Concepts of Mass Media and Popular Culture," gives you a framework for your studies and explorations throughout the book.

By the end of your study, you may be closer to that 15 000-hour mark of television-watching time, but you should also have a more critical perspective, not just on television but on all the media and popular culture products to which you are exposed. You will be well on your way to becoming "media literate."

Key Concepts
of Mass Media and
Popular Culture

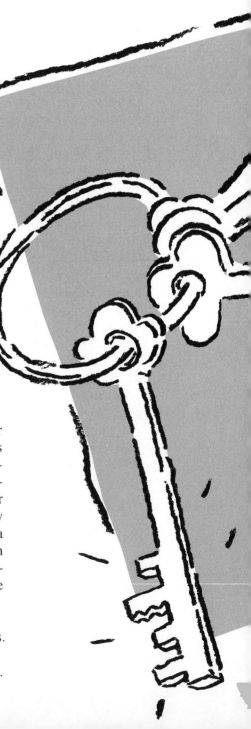

In many casual discussions about media and popular culture, people are often uninformed and their ideas are unfocussed. To make sense of the issues, a context or framework is necessary. The following principles or categories provide this framework for understanding mass media and popular culture and how they affect us. The four categories provide you with a basis for key questions to ask during your study of an issue. You will find that sometimes the categories overlap and some, at times, will be more relevant than the others. Here are the four principles:

1. The media construct reality.
2. The media have their own forms, codes, and conventions.
3. The media present ideologies and value messages.
4. The media are businesses that have commercial interests.

CONSTRUCTIONS OF REALITY

You are watching the news or a public affairs show on television. The pictures and the soundtrack seem very real; you are expected to believe what you see and hear, and accept the announcer or narrator as the authority on the events he or she describes. This is your "window on the world." Or is it?

Further investigation would reveal that most television news programs favour the visual; producers like to show film footage of war scenes, terrorism, fires, auto accidents, riots, and strikes. Events that were left out of the newscast could, ultimately, be as important as what was shown. As for that public affairs show, the producer may have used only a small proportion of the film footage shot by the camera crew. A 20:1 ratio of footage shot to footage used is not unusual. How did the producer decide what to use?

The point is that the producers of media "construct" their product, whether it is the 6 o'clock news, a TV drama, your daily newspaper, a magazine ad, or a record album, to create illusions or to make a world that is exciting and entertaining enough to keep audiences interested. Media products are shaped and given meaning through a process that is subject to a variety of decisions. What material looks best? How should the person, object, animal, or event be shown? What will grab—and hold—the audience's attention? The results may be anything but real.

An example from the television nature program *Wild Kingdom* will illustrate the concept of how media "construct reality." In wilderness areas inhabited by both wolves and cougars, these two predators stay out of each other's way. But the producers decided that their footage would be more interesting if there were a conflict between the animals, so they used a cougar and a wolf bred in captivity and provoked them to fight. The producers also decided to dub in more snarling and growling than what was actually recorded in the filming. The CBC's *the fifth estate*, the news documentary show that investigated this story, revealed that such fakery is a common practice in many nature programs.

We all have our own view of the way the world is "constructed," based on factors such as our culture, our social conditioning, and our unique experiences. It is important to realize that many of our notions of reality are reinforced or affected by what the media show us. For example, the dubbed-in snarls and growls of the cougar and wolf reinforce many people's preconceived notion that nature is either cute and cuddly or savage and ferocious.

Your task in studying the media and popular culture is to "deconstruct" the products—take them apart and examine how and why they were constructed that way, and determine their effects on the audience.

RESPONSES

1. If you have access to a video camera or a Polaroid camera, work in groups to construct a number of meanings by filming two people in conversation. Using a variety of camera angles, camera distance, audio effects, and lighting, discuss the different meanings that your constructions produce. You will learn more about these techniques in the Film and Television chapters. See page 209 in the Reference Section for tips on filming and videotaping.

2. Watch a scene in a TV show or film closely and list the ways in which meaning and atmosphere were constructed.

3. Clip some magazine ads that depict a constructed view of reality. For example, most travel ads depict an idealized vacation spot. How do ads such as these define happiness and the "good life"?

FORMS, CODES, AND CONVENTIONS

Consider the following:

- In a television show, the camera moves in for a close-up on a man and woman, the lighting is dim, and the music is soft and slow. What do you think the scene is about?

- In films such as the *Star Wars* trilogy or old westerns what codes are used to help you tell the bad guys from the good guys?

- What is the usual setting for television family sitcoms (situation comedies)?

- In the popular music industry, how can you distinguish a heavy metal fan from a new waver?

- According to advertising, what type of person drinks milk?

- How does the phrasing of sports news affect the interpretation of the events? For example, what are the implications of "Habs trounce Canucks, 5–0"?

In answering these questions, you have identified some of the customs or conventions in language and symbol that the media use. There are codes, or symbols, or ways of conveying information in the media that we understand without really being aware of them. Camera angles, sound, lighting, editing, language, design—all are used to construct meaning and create effects. Part of being media literate is being aware of these techniques and knowing the effects they are meant to have.

The meaning of an event is also shaped by the form of the medium and the biases that are a natural part of that medium. Because of each medium's unique characteristics, there will be inevitable differences. For example, television may stress the visual aspect of the story, radio may favour interviews, background sounds, and commentary, while the newspaper may be able to provide more detailed background information, interviews, as well as photographs. The televised presidential debate between Richard Nixon and John F. Kennedy in 1960 illustrates these differences. Those who heard the debate on radio were convinced that Nixon had won, while the television audience believed the opposite. Nixon was sweating profusely and appeared uncomfortable compared with Kennedy, who was cool and assured. More people watched the debate than listened to it on radio, and Kennedy won the election.

Canadian communications expert Marshall McLuhan made some important observations about how the mass media create their messages. He claimed that each medium codifies reality in a unique way, or that each medium has its own grammar, its own bias. Because of the built-in bias of each medium, the nature of the message differs in each medium we encounter. This notion was framed in his memorable slogan, "The medium is the message."

RESPONSES

1. Consider the following situation:
The government is considering new legislation that might increase unemployment. The local member of parliament has just made a speech in front of the city hall to justify the government's position. A fight breaks out between the government supporters, mostly well-to-do adults, and the protesters, mostly unemployed young people, a group of whom have spiked hair and "punk" clothes.

   Predict how this event would be covered by a newspaper, a radio station, and a television station. How do you think the media coverage would differ and why?

2. In groups, list some codes and conventions, or standard ingredients, that are often used in the following categories of media: Saturday morning cartoons, soap operas, movie magazines, heavy metal album covers, travel advertisements, horror films. Compare your list with those of other groups. How similar are they?

IDEOLOGY AND VALUES

We all have a set of assumptions about the world that shape our views on issues such as: the roles of men and women; discipline in schools; and the importance of authority figures such as government leaders, police, and teachers. We use this set of assumptions to define happiness, success, and morality. The term for this set of beliefs is "ideology."

A particular class or group of people may have its own ideology; for example, a church group may have a certain set of beliefs and a gang of bikers probably has a different set, or a different ideology. What about the ideology of the people who produce, own, or control the media, many of whom are middle or upper-class males? What kind of messages are we receiving through the media from this "dominant group"?

When we receive a message from the media, we usually interpret it through our own ideology and set of values. If we agree with the message that presents the dominant view, this is called the "preferred reading." It is important to note that "preferred" in this sense does not necessarily mean "better." If we disagree with the message, we have given it an "oppositional reading." For example, a newspaper photo of a scuffle between striking postal workers and management could be read two ways: the dominant, or preferred, reading might suggest that the fight is typical of strikers, that they are probably demanding more money, and that the strike is unwarranted. An oppositional reading might suggest that the reasons for postal strikes are often misunderstood, that perhaps there were other reasons for the strike besides a desired wage increase, and that maybe management provoked the scuffle.

Some messages sent to us by media are almost invisible—we are so accustomed to the medium that we may not be aware of any message. For example, in advertising, cars are often associated with beautiful women; beer is associated with a "partytime" lifestyle; women, not men, are usually the ones concerned with clean clothes and sparkling dishes. Are those accurate representations? Are the values suggested by those commercials ones that you accept? How are Canadians affected by American viewpoints? Recognizing these messages and identifying the values they uphold is part of being media literate. The following is a checklist to remember when analyzing media messages in any media product.

1. Are the beliefs of one particular group being represented?
2. Who is in a position of power? Who is not?
3. What stereotypes, if any, are used? To what effect?
4. What views of happiness, virtue, or morality are implied?
5. Is there a predominant liberal view or conservative view of trends?
6. If the viewpoint is American, to what extent does it apply to Canadians?

RESPONSES

1. Watch some TV shows and, if you see any current films, note the social groups that are noticeably excluded. What social issues are dealt with? If a different social class were included, how might the plot, the nature of the conflicts, or the ideological messages change?

2. Choose a) a Canadian television drama or comedy and b) a Canadian performer or band and discuss the ideological messages they send. Do these messages differ from those of comparable American shows or performers?

3. Select some ads from magazines and note who or what is excluded and then determine what the ideological messages are. How would these messages change if certain elements were added?

4. Give a preferred and an oppositional reading to the following: a news article, a rock performance, lifestyle ads, a popular TV program.

COMMERCIALISM

Many people believe that the media are intended only to entertain and inform us, and that easy access to the media is simply one of the privileges of living in a technological society. But it is not that simple. We are part of an economic system, a consumer society. Mass media and popular culture provide goods and services that are marketable. They offer commodities. There is an enormous financial investment in popular culture and mass media industries; they are multi-billion dollar businesses that employ thousands of people, ranging from the concert performer to the people who clean the stadium when the concert is over.

Television programs provide sponsors with audiences. Sponsors, then, are understandably concerned about the size of their audience and the rating of the programs. The cost of advertising increases as programs gain more viewers. In the pop music industry, a record company's financial success is directly dependent on the frequency of "plays" of their records on radio stations. Music videos can be regarded essentially as three-minute commercials to sell records. A band or performer's concert tours usually coincide with an album release; the concert promotes album sales.

One of the major concerns in media studies is ownership and control of the media. In both Canada and the United States, there is a concentration of ownership—a small number of corporations own most of the media industries. Such monopolistic tendencies can result in conflicts of interest. For example, a newspaper that is owned by the same company or person who owns the local television station may be reluctant to criticize that station's programs or sponsors.

The following facts will help you realize the relationships between various members and branches of the media, and the extent to which the media are "big business."

- Coca Cola Ltd. owns Columbia Pictures.
- Advertisers paid $650 000 U.S. for a 30-second spot during Super Bowl XXII, 1988.
- Bill Cosby's earnings in 1986–1987 for his television show were an estimated $84 million.
- The average cost of an American TV network's half-hour program is over $400 000 U.S.
- Gulf & Western, Inc. owns, in Canada, Coronet Films Inc., Famous Players Ltd., Paramount Productions Inc., United Theatres Ltd., Atlantic Theatres Ltd., Pocket Books of Canada Ltd., among other companies.
- Labatt's Ltd. owns 45 percent of BCL Entertainment, which owns Canada's largest concert presenter, Concert Productions International, and the world's largest rock merchandise company, Brokum.
- Cineplex Odeon Corporation, a Canadian-owned company, has 1650 theatre screens in North America.

Realizing that mass media are a business—a huge one—should help you in your "deconstruction" of media products. Being aware of the commercial interests of the media should make you question the values or messages that the media present.

RESPONSES

1. Exchange information with your class about any jobs or other experience you have had in media industries, e.g., being an usher in a theatre, delivering newspapers, working in advertising, television, or music production. Share any knowledge you have gained about the business side of media.

2. Have you ever had trouble finding a record because it is not mainstream— because it did not appeal to a large audience? Have you tried to buy a favourite style of clothing only to find that it is no longer marketed because of poor sales? Have you tried to rent a movie on video that was not available because it had a small audience? Discuss these and similar experiences with your class. How much are you affected by mass marketing of media and popular culture products?

CHAPTER 1

Popular Culture

What is popular culture? It's skateboards and Cabbage Patch Kids, *Miami Vice* and *60 Minutes*, leather jackets and acid-washed jeans, McDonald's and Burger King, teen films and Rambo, Marilyn Monroe and Madonna, Diet Coke and exercise videos, Trivial Pursuit and Barbie dolls, *People* and *Rolling Stone*, talk show hosts and TV evangelists, shopping malls and drive-in movies. It's jokes about Canadian identity and the Grey Cup and whether there is such a thing as a Canadian popular culture—it's all this and much, much more.

"In the simplest terms, popular culture is best thought of as mainstream culture—the arts, artifacts, entertainments, fads, beliefs and values shared by large segments of the society."—*The Popular Culture Reader*, 1983

Popular culture surrounds and affects us and our economy so much that it has become a kind of invisible environment—but one that we should train ourselves to see. There is probably no area of human activity that it does not touch.

Learning about popular culture helps us learn a great deal about our own values. We are sent hundreds of messages about pop culture daily, via the media. There are always new fads or trends: new fashions, or hair styles, new slang expressions, new toys mass marketed at Christmas, new films, new TV stars. What are the values that these trends or celebrities present to us? Are those values ones you believe in?

WHAT MAKES POPULAR CULTURE?

Mass media and popular culture are, first and foremost, businesses. Our economy is intimately connected with the marketing of the wares of media and pop culture. For example, $6 billion were spent on advertising in Canada in 1984, and an approximate $35 billion are spent each year on advertising in the United States. Television ratings are so important that if a network show does not have 20 million viewers, it could be cancelled. It is understandable, then, that we see so many sequels and spin-offs to successful TV shows or films such as *Police Academy V* and *Jaws 3-D*. The problem with using these formulas is the repetition and lack of daring that results. It could, however, be this very predictability that reassures audiences and sends them back for more of the same.

Formulas can lead to conservative popular culture trends. Since pop culture aims to appeal to as large an audience as possible, it tends to stake out the solid middle ground and preserve the "status quo" or keep things unchanged. In fact, social critics point out that it reproduces the structure and attitudes of the dominant social, political, and economic system. Views on social trends, the role of women, minority groups, and definitions of happiness—all are influenced by the dominant system's views.

What do we find when we get below the superficial meanings of the fads and trends of popular culture? A careful analysis reveals a system of beliefs, an ideology, or popular mythology, that conveys the desires, fears, and aspirations of the culture. In fact, much of our lives is lived according to certain myths. To help them fulfill their need for a meaningful role in life, some people use a hero or a celebrity as a stand-in. As media critic and teacher Jeffrey Schrank commented, "Clark Kent is what we know we are; Superman is what we dream we can become."

To look at the idea of myth in a broader perspective, consider the notions of freedom and individualism. They surface in our attitudes to the law, civil rights, and our free enterprise system. Our popular culture, however, contains countless examples in which freedom and individualism operate mythically. John Wayne as the great cowboy-liberator of oppressed settlers is myth. Rambo is myth. Sergeant Preston of the Mounties is myth. And, at a more subtle level, myth operates in our romance with the automobile and its promises of adventure. It operates in our financial dreams, symbolized by those plastic credit cards which in the mythic world offer endless freedom and in reality—endless debt.

By examining these ideologies in popular culture and their value messages, we take the pulse of our society or, to borrow another metaphor, take a cultural barometer reading. For example, listening to some of the pop songs of the 1950s or seeing television reruns of old programs such as *Leave it to Beaver* are ways to explore the trends and concerns of those times. You should remember, however, that although those media products can give you a barometer reading of the times, they may not give a true reflection of society—not all families were like the Cleavers. Other cultural barometers include (in films) the *Star Wars* trilogy in the 1970s and 1980s, (in music) the appearance of heavy metal and punk rock, and (in the toy business) the development of war toys such as *G.I. Joe, Transformers*, and *Gobots*.

WHOSE CULTURE IS IT ANYWAY?

". . . The U.S. has a knack for concocting and consuming entertainments that are quick, vivid, exuberant. Razzmatazz is a plentiful U.S. natural resource, like oil with no OPEC competitors. Americans are pop-culture vultures, profligate in the money and time they devote to making themselves giggle and choke up on cue, ooh and aah en masse. . . ."

". . . To a good part of the rest of the world, The U.S. is nothing but its global pop gush. . . ."

". . . Stopping for a big Mac in Singapore, says a young customer, is like walking into a bit of America. . . ."

". . . The '80s are a pop decade, no question, a reclining era of good tans, big parties, beach reading, girl-group music. The stars are bigger than they have been in a long time, selling more billions of dollars worth of records and movie tickets than ever before. Celebrities are more numerous, but their fame is briefer: the half-life even of putative superstardom can be as short as a year. Fads are announced, exploited and abandoned even before *Good Morning America* can cover them. . . ."

—TIME, JUNE 16, 1986

It is important for us to realize that most of the popular culture and media products we are exposed to are American. We should ask ourselves if those products and trends represent us as Canadians. Part of our responsibility should be to find the images that represent our identity and to understand the ways that constant exposure to American images can alter our self-perception and identity.

Studying media and popular culture will allow us to step back and observe critically those hundreds of messages they send. In the rest of this chapter and throughout the book, you can analyze the media and the products of popular culture by taking apart, or "deconstructing" their structures and techniques and finding the values they present. You can begin to understand how these value messages can affect your life.

RESPONSES

1. "Skateboards and Cabbage Patch Kids, *Miami Vice* and *60 Minutes*, leather jackets and acid-washed jeans. . . ." Using this style of listing paired examples of the features of current popular culture, create a class "pop culture catalogue poem." You could read one or more of your examples out loud followed immediately by the next student, and so on. You could tape the reading, and add to it during your study of this text.

2. In your media log, write an entry called "A Day in the Life of a Pop Culture Consumer." See page 214 in the Reference Section for information on keeping a media log. Keep a list of and describe all your encounters with pop culture over two days. Include radio programs, music, films, television shows, visits to shopping malls, billboards, observations on fads, fashion, hairstyles, decorating styles, architecture, slang, and any other features of pop culture. You might like to share your writing with other students. What did you learn about the nature of popular culture and your awareness of it? What did you learn about other people's tastes?

3. Sometimes we take a kind of guilty pleasure in a fad or trend—for example, we may enjoy a TV show that all our friends or members of our household consider immature. Describe any instances of this in your life.

4. Brainstorm with your class to make a list of images or features of Canadian popular culture. You could consider Canadian TV and radio programs, celebrities, sports figures, historical figures, literature, and even the articles sold in our souvenir shops. Think about Canadian stereotypes and discuss their validity as representations of our popular culture. Explain why you think Canada does or does not have a popular culture.

5. We can learn about history through popular culture. In groups, select and study a variety of popular cultural materials through videos, films, magazines, artifacts, and interviews that represent different decades from the '20s onward and make a presentation to the class. Each group could focus on a different decade. What did you learn about the times—the political, economic, and social climate?

6. Imagine that you are a writer, producer, or agent in the following situations. In groups, use your knowledge of popular culture and media trends and formulas to outline how you think each situation would be treated. Share your outlines with other groups to see if your ideas are similar.
a) A film director needs a script about a shy, awkward boy who falls in love with the most popular girl at his school.
b) A television producer of a sitcom wants a script concerning the conflicts arising from the parents' discovery that their teenage daughter and son are planning to cheat on the final exams in school.
c) The publicity agent for a Canadian rock star is expected to provide extensive publicity for a forthcoming tour that will coincide with the release of a new album.

TRENDS

Newspapers and magazines often review contemporary trends and fashions and predict future trends. Sometimes these trend-tracking journalists contradict each other; they are, after all, only guessing. The formula is simple: criticize the trends that are on the way out and cautiously welcome the new arrivals. Readers can either try frantically to keep pace with the trends, or ignore them.

The following is an excerpt from a newspaper article that appeared in 1985, in early January—a time when newspapers and magazines usually take stock of the past and predict what is ahead. 1985 may seem a long time ago. As you read the excerpt, think about what has changed and what has remained the same.

What's In and What's Out

by Rosie DiManno

Hats are in for both men and women. So are tartans and kilts, but only for women. (We know by now what men wear under their kilts and the discovery is hardly front page news.) Last year's bizarre flirtation with dresses for men in some corners of the planet (read California) is quite out.

Heavy chains that masquerade as belts, jewelry and bikinis are out and T-shirt dresses with social commentary stencilled across the front (CHOOSE LIFE!) are in.

The color black is out and all blinding neon colors are in, especially pink, though by the time you read this, they might be out. Paint-splattered patterns are also in. Status accessories, diamonds and other rocks which are the Real Thing are in, but so is el cheapo rhinestone jewelry in rainbow colors. . . .

Punk is kaput so you better take those safety pins out of your nose/ears. Mohawk cuts, spiky hair of all hennas, and the messy teased look are out. Long hair for both women and men is back in. Styling mousse, the greatest invention since the curling iron, is still in. So is the just-been-passionately-kissed stained lipstick look. . . .

Since being in entails not only what you wear on your body but also what you put in it, remember that nouvelle cuisine is out and down-home traditional is in. Smoked salmon is in but only the imported Scottish kind. Iceberg and romaine lettuce are out, endive and raddichio are in. . . .

After taking the genre to non-sensical extremes, rock videos are out, unless the musicians stick to old-fashioned filmed concerts, which are in. But no matter what they do or how they do it, some of the best-known stars will sink out of sight this year. Checking out are Duran Duran, The Clash, Boy George, and Frankie Goes to Hollywood, who will in fact be going nowhere but down the tubes. Also out, finally, is moonwalkin' Michael Jackson, who really should throw down the sequined glove.

Cabbage Patch Kids and other CP paraphernalia are still in. The board game *Kensington* is coming in fast but it's still not as in as *Trivial Pursuit*, which is hot in the States. Spotting the wrong answers is particularly in. . . .

Reading in/out lists is out. But not as out as writing them.

—*THE TORONTO STAR*, JANUARY 6, 1985

RESPONSES

1. Suggest reasons some of the trends listed in the articles have faded away and others are still here.

2. Working in groups, make a list of current "ins" and "outs." Include favourite expressions, the latest slang, fashion, new fads, toys and games, hobbies, films, television, music, and any other category you think of. Appoint a class editor to choose the best examples for a composite portrait of current trends.

3. In groups, write and perform a skit that features many of the trends from your "what's hot and what's not" list. How does "what's in" relate to "who's in"?

TRACKING TRENDS

Who identifies consumer trends? Where do words such as "yuppies" (young urban professionals) and "dinks" (double income, no kids) originate? They often come from marketing consultants or consumer analysts. John Elkins, president of the Naisbitt Group, attributes the amazing growth of companies such as his to the accelerating rate of change in the 1980s. The rate of change is now so fast that "new" doesn't last too long. New products typically take about five years to develop and the company that can best predict consumer behaviour and take advantage of the lead time will be the winner.

One of the most successful trend-trackers is Faith Popcorn, whose marketing consulting company called *BrainReserve* has annual revenues of $20 million. More than 200 companies have come to her with products that are not selling well. She "repositions" the products or connects them to a current trend that will attract consumers. To check the pulse of consumers, she and her colleagues interview at least 2000 people a year, monitor films and TV shows, and examine over 300 trade and consumer publications. Some of her observations on trends in the '80s led to her predictions that:

- The New Coke that appeared in 1985 would not be a success.
- An appetite for new sensations would increase experimentation with a variety of exotic products.
- The divorce rate would decline.
- The obsession with thinness would decline.

FAITH POPCORN

DINKS

YUPPIES

NEW!

- Salt-free food products would increase in popularity and North Americans would eat more grains, vegetables, and "Mom" or comfort foods—oatmeal cookies, mashed potatoes, and meatloaf—because people seek security and warmth to offset the depersonalization of modern living. There would also be a return to hard liquor, and fast food would include gourmet items, such as lobster at McDonald's.

RESPONSES

1. In light of current consumer trends, assess the accuracy of Faith Popcorn's predictions.

2. Discuss how Faith Popcorn might use the sources she lists as a basis for forecasting trends. Use those sources to try your own trend-tracking. In groups, you could interview people, read a variety of magazines which could reveal trends, or examine the trends in current films and television shows. Write an essay to summarize your findings.

FOLLOWING FADS

Discuss in class the meaning of "fads." What is the difference between a fad and an artifact that truly represents a culture? Is there a difference? In the introduction to his book, *American Fads*, Richard A. Johnson writes the following:

". . . Nothing mobilizes the population like a big booming fad that comes bustin' out all over. . . . We turn ourselves into coast-to-coast theater of the absurd every time someone creates a clever new plastic toy or thinks of a new way to wear blue jeans. . . .

"Fads are giant symbols for analysis. . . . The Hula Hoop® showed that "a child feels secure in a family circle." The Twist was "a proper cure for working off frustrations." Streaking was "an attack on dominant social values." The Pet Rock® caught on because "people were tired of all the gloom and wanted a good laugh.

"A fad is a form of energy, like thunder and lightning, and it is just as hard to bottle. No one can mastermind a fad. It grows out of all proportion to marketing strategies or publicity campaigns. It takes on a life of its own, coursing through the veins of the country like a wonder drug. . . ."

Cabbage Patch Kids were a fad. Handmade and sold in the late seventies for $125 to $1000 each, the real craze for them began in 1983 when a toy company began to mass market them. The following excerpt from Johnson's book, *American Fads*, describes how the demand for these dolls caused shoppers to go to great, even absurd, lengths to acquire them.

Cabbage Patch Kids™

by Richard A. Johnson

They looked something like the young actor who played Larry Mondello on *Leave it to Beaver*. With cheeks fat and floppy, lips pursed, nose pinched and eyes aglaze, Cabbage Patch Kids™ were the perfect comehither dolls. And they were sewed up in a spongy skin that made them more caressable than dolls molded out of cold, hard plastic.

Each was given a name pulled from 1938 Georgia birth records and packaged with a set of "adoption" papers. And thanks to computerized factories, no two Kids were alike.

In fact, Cabbage Patch Kids™ were quite unlike any doll in history when they arrived in 1983, and they got a reception like none other. America was heartsmitten. A nation of children wanted them to have and to hug.

Cabbage Patch Kids™ became the hottest store-bought babykin since Raggedy Ann. In the weeks before Christmas, 1983, demand reached an impossible fever pitch. Baby bedlam was everywhere. Competition for Kids even turned ugly as jostling, grabby shoppers engaged in one department store fracas after another.

At a discount house in Wilkes Barre, Pennsylvania, one woman suffered a broken leg when she was caught in the midst of a thousand shoppers who'd waited eight hours to get at the dolls. As the mob advanced, a department manager took up a baseball bat to hold his ground. At a hobby shop in Middletown, Connecticut, buyers waited ten hours for twenty-four dolls delivered by armored car. Uniformed guards, with side arms, kept the peace.

The manager of a Best Products store in Dallas was threatened by angry shoppers who pushed their way into the store's receiving bay. The rabble demanded that he break Cabbage Patch Kids™ out of crates and sell them on the spot.

Fearing a riot, the manager of an

F.W. Woolworth in Lawrence, Kansas, put the store's last seven dolls in a bank vault and held a drawing for the rights to buy them. . . .

The Cabbage Patch crop grew out of the fertile mind of a young Georgia sculptor named Xavier Roberts. After discovering similar soft sculptures at art and craft fairs in the South, he begat his own baby in 1977. . . . Roberts formed Original Appalachian Artworks to turn out diapered "Little People" by hand in a converted medical clinic in Cleveland, Georgia, dubbed Babyland General Hospital. Roberts was the hospital's "chief of staff." . . .

Cabbage Patch Kids™ were brought to mass market by Coleco Industries, the giant toymaker which began life in the 1930s as the Connecticut Leather Company. Coleco had been in the middle of a raging fad before, having cleaned up with Davy Crockett moccasin kits in 1955.

The company took shrewd control of the new doll after it was passed over by the likes of Fisher Price and Mattel. It manufactured a sixteen-inch, $25 version of Roberts's handmade dolls, replacing the cloth face with vinyl skin.

Coleco retained the "adoption" ploy, enclosing a realistic "birth certificate" and adoption papers which asked "parents" to raise their right hand in front of another person and say, "I promise to love my Cabbage Patch Kid™ with all my heart. I promise to be a good and kind parent. I will always remem-

ber how special my Cabbage Patch Kid™ is to me." Each doll came with a card describing "my special personality traits." A typical one read "I'm very shy but once you get to know me I'll tell you more about me." . . .

Unsure about overall retail sales prospects, department stores ordered modestly at first. But it turned out shoppers were rushing Christmas, 1983. Coleco's production sources, which consisted of eight factories grinding away in the Far East, were straining to keep up.

Jetliners brought back two hundred thousand dolls a week from the Orient. Emery Worldwide, the air freight company called on to speed deliveries to the States, ran ads heralding its Cabbage Patch connection. The company boasted that "to keep up with these kids you've gotta be fast." . . .

Coleco officials finally estimated that 3.2 million dolls were sold in 1983, and six months into 1984, 2 million more were delivered.

But even while shoppers clamored for the dolls, they remained puzzled by their attraction. "Why all the commotion?" went the refrain. "They're sooooo ugly!" For months, ugly was the issue. Dr. Joyce Brothers surmised that "it is comforting to feel the Cabbage Patch doll can be loved with all your might—even though it isn't pretty." But Cabbage Patch Kids™ grew on America . . . and fast. They became merely homely. Then cute. Then adorable. Then irresistible.

—*AMERICAN FADS*, 1985

RESPONSES

1. One commentator remarked that Cabbage Patch Kids appealed to "a universal need that children have to hold something and cuddle it." Discuss this idea with your class. What do you think is the appeal of some of the doll's features, such as its adoption papers and the fact that no two dolls are alike?

2. The author writes, "They became merely homely. Then cute. Then adorable. Then irresistible." How would you explain this progression in people's responses? Are these responses from children or their parents? Explain your answer.

3. In groups, research some of the big fads of the last twenty to thirty years. Some of these fads include: Frisbee discs, phone-booth packing, dances such as the Twist and the Limbo, go-go boots, skateboards, granny glasses, tie-dyeing, Mood Rings, video games. Each group could study a different period of time. In addition to reading about the fads in books and periodicals, you could also interview adults who may have experienced them. Be prepared to give a report to the other groups. You may want to present your findings in a short skit or play.

4. Make a list of recent fads and discuss how they serve as a mirror of the times.
   a) To what extent did their marketing and promotion cause a strong reaction in consumers?
   b) How has the advent of mass media affected the "staying power" of fads?

5. Explain why you agree or disagree with Richard Johnson's statement, "No one can mastermind a fad." Try inventing a fad. Decide on its appeal and suggest marketing strategies.
   Or
   Write a short story or play in a fantasy mode describing the effects of a bizarre fad that sweeps North America.

6. Document a current fad by using media such as videos, photographs, slides, or audiotapes. Present your work to the class.

FEATURING FAST FOOD

Pizza Pizza, Taco Bell
Howard Johnson's, Dairy Dell
A&W, Harvey's, Wendy's
D.Q., Arby's, Donutz, Friendly's
Pizza Hut and K.F.C.
Swiss Chalet and Grandma Lee's

"You deserve a break today, at McDonald's"

—MCDONALD'S ADVERTISING SLOGAN

"Since 1970 McDonald's has dramatically increased its marketing expenditures, to approximately $300 million, making it the fifth-biggest commercial user of television among American corporations."

—WILLIAM MEYERS, *THE IMAGE-MAKERS*, 1985

"Each man makes his own happiness and is responsible for his own problems." . . . Work is the meat in the hamburger of life . . . the history of McDonald's corporation is a dramatic refutation of all who believe that risk takers will no longer be properly rewarded."

—RAY KROC (FOUNDER OF MCDONALD'S),
GRINDING IT OUT:THE MAKING OF MCDONALD'S, 1977

"What does seem clear is that places like Disney World and Ronald World are microcosms of America—perhaps of the emerging Global Village—as we move toward the final years of the 20th century. We have seen the future and it is Donald and Ronald. Go for Big Mac!"

—MARSHALL FISHWICK, *RONALD REVISITED*, 1983

YOUR FAST FOOD HABITS: A SURVEY

To find out how often you eat in fast food restaurants, why you eat in them, and your fast food preferences, complete the following survey in your media log.

1. How many times per month do you eat in fast food restaurants?

2. What are your three favourite fast food restaurants? What are your reasons for choosing them?

3. a) What do you usually order at your favourite restaurants?
   b) How much does it cost?

4. How far away from home is your favourite restaurant?

5. Do you usually go with friends? / with family? / alone?

6. Do you usually go on: weekdays / weekends?

7. What time of day do you usually go?
   weekdays: 7 am – noon
   noon – 4 pm
   4 pm – 7 pm
   7 pm – midnight

   weekends: 7 am – noon
   noon – 4 pm
   4 pm – 7 pm
   7 pm – midnight

8. List three things you dislike about fast food restaurants.

9. Why do you go to fast food restaurants? Rate the following reasons, with 1 as your top reason: You like the food ____; To be with friends ____; The food is affordable ____; Service is fast ____; You like the atmosphere ____; Other ____.

10. How much does advertising influence your choice of restaurant?

As a class, compile the results of your surveys, and discuss your findings. What were the main reasons for going to fast food restaurants? What do your findings tell you about fast food and social needs?

Today, fast food restaurants are everywhere. Statistics tell us that the majority of North American families eat in them at least once a week. Fast food in general and McDonald's in particular are the essence of the American success story, and their influence is now worldwide. In recent years, we have witnessed "the burger wars" in which fast food franchises battle each other through their advertising.

The following excerpt is about McDonald's. Why study something so commonplace? Such a study will help us see how this "mythical wonderland" functions—its amazing growth and its marketing strategies, and its success in catering to many people's psychological needs. There is much to be found behind the golden arches; your explorations will offer some revelations about our popular culture.

The Psychology of Fast Food Happiness

by Gregory Hall

McDonald's eateries are as common as chewing gum under cafe counters, and more genuinely American. A few facts are in order. As of 1973 McDonald's hatched on the average one fledgling fast food diner each day. In the restaurant business this amounts to a population explosion. It's still happening. Even more staggering is the number of cows that have been ground up for the billion McDonald's burgers sold roughly every four months. Res-urrected, these herbivores would ring around an area larger than Greater London. But even this number is far exceeded by the number of American school children who adore Ronald McDonald second only to Santa Claus. Clearly, McDonald's is more than just another hamburger joint. It is a hamburger joint that wins people's hearts. It is itself the product of peculiarly American preoccupations. Its product is fast food happiness. . . .

Why do so many hungry Americans prefer McDonald's meals? Because McDonald's is a form of therapy. Like many modern technologies tailored to the consumer market, McDonald's wants to entertain. But the entertainment is subtle, almost imperceptible. "When you are in this business," says Ray Kroc, [founder of McDonald's] "you are in show business. Everyday is a new show. It's like a Broadway musical—if people come out humming the tune, then the show was a success." Kroc, one time barroom piano player and war cohort of Walt Disney, knows how to entertain. His fast food circus stars a clown and a bevy of energetic uniformed kids who welcome the hungry into a carefully designed atmosphere. "We offer people more than just fast food. It's an experience," says John Giles, national director for public relations. "It's an experience of fun, folks and food. We've sold 18 billion hamburgers, but we sell them one at a time." The McDonald's indoctrination begins with elaborate television

commercials that illustrate the joyous restaurant atmosphere. Under the arches, we may feel the commercial-related *esprit de corps*. We may be entertained and fascinated by a group of unskilled adolescents who have been miraculously mobilized into an efficient, cheerful, coordinated unit. We may feel the invisible but ubiquitous Ronald McDonald poke and make us vulnerable to happiness. . . .

Dr. Kottack, a U. of Michigan professor of anthropology, addressed the 1976 annual meeting of the American Anthropological Association. His claim: that McDonald's has become a virtual religious experience for millions of Americans. Kottak believes that McDonald's eateries, much like churches or temples, offer uniformity in an otherwise chaotic world. He says: "From the rolling hills of Georgia, to the snowy plains of Minnesota, with only minor variations, the menu is located in the same place, contains the same items and has the same prices." According to the professor, "We know what we're going to see, what we are going to say, what will be said to us and what we will eat." From that first request for a Big Mac to the final "Have a nice day!", every move is ritualized much like a religious service.

But the religious experience of McDonald's goes deeper than ritual. McDonald's is the Messiah carrying the new theology into a world of chaos: the Messiah whose Golden Arches are symbols heralding the new age of Yankee fast food technology. Eateries which are the same everywhere destroy the artificial boundaries of local custom and become a unifying force, bringing together all believers in a common personhood of those who have been cured of a Big Mac attack. This applies to the people of Europe and the Orient as well as Americans, because everyone must have a chance to believe. It is understandable why Steve Barnes, head of McDonald's International Operations, says of the European campaign, "It's corny, but I feel like a missionary over here."

The McDonald's canon is one of basically Puritan values: law and order, cleanliness, purity, hard work, self-discipline and service. The jingle, "We do it all for you," is meant to characterize the selfless aspect of the religious McDonald's. Cleanliness is a personal fetish of Ray Kroc's. It is well known among franchise owners that Kroc is a self-assigned, plain-clothes policeman who patrols his empire on periodic inspection tours in order to catch deviants. . . .

Inspiring values of power, dominance and mastery which produce kingdom, McDonald's is the perfect embodiment of American military prowess. Accordingly, McDonald's has captured the suburbs and, in the language of *Time* magazine, conquered the country. Advertising *campaigns* are waged to win the populace and deliver lethal blows to the competition. . . . Armed with a variety of "secret" sauces and jingles, the fast food brigadiers engage in pitched battle for a bigger cut of the market. The artillery is in the form of jingles, musical ammunition which lodges in the psyche of the consumer and prods him or her continually. The roots of this mobilization and expansion are at the heart of the American movement itself, the exploration and colonization of the remaining frontiers. It is Commander Kroc who leads the fast food army into fertile territory, current exploitable American preoccupations, winning the natives with Ronald McDonald straws and napkins. . . .

The McDonald's phenomenon is not necessarily a sign of declining culture. It is more a reflection of basic American values and as such may be a symptom of stresses. Centuries from now, when historians and anthropologists sift through twentieth century artifacts, they will try to make sense of a hamburger joint that inspires religious fervor. If we could hold it up to ourselves like a mirror, we might experience a moment's astonishment. But almost as quickly we might see the signs of hamburger addiction: the gaunt, harried look that precedes a Big Mac attack. Like Faust before the Mater Gloriosa, an irresistible power draws us on and we may find ourselves in the sanctum of a McDonald's kitchen. Although we may not genuflect after receiving the great beef cure, we may feel the urge to glance skyward, giving thanks that we do not need to leave a tip.

—*RONALD REVISITED*, 1983

RESPONSES

1. Ray Kroc, the founder of McDonald's, stated that, "When you are in this business, you are in show business." What are the show business aspects of McDonald's?

2. Explain why you agree or disagree with the author about the religious and ritualistic aspects of McDonald's. What other features of our popular culture do you think have religious and ritualistic dimensions? Consider such activities as watching favourite TV programs, buying fashionable clothes, or attending a concert.

3. The advertising campaigns for McDonald's have been remarkably successful. According to William Meyers in *The Image-Makers*, "Madison Avenue and McDonald's had redesigned the hamburger, but more important, they had transformed it from a mere sandwich into a symbol of family unity." Discuss the appeal of the McDonald's advertising campaigns.

4. Fast food restaurants have their critics—often people who are concerned about good nutrition and the effects of the waste materials on the environment. What suggestions might you offer these restaurants so that they remain competitive? Be sure to consider the food, packaging, and advertising strategies. You could write your answer in the form of a letter to the president of a fast food restaurant.

5. Brainstorm with your group on the topic of other merchandisers that use entertainment to help sell their products. Report your findings to the class.

6. Write a letter to a family with two teenagers who are planning to emigrate to Canada from a village in a Third World country where there are no fast food restaurants. Explain what they could expect from Canadian fast food restaurants.

SHOPPING MALLS

Since the 1960s, shopping malls, like fast food restaurants, have become part of our landscape. In this timeless, enclosed environment, we have a kind of wonderland which is the most popular place in North America for teenagers to gather and where shopping has become a form of entertainment. Malls may best typify North American civilization in the twentieth century. As a kind of "main street of suburbia," they symbolize many of our desires and aspirations. The mall is an ideal place to explore trends in the media and popular culture. On your next visit, alone, or in pairs, take along a notepad or, if you have access to them, a camera and tape recorder, or a video camera to observe and record the world of the mall. If you use a camera and tape recorder, you should first get permission from the mall manager and from the people you interview. The following are suggestions for your study:

1. What is the layout of the mall, and how does it influence people's behaviour? Note the location of the entrances, fountains, directories, greenery, benches, food areas, washrooms, telephones.
2. How many stores are there? How are they situated?
3. Do the stores try to appeal to a variety of customers or to a specific type of customer? How can you tell?
4. Note the colours, lighting, and sounds. What feelings does the atmosphere evoke?
5. How do the stores reflect recent popular culture trends and advertising campaigns?
6. You might want to interview shoppers or store clerks to get their opinions of malls. See page 212 in the Reference Section for tips on conducting interviews.
7. Share your perceptions and data with the class.

In the following excerpts from the first part of his book, William Severini Kowinski offers reasons for the popularity of malls. As you read, see if the results of your mall study support or refute his ideas. Ask yourself if the reasons he offers apply to you or your friends.

The Malling of Main Street

by William Severini Kowinski

The mall is Our Town's year-round carnival, the cathedral of the postwar culture, the Garden of Eden in a box. It is a mirror held up to contemporary American dreams and a fantasy haven from American nightmares—a circus in a fallout shelter. It is the strange achievement of the American Way: a utopia fashioned by the not-quite-invisible hand of merchandising. It is our latest attempt to cure the great endemic American disease of loneliness. Malls are everywhere, and everywhere they are, they are expressive and emblematic. . . .

This is the culmination of the postwar Highway Comfort Culture which has matched the aspirations, obsessions, social mores, and upward mobility of the middle class every step of the way. Quick'n Easy isn't enough anymore: The Highway Comfort Culture has gone beyond mere hamburgers and wash 'n wear to a veneer of sophistication. So even on the outskirts of a town like Greensburg, you will find the Naugahyde restaurants with ersatz Tiffany lampshades, antiqued mirrors, and the bric-a-brac of mass-produced nostalgia, selling foreign beers and exotic foods that a decade or so ago were the exclusive preserve of the big-city life. It's lobster and Löwenbräu out here now, although the lobster is microwaved and the German beer is made in Texas. Even the fast-food places have hanging plants and salad bars; the discount stores have designer labels. The stores and restaurants

have dressed up their interiors with motifs that suggest high fashion and *haute cuisine* and sometimes they even deliver it, but they do so while maintaining and refining the same basic delivery system as McDonald's. The highway has created new forms that continue to mold the culture while responding to changing wants and needs. . . .

Its space is special because it is *protected*. The mall banishes outside threats of disruption and distraction. No cars are allowed in the mall, no traffic, noise, or fumes. The natural world can't even intrude; there's no rain or snow, heat or cold, no seasonal changes—not even

gathering clouds to cause concern. This space is protected so that people will not be distracted or feel threatened; they'll relax and open themselves to the environment, and trust it. That must be part of the reason why very little is allowed in the mall that is larger, faster, or more powerful than a person.

The mall is also *controlled* space. This essential element is clearly implied in the official definition of a shopping center that I read in a publication of the Urban Land Institute, an organization that works closely with the mall industry. The operative part of that definition is: "a group of architecturally unified commercial establishments built on a site which is planned, developed, owned and managed as an operating unit. . . . '' Unity, preplanning, single and centralized management . . . are the instruments by which the mall creates its special conditions, by which it controls the environment created by enclosure and protection. . . .

The mall environment is itself a magic theater—trees grow out of the tiled floor! Plants flourish without sun or rain!

But even before the theatrical effects, the conditions for theater are set by design and management. For a space to be a theater, the outside rules of time and space must be banished. The mall keeps out such reference points—not only its windowless enclosure but its very uniformity (one mall resembling

The mall doesn't allow the appearance of aging—the stores are forever new . . .

another) means it could be anywhere. It is placeless. Many malls banish all sense of time by eliminating clocks, and although Greengate [Mall] has a large but unobtrusively decorative clock above center court, it neutralizes time by controlling light and sound—morning, noon, and night, they are the same. The mall doesn't allow the appearance of aging—the stores are forever new in an environment that is forever now. It is timeless.

The mall is kept squeaky clean, the stores bright, the fountains gushing, the greenery fresh—or at least those are management's goals. The effect is one of almost unreal perfection. Moreover, this continuous, flowing environment with no reference to the outside—this sense of a special world—permits a kind of unity of experience within an effortless enclosure that is something like the classical theater's unities of time, place, and action. It's all here, now. The mall concentrates the drama, suspends disbelief. . . .

Like Disney's street, the shopping mall plans and carries out a consistent design so that the mall's street looks unified, quaint yet familiar. The mall also excludes the rougher elements of real downtowns—no dives or pool halls here—and like the Disney versions, the stores are smaller than stores on town streets.

So the resemblance goes beyond enclosure, protection, and control. It struck me that the basic image the mall delivers—what this stage was set up to be—is a simplified, cleaned-up, Disneyfied fantasy version of Main Street U.S.A. . . .

The mall is a visual experience. It's TV that you walk around in. "People-watching" is what people do in the mall when they aren't "looking for something" to buy. The images they see in the mall are from television; and how they see and accept these images has been conditioned by watching television.

"People have gotten used to two-dimensional effects, to cardboard reality," [Ralph] Keyes [author of *We, the Lonely People*] maintained. "That's what they see on television, and they accept it."

In particular, television shows from *Ozzie and Harriet* to *Happy Days* produced visual, dramatic images of small towns. They were simplified and cosmeticized: a few endlessly repeated sets, characters, and relationships, all encased in squeaky-clean nostalgia, but since they all appeared complete, in everybody's living room every week, they assumed an undeniable reality. It was all there, scaled down to the small screen.

From family sitcoms and homey westerns to the sixty-second and thirty-second dramas of commercials, television makes the mall's relentlessly upbeat and minimalist Main Street easier to accept. For millions of urban and suburban viewers, the television image may be the only visual idea they have of small-town Main Street. For residents of real small towns, this Main Street may be equally convincing on another level: It may be what they wish their reality was, and they wish it hard enough to make it so.

Advertising uses this kind of suggestion (as opposed to suggestiveness) even more extensively, and more pointedly. TV commercials try to communicate quickly with a repertoire of visual images that suggest places and the feelings associated with them. They didn't invent all these images and associations, but through repetition they've made a virtual iconography of them. In advertising talk, the image "says" something. If you want to "say" glamour and romance, you "say" Paris, and if you want to "say" Paris with an image, you show the Eiffel Tower. The Eiffel Tower "says" Paris, which "says" all kinds of glamorous and exciting things about the product, and what will happen to you if you buy it.

All these places have been seen in movies and on television and perhaps only there.

The mall shrewdly makes use of these perceptual habits created by TV. It "says" Main Street with some Disneyesque design elements and a few props. The same technique is used in theme restaurants and shops. It's relatively cheap to do, and it works great.

What is true of the perception of Main Street is also true of the perception of many other kinds of places, from western towns and sailing ships to grand hotels and space ships: All these places have been seen in movies and on television—and perhaps *only* there. Media images dominate ideas about these places. The mall can make use of these simplified images to create its own fantasies, even beyond the principal one of Main Street.

It occurred to me that perceptual habits learned through hours and hours of television watching may also account for something else the mall seems to manage easily: its incongruities. The mall jumbles so many kinds of stores and services, from brokerage offices to cotton-candy stands, singles bars to interfaith chapels, that otherwise don't go together. But to a population used to seeing a bloody murder followed by a candy-bar commercial, followed by soap opera sex, a religious revival, and a public TV fund drive, nothing much would seem incongruous. Compared to what is shown in sequence on one TV channel, or what is available at any moment on many channels as the viewer switches through them, the eclecticism of the mall has to be considered mild.

The similarities of television and the mall go on and on. Both of them lull and stimulate simultaneously. Watching TV, we can be everywhere without being anywhere in particular. And basically, television and the mall are in the same business: entertainment in order to sell products. Advertisers pay for TV programs so people will watch the commercials, and the commercials themselves try to sell products by being entertaining. In the mall, product sales are also based on how attractive and entertaining the mall environment and its stores are. The mall is like three-dimensional television.

Television advertises attractive ways of life and the products associated with them in its programming, and its commercials tell little stories; the line between programs and ads is therefore often blurred. At the mall, the line between "programs" and "advertising" is almost nonexistent. The fantasy of Main Street is there to sell products. Because that's what all of this—the theater, the sets, the costumes and props—is for. The mall industry even has a name for what it's all about: They call it The Retail Drama. . . .

—*THE MALLING OF AMERICA.*
AN INSIDE LOOK AT THE GREAT
CONSUMER PARADISE, 1985

RESPONSES

1. William Kowinski discusses the mall's sense of timelessness and its banishment of outside threats. What is the importance of these factors in our perception of reality in a shopping mall?

2. Summarize the author's description of how malls resemble television and try to make some of your own parallels.

3. The author refers to Disneyland amusement parks in his essay. Research these parks in books and magazines, or talk to someone who has visited one. What are the similarities between the appeal and organization of these parks, McDonald's, and shopping malls? Consider aspects such as marketing, atmosphere, appeal of fantasy and wish-fulfillment, crowd management, order, efficiency, and cleanliness.

The concept of shopping as entertainment seems to have been accepted by the Ghermezian brothers, the developers of the world's largest shopping centre—the West Edmonton Mall. After you have read the following excerpt from *Saturday Night*, have a class discussion about this mall. If you or any of your classmates have been there, share your experiences with the rest of the class.

Shop Till You Drop

by Ian Pearson

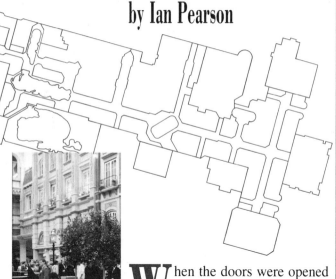

When the doors were opened to the third phase of West Edmonton Mall in September 1985, a curious crowd left a windy prairie evening outside and found itself in an enclosed street that simulated a Parisian boulevard. The pastel-coloured façades, patterned after the shops of Faubourg St-Honoré, held the visitors' attention briefly, but they were eager to discover the even greater artificial wonders that the mall promised around every corner. Here was a miniature golf course modelled on Pebble Beach. Over there was a lifesized replica of Columbus's galleon, the *Santa Maria*. Beyond that, four submarines slowly followed a track on the edge of an emerald pond next to a saltwater tank that held four dolphins. And below the visitors' feet in an underground aquarium, huge lemon-coloured sharks swung in slow restless arcs.

The incongruities were startling: sharks, ships, and submarines seemed out of place against a backdrop of more than 800 stores and 110 food outlets. But as the crowd wandered through the world's largest shopping centre it became increasingly difficult to separate retailing from razzle dazzle. By merging entertainment with shopping, West Edmonton Mall had created a carnival atmosphere about the marketplace: a trip to Fairweather or Big Steel had been transformed into a celebration. The 100 000 Edmontonians who poured into the mall at the opening were inspecting more than a suburban mall with elephantiasis—they were bearing witness to the future of retailing.

West Edmonton Mall is eight city blocks long and three blocks wide, a two-level, yellow-brick structure that houses a miscellany of modern recreation. There's an indoor amusement park called Fantasyland with carousels, water rides, a miniature train, and a thirteen-storey high, triple-loop roller coaster. There are hundreds of video games in two giant arcades which serve as social centres for thousands of teenagers.

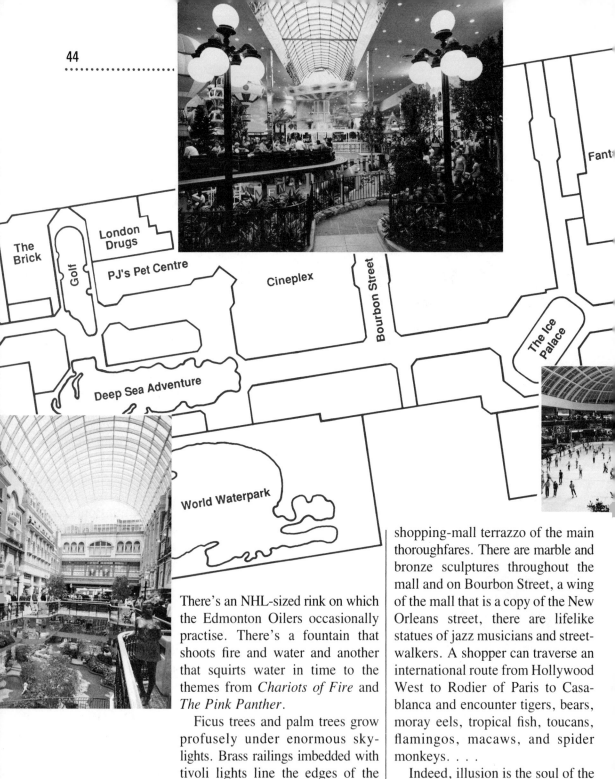

The Brick

Golf

London Drugs

PJ's Pet Centre

Cineplex

Bourbon Street

Fant

The Ice Palace

Deep Sea Adventure

World Waterpark

There's an NHL-sized rink on which the Edmonton Oilers occasionally practise. There's a fountain that shoots fire and water and another that squirts water in time to the themes from *Chariots of Fire* and *The Pink Panther*.

Ficus trees and palm trees grow profusely under enormous skylights. Brass railings imbedded with tivoli lights line the edges of the rink, the submarine pond, and the upper level of the mall; slabs of Italian marble border the standard shopping-mall terrazzo of the main thoroughfares. There are marble and bronze sculptures throughout the mall and on Bourbon Street, a wing of the mall that is a copy of the New Orleans street, there are lifelike statues of jazz musicians and street-walkers. A shopper can traverse an international route from Hollywood West to Rodier of Paris to Casablanca and encounter tigers, bears, moray eels, tropical fish, toucans, flamingos, macaws, and spider monkeys. . . .

Indeed, illusion is the soul of the mall. It is a contrived paradise that jumbles together intriguing bits of the world. Walking through the

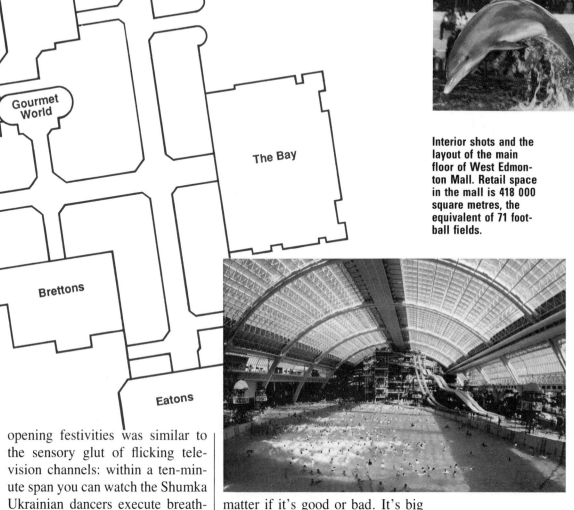

Sears

Gourmet World

The Bay

Brettons

Eatons

Interior shots and the layout of the main floor of West Edmonton Mall. Retail space in the mall is 418 000 square metres, the equivalent of 71 football fields.

opening festivities was similar to the sensory glut of flicking television channels: within a ten-minute span you can watch the Shumka Ukrainian dancers execute breathtaking leaps, a muscular man caparisoned in leather and sequins twirl a flaming baton, and an imported dance troupe called California Dreamin' Girls preen suggestively in their bikinis to Bruce Springsteen's *Born in the U.S.A.* Rushed and out of context, the entertainment was at once exhilarating and meaningless. Like the mall itself, much of it demonstrated colossally bad taste, a bullying self-aggrandizement that said, "It doesn't matter if it's good or bad. It's big and it's unlike anything you've ever seen before." . . .

The architecture of West Edmonton Mall follows the lessons of more than fifty years of shopping-centre history. The main pedestrian thoroughfares are laid out in straight lines, meeting side "streets" at right angles. Nothing twists or turns: the layout resembles a street system more suitable for automobiles than people, and ensures that customers will pass the greatest number of stores as they move from one attraction to another. The dearth of escalators and elevators—positioned only at the ends of long rows of shops—adds to that effect. The fountains in the middle of the thoroughfares divert the shoppers close to the open doorways of the stores.

> *"If you walked around and got people's first impressions, it would be interesting," says Ron McCarthy . . .*

To keep shoppers coming back to such a constrictive atmosphere, developers continually scramble for new forms of stimulation. As a means of drawing people to the vastly increased number of shops, the theme-park/shopping-centre hybrid of West Edmonton Mall is as significant in shopping-centre evolution as Southdale [the first enclosed mall, in Minneapolis] was thirty years ago. The Toronto architectural firm of Moorhead Fleming Corban McCarthy, the landscape architects for West Edmonton Mall, is so certain that recreation has become an essential component of shopping that it has created Forrec, a separate company to design, build, and operate theme parks, mostly for the shopping-mall market. Forrec is building smaller versions of West Edmonton Mall's amusement facilities in shopping centres around the world. At Woodbine Centre in Toronto, a Forrec-built amusement park called Fantasy Fair fills the space that would normally belong to a department store "anchoring"

one end of the mall. . . .

"If you walked around and got people's first impressions, it would be interesting," says Ron McCarthy, as he shows off the Woodbine Centre. Under a slowly revolving Ferris wheel, which spins with a momentum it gained from West Edmonton Mall, a man and woman are taking photographs. When McCarthy spots the couple, he says, "Sometimes you can tell the foreigners, people from the U.S. or Europe." He approaches them and inquires, "Hi, where are you from?"

"Edmonton," the man replies, "or at least a little north of there." They turn out to be from Westlock, Alberta, seventy kilometres north of Edmonton, and they speak proudly of the mall back home. "West Edmonton Mall is much bigger," says the woman. "It seems more elaborate. This is done up well too, but West Edmonton is really something to see."

"There's more marble and that type of thing at West Edmonton Mall," adds her husband. "It's on the floor and the walls. . . . "

"And they have subs and a great big ship like they have at Disneyland."

The man explains that he runs a drugstore in rural Alberta. The malls have made him realize that he has to keep up. "I'm thinking of knocking out a wall in the store," he says, "and putting up a stage or something. These days, you've just got to have a show."

—SATURDAY NIGHT, MAY 1986

RESPONSES

1. What do you enjoy about shopping malls? What do you dislike? Why do you think malls are appealing to teenagers? to parents with small children? to senior citizens?

2. Write an essay on the topic, "The shopping mall: the embodiment of twentieth-century civilization." William Kowinski's opening paragraph contains ideas which may stimulate your own reflective essay. Notice his use of imagery: "cathedral," "circus," "Garden of Eden," "utopia."

3. Write a film script, short story, or poem set in a mall. Try to suggest the mall's atmosphere and some of its pop culture dimensions. Your writing might include actual phrases you have heard in the mall or names of stores and products.

4. Working in groups, prepare a short media documentary on a mall. You could use film, video, photographs, slides and audiotape, or a combination of these. Present your documentary to the class.

THE NATURE OF CELEBRITY

As a class or in groups, make a list of this year's top ten celebrities and discuss the reasons for your choices. What makes them celebrities? What do you like and dislike about these people? What qualities do they have that might make them good role models? How many of your choices are Canadians?

In the book *Celebrity*, James Monaco defines four categories of celebrities:

1. **Heroes**   People who gain celebrity status for what they do: Terry Fox, Mother Theresa.

2. **Stars**   People who are known for what they are: Cher, Bryan Adams, Michael Jackson.

3. **Paracelebrities**   People who are known because of their association with celebrities: Bianca Jagger, Ronald Reagan Jr., members of the Kennedy family.

4. **Quasars**   People who are famous for what we *think* they are. They usually have no control over the image they project: Greta Garbo. Quasars can also be those "people made strangely important," mainly because of the media: Oliver North.

Place the people on your list of top ten celebrities in these categories. You may wish to categorize them in chart form. Discuss and compare your choices with the class.

Read the following observations about celebrity and discuss your reactions to them.

The quality of being a celebrity—"being well-known for their well-known-ness."

—DANIEL BOORSTIN, SOCIOLOGIST

"In the future everyone will be famous. For fifteen minutes."

—ANDY WARHOL, NEW YORK ARTIST

"People tune in, not to hear the news or the stories, especially, but simply to spend time with the personalities. Hence the rise of the talk show, true home of the celebrity."

—JAMES MONACO, AMERICAN FILM CRITIC

"It's better to look good than be good."

—BILLY CRYSTAL, ACTOR AND COMEDIAN

"No one presents himself directly, even among friends. Everyone is more or less fictional, made up, constructed. The larger the audience, the greater the fictional quotient."

—JAMES MONACO

What do the quotes tell you about the nature of celebrity? List any other aspects of celebrity you can think of. Refer to your list of top ten celebrities and see if these quotes apply to the people you chose.

Left to right: Vanna White, Yoko Ono, Michael J. Fox, Rick Hansen. In which of James Monaco's four categories, listed on the opposite page, do you think each of these celebrities belongs?

Just what does it take to be a "star"? As you read the following excerpt by Barbara Goldsmith, an American author and social historian, think about your discussions of celebrity. Ask yourself why and how celebrities get our attention. What role do the media play in the making of celebrities? Do the Canadian media play the same role in celebrity-making as American media? Do Canadians treat celebrities in the same way or differently than Americans treat celebrities?

The Meaning of Celebrity

by Barbara Goldsmith

At a recent Manhattan dinner party, the celebrity guests included a United States Senator, an embezzler, a woman rumored to spend $60 000 a year on flowers, a talk-show host, the chief executive officer of one of America's largest corporations, a writer who had settled a plagiarism suit and a Nobel laureate.

The line between fame and notoriety has been erased. Today we are faced with a vast, confusing jumble of celebrities: the talented and untalented, heroes and villains, people of accomplishment and those who have accomplished nothing at all, the criteria for their celebrity being that their images encapsulate some form of the American Dream, that they give enough of an appearance of leadership, heroism, wealth, success, danger, glamour and excitement to feed our fantasies. We no longer demand reality, only that which is "real seeming." . . .

Synthetic celebrities are our own creation, the modern equivalent of biblical graven images. In bowing down to them, we absent ourselves from the everyday ethical and moral judgments that insure the health of a society. . . .

Earlier this century, the proliferation of magazines, newspapers, network radio and Hollywood movies propelled celebrities into prominent positions in the national psyche. Now images can be instantly transmitted across the nation, indeed, the world, sometimes with disastrous results. Marshall McLuhan, the late masscommunications expert, credited television with turning terrorism from an isolated phenomenon into an international spectacle by allowing its practitioners to make free use of electronic facilities to publicize their causes. Political protesters inform the news media of their intentions, then stage demonstrations in front of the cameras. Even intimate tragedies become public events, turning those involved into momentary celebrity performers.

In today's highly technological world, reality has become a pallid substitute for the image reality we fabricate for ourselves, which in turn intensifies our addiction to the artificial. Anyone who has attended a political convention or a major sporting event knows that watching the proceedings on television, where cameras highlight the most riveting moments, then replay and relate

> *Synthetic celebrities are our own creation, the modern equivalent of biblical graven images.*

them to similar situations, provides us with more stimulating and complex perceptions than being there does.

Next year's visitors to the Grand Canyon need not see it. One mile from the boundary will be a $5 million complex where they will be able to view a film of the way the canyon looks during all four seasons and take a simulated raft ride through artificial rapids. . . .

Though our deep-seated need to

have individuals to celebrate has remained stable, our society has not. Many people wish to be admired, not respected, to be perceived as successful and glamorous, not as hard working and righteous. Among the worthy now are synthetic celebrities, famed for their images, not their deeds. They need not have a sense of moral or ethical obligation, and often use our approbation for their own cynical purposes. The trade-off is no longer fair.

In a society where the details of private lives are subjected to public scrutiny, role models have all but vanished. In the past, we often provided those we celebrated with a protective cloak to cover their fallibilities and frailties. It was an unwritten law, for example, that the press never photographed President Franklin Delano Roosevelt except from the waist up, so that the dispirited society of the 1930s would not be reminded its leader was physically disabled. Today such amenities are not practiced, nor are figures from the past spared. Long after their deaths, we are informed that Presidents Franklin D. Roosevelt, Eisenhower, Kennedy and Johnson all were unfaithful to their wives.

The public appetite for celebrity and pseudo-event has grown to extravagant proportions, and for the first time in history, the machinery of communications is able to keep up with these demands, even to outrun them, creating new needs we never knew existed.

To one extent or another, all the branches of the media have become complicitous [partnered] to this pursuit. *People* magazine is prototypical. In one issue, novelist E. L. Doctorow is mentioned, but so are Joanie and Gary McGuffin, an Ontario couple on a 6 200-mile canoeing honeymoon across Canada. Elizabeth Taylor appears, but so does Frank Spisak, a neo-Nazi murderer. The ersatz [synthetic] and the real appear side by side, and the willingness to distinguish between them has been abdicated. . . .

The rise of synthetic celebrity coincides with what the writer Jules Henry calls "the erosion of the capacity for emulation, the loss of the ability to model oneself consciously after another person." When Lisa Birnbach, a young writer who is currently preparing a comprehensive guide to American universities, asks students to name their heroes, many say they have none. A typical explanation is that they are no longer willing to admire any person. (Indeed, Marilyn Monroe, James Dean, Elvis Presley, Humphrey Bogart and the like may have become enduring deities precisely because they are dead and can no longer manipulate or disappoint us.) Those students who do name their heroes often include the name of Blake Carrington, the unprincipled tycoon character in the television series *Dynasty*.

Daily, the concept of the melding of heroes and villains plays itself out on prime-time television where notorious, immoral, self-centered individuals, often the perpetrators of heinous crimes, are pseudo-heroes. J.R. Ewing of *Dallas* is a scoundrel, but he is vigorous, rich, powerful and successful.

George Gerbner, Dean of the University of Pennsylvania's Annenberg School of Communications, estimates that by the time a typical American child reaches adulthood, he or she will have absorbed more than 30 000 electronic "stories." These have, he suggests, replaced the socializing role of the pre-industrial church in creating "a cultural mythology" that establishes the norm of approved behavior and belief. Gerbner concludes that watchers of prime-time television are receiving a highly synthetic picture of the real world, but that they accept it *more readily* than reality itself. . . .

Image is essential to the celebrity because the public judges him or her by what it sees—his or her public posture as distinguished from his or her private person. Entertainers are particularly adept at perfecting their images, learning to refine the nuances of personality. Indeed, the words "celebrity" and "personality" have become interchangeable in our language. Public-relations people, who are paid to manufacture celebrities for public consumption, are often referred to as image makers.

Celebrities are invariably accepted as instant authorities. Advertising takes advantage of this, fusing the celebrity with the product to be sold. Robert Young's long association with a physician role on television helped solidify his image as a medical authority, adding credence to his endorsements of Sanka. A similar case is the endorsement of Scoundrel perfume by the actress Joan Collins, the bad girl of television's *Dynasty* series. . . .

Synthetic celebrities are, after all, but reflections of ourselves and in deifying them we are holding a mirror to our own foibles. This reflected image cannot illuminate, it can only

> *Image is essential to the celebrity because the public judges him or her by what it sees . . .*

destroy our capacity to take an interest in anything outside of ourselves. A society that exalts flights from reality sets a dangerous course. Only a culture that acknowledges power without moral obligation could spawn such celebrity monsters as Charles Manson and the Rev. Jim Jones. John Lennon's assassin, Mark David Chapman, wanted nothing more than forever to be identified with the singer he idolized. Now he is. . . .

As our lives become more and more difficult to comprehend, we become so accustomed to retreating into our illusions that we forget we have created them ourselves. We treat them as if they were real and in so doing we make them real. Image supersedes reality. Synthetic celebrities become the personification of our hollow dreams.

—THE NEW YORK TIMES, 1986

RESPONSES

1. State three of Barbara Goldsmith's major criticisms of celebrities. Give some current examples to support the criticisms.

2. In the concluding paragraphs, Goldsmith makes some strong criticisms of our worship of celebrities. Put her basic criticisms into your own words. What is she suggesting in her statement that celebrities are "reflections of ourselves and in defining them we are holding a mirror to our own foibles"?

3. There is clearly a bond between the media and the rise of celebrities. How does each depend or feed on the other? In groups, consider how the following contribute to the celebrity industry: magazines such as *People*; the "people" section in newspapers and in magazines such as *Time* and *Maclean's*; television talk shows; advertising; television programs that examine the lifestyles of "the rich and famous"; docudramas that recreate the life of a celebrity. Each group could study one aspect and report to the other groups.

4. Celebrities are often used to endorse products. The celebrity's style and image become an endorsement for attitudes and values and the products often sell very well. By referring to several current examples, discuss the pros and cons of this practice. Try acting out some of these examples. Discuss ways in which student behaviour in your school has been influenced by celebrities.

5. Discuss the style of some celebrities. In groups, use the following list of elements of style and do a celebrity profile of some current celebrities as well as some from the past, such as Marilyn Monroe, Elvis Presley, or Humphrey Bogart. Study their appearance, style of dress, mannerisms, speech patterns, favourite expressions, typical settings or props with which they are identified, and what you think their values and/or "lifestyles" are like. Be prepared to present your profiles to the class. You could use photos, or play the role of the celebrity and have the class guess who you are portraying.

6. Imagine that you are a celebrity. Write a page for your diary or some dialogue that would support your public image. Read it to the class and see if they can guess who you are.

7. What advice would you offer to help a friend be aware of the negative aspects of celebrity or celebrity worship? You might want to present your advice in letter form, or record your thoughts on tape.

8. Interview someone who is a member of a fan club for a rock star or actor. What personal satisfaction do fans get from these clubs? Assess some of the literature these clubs send to their members and report to the class.

9. The British royal family has been covered extensively by the media. How do you account for some people's fascination with them? How is the royal family usually presented by the media? Find a variety of articles and photos portraying the royal family and assess the coverage. For example, how much of the coverage centred on the political aspects of royalty?

ISSUES FOR FURTHER STUDY

This chapter has identified a few features of popular culture and its media, and has introduced you to what you will be doing throughout the text: taking apart, or deconstructing, media and their techniques, and analyzing the messages they send.

Being able to recognize the trends and features of popular culture and trying to account for them—why they have appeared and what effect they have on us—is what the study of popular culture is about.

The following questions allow you to explore in more detail some of the issues raised in the chapter. You might want to brainstorm with other students to propose some other issues you could research.

1. We live in a society that is supposed to support freedom and individuality, but to what extent are we controlled by fads and trends? Does pop culture emphasize individuality or does it ask you to conform? Using examples from your own school and personal experience, write your answer in a brief essay.

2. The theme of "love at first sight" is a popular one in today's films and some television movies, but it is not a new idea—think of *Romeo and Juliet*. Some critics have suggested that what appears to be a novelty is actually an update of the same old thing.
a) Compare some fads and trends from the past with today's popular culture to see if any patterns are repeated.
b) Have a debate on the following statement. "Resolved: That popular culture does not lead trends; it follows them."

3. In groups, choose a popular American television series and try to "Canadianize" the content. You should go beyond superficialities such as geographical locations and occasional Canadian references—try to incorporate Canadian concerns. Think of some Canadian actors you would choose for the roles in the series.

4. Barbara Goldsmith's essay "The Meaning of Celebrity," and the essays on malls suggest that fact and fiction, the real thing and the artificial, become almost indistinguishable. Using the ideas from these essays as well as your own ideas, write an essay on the topic. "Our addiction to the image: a major problem in twentieth-century life."

5. Our society undergoes frequent major changes. The media have the power to make us aware of these changes, to make these changes accessible, and to make them part of popular culture. For example, AIDS was made real to many people only after actor Rock Hudson's death from the disease became front page news. In the 1970s, television shows began to deal with social issues such as feminism, gay rights, and racial prejudice. The following are some issues we deal with today: abortion, euthanasia, wife-battering, lack of affordable housing, free trade, unemployment, Native People's rights, and nuclear threats. Refer to a variety of media to examine how some of these issues, or others that you think of, have been treated. You might ask yourself questions such as: Was the issue made accessible to a wide audience? How? Was the issue sensationalized, romanticized, or made trivial?

6. Because popular culture is such a colourful topic, the writing associated with it is often characterized by a lively, vivid, and descriptive style. Choose an aspect of pop culture and write about it in such a style. You could describe: a toy store, a rock concert, a hairstyle, fashion, a fad, audience behaviour at a popular film, a social group such as "new wavers" or "preppies," or a topic of your choice.

CHAPTER 2

Television

Television is a powerful force in our lives. It shows us the best and worst of ourselves, and almost everything in between. It teaches us about other cultures and about the world we live in. It has helped to make stars of some people and has hurt the careers of others. It helps to set the agenda for our consumer society and establish the topic of conversation for the next day.

Perhaps because it is so powerful, people have always had a love-hate relationship with television. We can gain great personal satisfaction from watching TV, but at the same time curse it for consuming our time and catering to our most uninspired thinking skills and abilities. We use it to learn about other people, but also blame it for isolating people from their family and friends.

Understanding how television works can help us watch TV more critically: it will help us understand how we look at TV, what we see, and why we see it. Television contains a value system, an ideology that is only visible when we take the time to look beneath its surface. It is important to be aware that commercial TV is first and foremost a business, and that the programs are made to attract customers for sponsors' products. The commercial aspect of television inevitably influences how television constructs reality, but there are other factors at work, too, such as the technology of the medium, the content of the programming, and the dominance of American shows. By taking a closer look at TV, we can begin to understand both what affects our perception of TV and how TV affects our perceptions of our world.

YOUR VIEW OF TELEVISION

What is your opinion of television? In groups, read and discuss the following comments:

"What is the role of television? It's difficult to define. At its most ordinary it acts as an extension of vision: it relays routine information, routine entertainment, routine education into drawing rooms of the audience. At its best, it bestows insight, it heightens perception, reveals new relationships and brings with it a new view of our daily lives."

—AUBREY SINGER, *TELEVISION: WINDOW ON CULTURE*

"Television is a socializer: it presents role models to children, influences opinions, forms attitudes and molds minds. Even the votes that are cast for candidates are influenced by television. The very tilt of the camera and the angle of the picture can alter our perspective. The effects of television can range from the trivial to the extremely significant."

—HEREMENE D. HARTMAN, *TELEVISION IN AMERICAN CULTURE*

In your media log, write your opinion of television in 300 to 500 words, answering questions such as the following:

• What do you gain from watching television?

• What do you enjoy about it?

• Has it ever disappointed you?

• How do you think television has affected you?

• What role does it play in your household?

• How much are you influenced by what your family and friends like to watch?

As you continue this chapter, refer to what you have written. Add any new perceptions or opinions you may have.

YOUR TV VIEWING HABITS: A SURVEY

To find out how much TV you and your classmates watch, your reasons for watching, and your likes and dislikes, complete the following survey in your media log.

1. When do you watch television? In your log, create a chart similar to the one below and fill in the number of hours you watch TV in each time slot.

	Mon	Tues	Wed	Thurs	Fri	Sat	Sun
7am – noon							
noon – 4pm							
4pm – 7pm							
7pm – 11pm							
late night							

2. How much TV do you watch? From the data on your chart, calculate the total number of hours watched per day and per week.

3. Do you do other things while you watch television? Of your weekly viewing time, how much is spent watching television as the main or only activity?

4. Do you have a part-time job? If so, what hours do you work? How does your job affect the amount of television you watch?

5. Refer to the following list to help you rank, in order of preference, your favourite types of TV shows. Add any types that are not listed. Do not rank shows you do not watch.

sitcoms (situation comedies)
talk shows
variety shows
sports
news

crime/detective shows
game shows
soap operas
documentaries/public affairs
music shows

CONTINUED...

6. List your favourite shows (up to ten).

7. Indicate the main reasons for watching your favourite shows by matching each of them with one or more of the following:
   a) information, education
   b) topics for conversation
   c) companionship (TV as company)
   d) entertainment
   e) to watch a sport or sports team
   f) to get away from problems
   g) to gain insights into human relationships
   h) to pass the time
   i) other

8. List the Canadian shows you watch regularly.

RESPONSES

1. When you have finished the survey, summarize the information:
   a) What is the average viewing amount from Monday to Friday? On Saturday and Sunday?
   b) What are the most popular viewing times during Monday to Friday? On Saturday and Sunday?
   c) How many students have part-time jobs? What is the average number of hours worked per week?
   d) List the three favourite types of shows and the percentage of students who liked each.
   e) List the three favourite shows and the percentage of students who liked each.
   f) What were the three most frequently given reasons for watching TV?
   g) List the top three Canadian shows.

2. Discuss the patterns your survey results reveal.

3. Find the most recent television ratings. How do your favourite shows and those of the class compare with the top-rated American and Canadian shows?

As you may have found from your survey, people's reasons for watching television vary widely. Our age, background, character, and personal interests are all factors affecting what we watch and why we watch it, as well as what we gain from it.

The following excerpt from the article "Television and Our Private Lives" is a compilation of oral reports from various people about the nature of their television viewing. The author, Jeanne Betancourt, is a contributing editor to *Channels*, a magazine about the television industry. As you read these selections, consider what role television plays in your life.

Television and Our Private Lives

by Jeanne Betancourt

1. I watch baseball with my dad. Then sometimes we play baseball together and sometimes my cousins come too. I play in the park and in school. When you play sports you run or you're always doing exercise, keeping your body in shape, but when you watch TV you always have to stay there and stare at the TV. Sometimes you could get tired. Your eyes hurt. When I stop watching TV I feel like I want to keep seeing it. Watching TV is a lot of fun. But when my mother, she tells me sometimes we have to eat, I say, "Uh-uh. I don't want to eat." And she says, "You gotta eat, right now."

I feel like saying, "Man, I want to keep on watching." She says, "No. When you finish eating you go and see it." But I know when I go back the show will be finished. Then when I eat I don't feel like eating. Sometimes she gives me a chance and she says, "You can eat later."

2. Television has been very positive for me and I get very annoyed with people who pooh-pooh it and feel it's bad. It's so fabulous. There's a lot of junk on TV, but it's still such a miracle.

In the evenings as soon as I walk in the door, I turn on that TV in the living room. Just to have sound in the apartment and also to get the news. I'll watch TV while I prepare my dinner and often while I'm having it.

I enjoy the interview shows. It's a way to keep up with things and be with interesting people, people who are making the laws, who are important. I don't socialize as much as I used to and I miss the interesting dinner conversation that I used to have. This way I can choose my company.

You know television has made me more tolerant. For example, of homosexuality. I really never had contact with homosexuality. Discussions about it on TV have enlightened me and made me more tolerant and understanding. Now, if homosexuality happened in our family, I would not consider it that devastating at all. I would be much more compassionate and understanding.

3. About a year ago, I tried to make my life like a television show. When I get mad at my sister I try to make it feel like a soap opera and I'll say something and I'll storm out of the room. If I have a fight with my mother and I get really mad, a few minutes later I'll get sad and come in and hug her and say I'm sorry, real dramatic like TV.

In school I learn about math and spelling and things like that. When I watch TV I learn more about life. Certain shows teach you how to handle telling your parents that you don't want to do what they want you to do. You have to make sure that they understand that you probably won't be happy with your profession when you get older if it's not something you want to do. It seems like the people on TV solve their problems easier than me.

4. TV was nothing like my life. And I didn't expect it to be like life. TV was my mythology. It was never a source of information for me. It was entertainment. But I wouldn't go to it to learn about the world in any purposeful way. And to this day I can't take news on television seriously.

By the time I was a junior in high school I became a voracious reader. When I got to college my life picked up and I tapered off my TV viewing to the point where I just stopped watching altogether. It always struck me as being a natural transition. You're not a kid anymore and you read books.

Now I watch on Sundays. I sit in front of a TV all day so I can watch football games. I watch baseball games during the week sometimes, but outside of that I watch

FEIFFER © 1981 Jules Feiffer. Reprinted with permission of Universal Press Syndicate. All rights reserved.

very little television now. Since everything on TV is aimed at fifteen-year-olds and I'm not fifteen anymore, there's very little for me to watch. I'm a backslider like everybody else is and there are moments when I think, "Ah, I'll just turn on the TV," and I start watching one of those TV movies. After, I think, "You dope, you just wasted two hours watching some mediocre movie."

5. When I was about five years old I mainly watched cartoons and then all the regular shows. As I got older I watched the reruns in the afternoon. Sometimes I'd just stare at it. I don't know if I really understood what was going on. It was just an interesting thing to look at it. My mom said that whenever us kids watched a lot of TV we were really ornery to her.

When I watch now I'm really selective. Real easygoing shows are okay—*Little House on the Prairie*, stuff like that. I used to watch *M*A*S*H*. Mainly my sister really liked it and she got me hooked on it. But now I don't appreciate the language and stuff on there. I'm a Christian person and it just bugs me when they cuss and cut each other down. It's funny, it's humorous, people laugh, but I still think it puts that same critical spirit into your values and other things.

6. [We] talk a lot about television. Maybe it's because we work together so closely as a team—two fellows riding together hour after hour. For the sake of conversation one fellow will say, "Did you see this show last night on television?" You build a whole discussion around what you saw on television the night before. You'll start out usually talking about a show both of you have watched.

Whatever they're doing on television, in the media, they're going to do it on the street.

Then you talk about a show he watched and you didn't. It's great, especially if you're following a series.

Kids today watch a lot of TV. You could say they're addicted to it. I find that boys twelve to fifteen are very influenced by television. They pick up the macho image, not so much from their friends, but from television. And the girls all want to look and act like Brooke Shields. Whatever they're doing on television, in the media, they're going to do it on the street. I know this from working with people. TV doesn't really face reality. I don't see myself at all in any television program. Boy, I'd love to be able to cope with problems the way they do on TV. They can knock a problem out in twenty minutes or a half-hour.

I find television sometimes an escape from the hard, cold reality on the outside. For that hour you can lose yourself in a television program.

—*CHANNELS*,
DECEMBER/JANUARY 1987

RESPONSES

1. The following are brief biographies of the people who gave these accounts. Match the biography with the account and discuss how you reached your decisions.

a) Karen, 16, lives in Sacramento, California. Her father is a computer typesetter and her mother teaches English in the small Baptist school that Karen attends. There are two other children in the family.

b) Sandy, 12, lives with her mother and her 15-year-old sister. Her parents were divorced when she was 2.

c) Herbert, 10, is in the fifth grade in a New York City public school. His family is Puerto Rican and he is bilingual.

d) James, 27, is a journalist. He is a graduate of Harvard and spent one-and-a-half years teaching and writing in India. He lives alone.

e) Tim, 38, is a police officer in a small town. He is divorced and lives alone.

f) Martha, 59, has been widowed for 16 years, and lives alone. She is an assistant librarian at a suburban university. She earned her bachelor's degree when she was 56.

2. How do these accounts compare with your own?

3. Which comments surprised you? Did you notice any contradictions in the comments? If so, suggest possible reasons for them.

4. People often say they feel guilty about watching TV. Put together a class list of "guilty pleasures" by naming shows you like to watch but feel guilty about watching. Think of reasons people feel guilty about watching these shows and discuss your findings.

5. Interview two or three people in your community about their television viewing, asking questions similar to the ones you think Jeanne Betancourt asked. See page 212 for tips on how to conduct an interview.

Answer to Question 1: a – 5; b – 3; c – 1; d – 4; e – 6; f – 2.

Why You Watch What You Watch When You Watch

The following excerpt from an essay, written in 1971, offers an insider's view of why we watch television. The author, Paul Klein, is a former NBC (National Broadcasting Corporation) research chief. As you read the excerpt, note the points Klein makes. Decide whether you agree or disagree with his arguments, and why.

by Paul Klein

I t is about time that you all stop lying to each other and face up to your problems: you love television and you view too much.

I used to be the guy in charge of the ratings at NBC, and my waking hours were filled with people either complaining about how inaccurate the ratings were or, without my asking them, volunteering that they "never watch TV, because the programs stink, particularly this season."

Let's look at the facts, because only by examining the nature of the disease can we cure it, or at least make peace with it.

The Census Bureau tells us that 97.8 percent of U.S. homes have a television set (and about one half of those have two or more sets, with the number of homes and sets growing each day). The Census Bureau also shows that TV penetration is highest among the more affluent and better-educated segment of the population. In fact, 99 percent of the homes with $15 000-$20 000 annual income have at least one TV set— the majority of them have more than one—and most of them have a color set. And also we all know how they complain about the programs and how they say they never watch the stuff.

The truth is that you buy extra

sets, color sets, and even pay a monthly charge for CATV [cable television] to view television. Yet when you view an evening's worth of TV you are full of complaints about what you have viewed. But the next night you're right back there, hoping against hope for satisfying content, never really learning from experience, and another night is shot. Instead of turning the set off and doing something else, you persist in exercising the medium.

With more TV sets and clearer, more colorful pictures on those sets, you are tuned to TV *more* this year than last year and last year more than the previous year, etc.

The fact is that you view TV regardless of its content. Because of the nature of the limited spectrum (only a few channels in each city) and the economic need of the networks to attract an audience large enough to attain advertising dollars which will cover the cost of production of the TV program, pay the station carrying the program and also make a profit, you are viewing programs which by necessity must appeal to the rich and poor, smart and stupid, tall and short, wild and tame, together. Therefore, you are in the vast majority of cases viewing something that is not to your taste. From the time you bought a set to now, you have viewed thousands of programs which were not to your taste. The result is the hiding of and lying about, all that viewing. Because of the hiding and lying, you are guilty. The guilt is expressed in the feeling that "I

should have been reading instead of viewing." It is of course much more difficult to read than to view, even for people making $15 000– $20 000 a year. Reading requires a process called *decoding*, which causes a slowdown in the information taken in by the user. TV viewing is very simple to do—kids do it better than adults because they are unencumbered by guilt—and the amount of information derived from an hour's viewing is infinitely more than is derived from an hour's reading.

But print has been around for a long time and it has attracted people who have learned to express themselves in this medium, so the printed content, on the whole, is superior to the TV content. Still, most of us prefer television.

Despite the lack of quality content, the visual medium is so compelling that it attracts the vast majority of adults each day to a progression of shows that most of these people would ignore in printed form.

The process of viewing works like this: A family has just finished dinner and one member says, "Let's see what's on TV tonight." The set gets turned on or *TV Guide* gets pulled out. If it's *TV Guide*, then the list of programs (most of which are repeats) is so unappealing that each member of the family says to himself or herself that he or she remembers when *TV Guide* made an awful error in its program listings back in 1967 and maybe it has happened again.

The set is on whether a good program is listed or not at that time. Chances are over 100 to one that there is nothing on that meets this or any family's taste at that moment. But the medium meets their taste.

The viewer(s) then slowly turns the channel selector, grumbling at each image he or she sees on the channel. Perhaps he or she'll go around the dial two or three times before settling on one channel whose program is *least objectionable*.

"Well, let's watch this," someone in the family says. "There's nothing better on." So they watch. No one thinks of jogging a couple of laps around the block or getting out the old Parcheesi board. They watch whatever is least objectionable.

The programmers for the networks have argued that this is a "most satisfying" choice—not LOP (least objectionable program). But it it were, then why would everybody be complaining and lying about TV viewing? I don't deny that in some rare time periods, "least objectionable" is actually most satisfying, but the bulk of the time people are viewing programs they don't particularly consider good and *that* is why the medium is so powerful and rich. . . .

We view content we dislike, content that is frivolous, unsatisfying, unrewarding. We state that what we want from TV is more important content—like public affairs. Well, when public affairs is on, we really want to see it, we really should see it, but it's too objectionable compared to the entertainment programs opposite it. . . .

It is very rare that viewing in any time period is lower than normal. It is very difficult to either raise or lower the "sets-in-use" in a time period, indicating once and for all that viewing has little to do with content. When *Bridge on the River Kwai* was on (first time), sets-in-use rose five points—and when *Laugh-In* was a national phenomenon sets-in-use were up somewhat. But when the number one-rated *Marcus Welby* was preempted for a public-affairs-type program . . . on a night when public affairs shows were on the other two networks, more people saw public affairs than had seen that kind of beloved program since the same thing happened many years ago in the same time period. All three networks enjoyed greater viewing in the *forced* viewing situation—you either watched public affairs or you did not watch any network programs—than they would have had each program been opposite entertainment. All three of the programs were repeated later and they got very small audiences. Apparently no one felt so bad about missing the two he or she didn't see that he or she searched them out when they were repeated. . . .

People love TV. They love the ease of viewing and the ease of distribution; video pictures delivered right to the home. Somebody's going to figure out how to give this medium more satisfying content as we head toward a completely visual culture.

—TV GUIDE, 1971

RESPONSES

1. Why do you think Paul Klein starts his essay so bluntly? Do his credentials as a former NBC research chief make his observations more convincing to you? Explain your answer.

2. Explain how the principle of LOP—least objectionable program—operates. Write a brief description of a recent night of your own TV viewing to show how LOP does or does not apply to you or your household.

3. Do you agree with these statements by the author? In groups, discuss each one.
   a) "The fact is that you view TV regardless of its content."
   b) "It is, of course, much more difficult to read than to view."
   c) "The amount of information derived from an hour's viewing is infinitely more than is derived from an hour's reading."
   d) "The medium meets their taste."
   e) "They watch whatever is least objectionable."

4. List the reasons the author gives to explain why TV viewing is compelling. Explain why you do or do not agree.

5. The "limited spectrum" that Klein refers to in this 1971 essay has expanded; many communities have access to more than just a few channels. Do you think the author's argument is still valid? Why?

6. Refer to your own reasons for watching TV and those given by people in Betancourt's article, "Television and Our Private Lives." Do you agree with Klein's statement that most people love television and watch it too much? Explain your answer.

Some critics charge that TV viewing limits children's imagination. Bruno Bettelheim is a psychiatrist who emphasizes the importance of imagination for children. In the following excerpt he says that television, rather than inhibiting imagination, helps address children's needs for fantasy.

A Child's Garden of Fantasy by Bruno Bettelheim

Among the concerns about television's effects on our children, none is greater than that it may induce them to violence. Probably none has been more thoroughly investigated. I personally dislike watching violence on the screen, and would be favorably impressed with broadcasters if they restrained their desire to exploit it. But I cannot deny that as long as it is not vicious or cruel—which it very often is—it holds a certain fascination. . . .

Television offers a wide variety of models to fantasize about and try out, as if for size. Children tend to dress, walk, and talk like the TV characters they admire. Whether this helps or hurts a particular youngster seems to depend on which television figure he or she emulates. And this is determined much more by his personality and the problems he or she faces at the moment than by what is shown on the screen.

As Wilbur Schramm and other researchers recognized more than two decades ago, "The chief part television plays in the lives of children depends at least as much on what the child brings to television as on what television brings to the child." And the younger the child is, the more this is so.

In an experiment reported in 1978 in *Child Development* magazine, second graders viewed a program and then were asked to retell its story so that "someone who has not seen it would know what happened." In response the children strung together random occurrences, showing no recall of relationships among the events they had observed. But children several years older were able to recall fairly well what they had seen. Thus, the younger the child, the less responsive he or she is to the actual content of the program; he or she responds to it in terms of his or her inner life.

Only the child whose emotional life is barren, or whose conditions of life are extremely destructive, will "live" in the world of TV programs. Doing so may be preferable to facing his or her actual life, which would lead [the child] to give up all hope, or to explode into violence against those who make his or her life miserable.

In fact, most children seek refuge at times in television-fed fantasy, although they do not permit it to engulf more than a very limited part of their lives. Television is truly an ideal medium for the purpose of fantasizing because it permits the child to return immediately from the fantasy world to real life, and also to escape as quickly into the television world when reality becomes too much to handle. All it takes is turning a switch.

We ought to remember how restricted children's lives have become. It used to be possible to let children roam all by themselves for much of the day, or in the chance company of other children. They used to play somewhere in the neighborhood, in an empty shack, or wander the woods and fields. There they could dream their own daydreams, without parents nearby demanding that they use their time more constructively. Today, for our children's security, we cannot permit them to fend for themselves in that way. Yet, to grow up well, children need time and space to be themselves. Watching television gives them this chance. Being able to choose the program that will spark and feed their dreams has become a way for modern children to exercise their self-determination, an important experience in growing up.

—*CHANNELS*, SEPTEMBER/OCTOBER 1985

RESPONSES

1. By referring to your own childhood memories of television, respond to Bruno Bettelheim's assertion that TV plays a necessary role in allowing children to fantasize. When you watched TV as a child did you develop a fantasy world? If you did not watch TV as a child, did you still have a fantasy world? Have a group discussion about your experiences.

2. What was Bettelheim's observation about the value of television for children who are forced to live restricted lives? Do you agree? Why?

3. Ask two children you know under the age of 10 about their TV viewing habits. What are their favourite programs? If possible, observe them while they watch TV. How do they behave? Do they interact with the television characters? How do they respond to commercials? Present your findings to your group or class.

4. Bettelheim states that, "Being able to choose the program that will spark and feed their dreams has become a way for modern children to exercise their self-determination, an important experience in growing up." In groups, choose a popular children's show and watch it at home. Each group could watch a different show. Describe the show to the other groups and discuss how it may have helped to feed children's dreams.

5. Read some of the research that has been done on the effects of television on children. Report your findings to your group.

PROGRAM TYPES

Television has an enormous need for material. This need has led to the creation of a variety of formats and formulas. The wide range of types of television programs reflects the attempt to reach as large and varied an audience as possible. From police shows to documentaries, there is something for everybody.

Make a class list of the types of programs on TV, using question 5 of the survey on page 61 as a guide. In groups, use these categories to make a chart similar to the one following. Have each group prepare a chart for one day of the week. Study a television listing from a TV guide or newspaper for your day and complete the chart by filling in the names of all the programs listed. Indicate the length of the programs. (You might want to use abbreviations to save space.)

Time Slot					
Program Type	7am – noon	noon – 4pm	4pm – 7pm	7pm – 11pm	late night
Sitcom					
Soap					
Game Show					
(and so on)					

Calculate the total number of hours per day that are spent on each category. Report your findings to the other groups and, as a class, determine how many hours per week are spent on each category. Analyze the patterns that your charts reveal.

a) As a class, make a list of types of TV audiences—preschool children, people at home during the day, sports fans, and so on. Have each person in the class watch a different program. While you watch the program, record the following information in your log:

• name of program
• type of program
• time slot
• products advertised/sponsors

b) Decide what audience this program is intended for. Explain how the program and its sponsors try to reach that target audience.

Left page: top, left to right, *Archie Bunker's Place, Hockey Night in Canada, the fifth estate.* Bottom, left to right, *Wheel of Fortune, The Raccoons.* Right page: left to right, *Degrassi Jr. High, The Beachcombers*

SITCOMS

The situation comedy or "sitcom" is one of the most popular types of programs. With *The Honeymooners* and *I Love Lucy* in the '50s; *The Dick Van Dyke Show* and *The Beverly Hillbillies* in the '60s; *All in the Family* and *M*A*S*H* in the '70s; and *The Cosby Show* and *Family Ties* in the '80s, the sitcom has often reigned supreme in the television realm. Usually sitcoms are a half-hour in length and feature the same characters and setting every week. Generally, the show is about a problem that threatens the sense of normalcy. By the end of the show, the problem is resolved. Each sitcom has a premise—some basic idea, point of view, or philosophy. Characterization makes sitcoms especially appealing; the characters are usually very warm, friendly, and likeable. In some shows, they are capable of change and personal growth. As comedy writer and actor Carl Reiner said, "warm" is an important word. "You laugh easier when funny things are happening to nice people."

RESPONSES

1. What is your favourite sitcom? Write a short review of the show and share your opinion with others. See page 215 in the Reference Section for tips on writing reviews.

Top to bottom: Mork and Mindy, Newhart, Gimme a Break, Newhart, Happy Days

2. After watching two or three sitcoms:
a) Write a brief biography or description of the character you enjoyed the most in each show and state why you found him or her appealing.
b) Write a plot summary for each show and describe its basic premise or philosophy.

3. In groups, try playing the roles of the actors in a popular sitcom. Choose a director and re-enact a scene from a sitcom you have all watched, or write your own scene for the show and enact it.

The "soaps" claim large audiences who are often fanatically loyal to their programs. What do people obtain from these programs? Some critics have found socially worthwhile qualities in soaps, while others say that they are no more than predictable formulas which showcase inferior acting. What is your opinion?

Soaps' Search For Tomorrow

by Brian D. Johnson

Beneath the lofty glass dome of the suburban mall, he stood on display like a visiting deity. Hundreds of fans pressed around the lip of the stage with arms outstretched. There were housewives, career women, preteen girls, grandmothers—and even some men—all struggling to get closer to Eric Braedon, star of TV's daytime soap opera *The Young and the Restless*. Most of them knew him simply as Victor—the show's ruggedly handsome millionaire who is divorcing Nikki, the sultry and sad-eyed model who is now involved with Victor's brother, unaware that she suffers from a potentially fatal disease. . . .

Soap opera continues to be one of the most populist—and profitable—areas of television. Daytime television generates more than 50 percent of all earnings. Audiences are surprisingly large—an estimated 50 million North Americans follow the daytime soaps. . . .

Daytime soaps offer an intimacy unavailable in the fast-paced action of prime time. Soap scenes are designed to be savored rather than consumed at a gulp. Dialogue is stretched out with pregnant pauses and meaningful glances. *The Young and the Restless*, the most popular afternoon soap in Canada, relies heavily on lingering close-ups of faces transfigured by makeup, lighting and emotion. . . .

Frank M. Benard and Eileen Davidson star as Marc Mergeron and Ashley Abbott in the popular series, *The Young and the Restless*.

Such evening serials as *Dallas* and *Dynasty* have streamlined the soap formula and given it a glamorous sheen. . . . But unlike the durable daytime soaps, the evening's luxury products are prey to fickle prime-time trends and fierce competition. Ratings are slipping, and the evening dramas are resorting to high-powered injections of intrigue to pump them back up. . . .

Network executives once feared that the entry of women into the work force would wash away the audience for daytime soaps. Instead, the traditional daytime soap fan . . . has been joined by a surprising assortment of other addicts. About 30 percent of the audience is now male. . . . And technology has broadened the market further, allowing female viewers with full-time jobs outside the home to tape their favorite shows on VCRs and watch them at night. . . .

As the market grows and daytime serials become a respectable subject for gossip in the workplace, soap addicts are coming out of the closet. Even celebrities—from Elizabeth Taylor to Wayne Gretzky—have gone public with their addictions and made guest appearances on their favorite serials. Lorraine Segato, 30, lead singer for the Toronto-based band the Parachute Club, has watched *Another World* since she was 15. "What I find interesting about soap operas," she said, "is that they are based totally and utterly on deceit. It's not what's said that counts. It's what isn't said. And that fascinates me because a lot of the sordid part of relationships—and politics—has to do with what is left unsaid."

It is a sign of soapdom's new respectability that, although its long-tressed heroines hardly serve as symbols of female liberation, feminists find redeeming virtues. Agi Lukacs, an adult-education teacher at the University of Toronto, describes the daytime serials as "a secret communications channel among women that tells them how to handle their men and their kids." Lukacs, who has watched soaps since she was 14, says that "the soaps' treatment of class and race stinks. But the depth in which they develop relationships is very good." Harriet Rosenberg, who teaches social sciences at York University in Toronto, described soaps as "a guilt-free form of gossip." One reason why women are so attracted to soapdom, she said, "is that it's the only place where men pay attention to women and relationships. They're willing to drop their work at a moment's notice. And that's completely untrue in the rest of the world."

The plots that dominate soaps do indeed strain credulity. Story lines expose their characters to heartache, disease, murder, rape, adultery, abduction, amnesia, and incest at an absurd rate. But increasingly, shows are using emotional realism to grapple with social issues. With the fervor of a moral crusade, *The Young and the Restless* has taken a soapbox stand against targets ranging from drug abuse to wife-batter-

ing. And last summer *Y&R* overtook North America's No. 1-rated *General Hospital*, with a highly popular story line about teenage pregnancy.

Although the pregnant girl's final fate was left unresolved, the story climaxed with a concert in which the show's resident rock star,

> *Compared to prime time's thorough-breds, soap operas have been the workhorses of network television.*

Michael Damian, led the audience in a chant of "It's okay to say no." . . . Many younger fans take such soap sermons very seriously. . . .

Compared to prime time's thoroughbreds, soap operas have been the workhorses of network television. Many evening dramas are so expensive to produce that they usually do not turn a profit for their producers until they go into syndicated reruns. But the top-rated daytime serials, manufactured at a fraction of the cost, generate a healthy revenue even with lower advertising rates. Although exact figures are unavailable, *Y&R* producer Edward Scott concedes that his show is "a very efficient money-making machine."

The largest single owner of soap opera is, in fact, a soap company—Procter & Gamble. It owns four vintage serials—*Guiding Light, As the World Turns, Another World,* and *Search for Tomorrow*. And the company is involved in every level of production, from scripts to cast-

A scene from Dynasty. Why do you think the ratings for night-time soaps are falling?

ing. Resisting the trend to spice up story lines to lure a younger audience, Procter & Gamble remains devoted to an image of physical and moral hygiene. "Their products are notoriously clean," said Steve Schnetzer, who plays Cass Winthrop on *Another World*. "And our show is very conservative in its philosophy."

Still, with their sanitized moral code and fast-food production values, the soaps carry a certain stigma within the acting profession. Top stars earn $2500 to $3000 a day, but their work can be frustrating. Said Schnetzer, "The soap formula demands a constantly heightened sense of emotion, and that violates my actor's sense of truth." . . .

For generations, people have been searching for the alchemy that turns simple melodrama into successful soap opera. . . . With techniques of modern marketing, soap producers are constantly remolding their stories and characters to the tastes of a changing audience. But the questions they pose are eternal. Will tomorrow ever come? How long can the young stay restless? Will they find true happiness in another world? As long as the world turns, soap fans will keep searching for answers in a wishing well that, for now at least, appears to be bottomless.

—*MACLEAN'S*,
OCTOBER 6, 1986

RESPONSES

1. How are soaps a blend of fantasy and reality? If your class meets while a soap is telecast, watch it together and talk about your ideas.

2. Discuss the following observations from the article.
a) "What I find interesting about soaps is that they are based totally and utterly on deceit."—Lorraine Segato, lead singer for *Parachute Club*.
b) "The soap formula demands a constantly heightened sense of emotion, and that violates my actor's sense of truth."—Steve Schnetzer, who plays Cass Winthrop on *Another World*.

3. In your group, brainstorm to develop some criteria for evaluating soaps, such as quality of acting, kind and frequency of social issues dramatized, complexity of plots. Rate two or three of the current soaps based on these criteria and share your observations with the class.

4. Some universities are now offering courses about soaps. Based on your knowledge of soaps, compile a list of suitable study topics for this course. The inquiry model in the Reference Section, page 211, may help you.

5. Are soap operas inferior to other shows? Do they offer anything worthwhile to their audiences? Have a class debate between loyal fans and critics of these shows.

6. In groups, think of a story line for a soap opera that has your school as its setting. Think of a title for the show, design the title as it would appear on the TV screen, select opening music, and choose the time spot you would like to have. Make a presentation to the class. Discuss which soap opera you find most interesting and why. As a class, decide which soap would be most likely to succeed on television and why.

OTHER PROGRAM TYPES

Since commercial television is aimed at a mass audience, there is a need for a variety of types of programming to attract as many people as possible. Ratings are crucial to the survival of a show. Unless a program attracts millions of viewers, it is not likely to be renewed for the next season. Thus, the complexity of plot, ideas, and style are geared to an average intelligence, and the kinds of programs available are aimed at a wide range of "average" interests.

RESPONSES

1. Examine the following program types. Think of two or three current shows that fit these categories and identify their target audiences.

talk show

televangelism

educational program

nature show

made-for-TV movie

TV mini-series

family drama

music show

police/detective show

western

medical drama

docudrama

sports telecast

game show

variety show

2. Working in groups, choose one type of program and watch several shows of that type. Compare the shows to determine similarities and differences; for example, characterization, setting, pacing, plot, use of special effects. Present your findings to the class. You may wish to write an outline that parodies a typical show of that type.

3. Watch two or three types of TV programs and the commercials that accompany them. In your log, record the following information:

- type of program

- target audience for show

- who advertised during show and what products or services were advertised

- target audience for each commercial

- when commercials occurred

- your reaction to commercials, e.g., whether they were a welcome break or annoyed you

- what happened during the commercials, e.g., whether viewers discussed the show, left the room, or changed channels

4. List four or five current television commercials and identify the target audience for each. Suggest the type of program whose target audience matches that of the commercial. Watch for these commercials on TV to see if they are shown with the type of program you chose.

5. Television ratings usually decide the fate of programs. Make a prediction about three shows you think will remain on the air and three you think will be cancelled. Discuss how you made your decisions.

TV LANGUAGE AND TECHNIQUES

Television uses certain codes and conventions which the viewer interprets, or "decodes." We understand and accept this "language" without being aware of it. When one scene fades into another, for example, our experience tells us that there has been a lapse of time. Low angle shots in which the camera is aimed up at a person will inevitably make the person seem bigger or more important. The following glossary of terms used in filming and in television scripts is a guide to the language the industries use. As you read them, discuss how they might be used in a television show or commercial and what their use might signify. You can also refer to page 137 in the Film chapter for more information on film and video techniques:

TECHNICAL TERMS

Camera Angles (refers to the angle of the camera in relation to the subject)

HIGH ANGLE   The camera looks down on the subject.

LOW ANGLE   The camera looks up at the subject.

NORMAL OR STRAIGHT ANGLE   The camera is on the same level as the subject.

NARROW-ANGLE LENS   A camera lens that makes a subject seem closer to the viewer than it really is (like a telephoto lens).

REVERSE ANGLE   A shot showing the subject from the reverse direction; a shot showing a character from behind is the reverse angle to a full face shot.

WIDE-ANGLE LENS   A camera lens which shows a wide view of a scene.

Camera Distance

CLOSE-UP (CU)   A shot in which the camera is close to the subject. Often used to show emotion. When the close-up is on a person, only the face, or face and shoulders are shown.

EXTREME CLOSE-UP (ECU)   A shot in which the camera is very close to the subject. If the subject is a person's face, only features such as the eyes or mouth are shown.

EXTREME LONG SHOT (ELS)   A very long shot, e.g., a shot of characters who appear very small in the distance.

LONG SHOT (LS) (sometimes called a full shot)   A shot that uses the camera's full angle of view, so that the subject is a long distance away from the camera. MLS is a medium long shot, closer (or tighter) to the subject.

MEDIUM SHOT (MS)   The distance between a long shot and a close-up. With characters, it usually shows them from the waist up.

Camera Movement

ARC   Movement of the camera in an arc, or curve.

CRANE   A shot in which the camera moves up and away. It is often used to end films.

DOLLY   A dolly is a cart or truck that the camera is mounted on so that it can move smoothly. DOLLY IN means the camera moves toward the subject. DOLLY OUT or dolly back means the camera moves away from the subject.

PAN   The camera moves horizontally (left or right movement).

PULLBACK DOLLY   The camera moves back from a scene to surprise the viewer by revealing a subject that was previously off frame.

TILT   The camera moves vertically (up or down).

TRACKING SHOT (also called a travelling shot, or a follow shot)   A variation of the dolly shot, the camera moves along with the subject, e.g., to film a character who is running. For a smooth shot, tracks are laid down on which the dolly runs.

ZOOM IN, ZOOM OUT, (ZI, ZO)   The zoom lens changes its distance from the subject quickly, so the movement toward or away from the subject is apparent to the viewer.

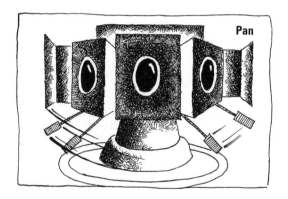

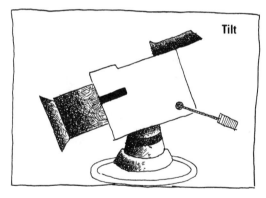

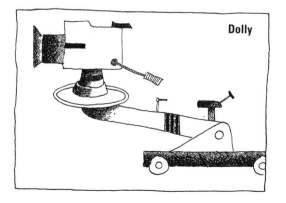

Shots and Shot Transitions

DISSOLVE   A transition from one shot or scene to another in which one shot fades away while the other begins. One shot is superimposed on the other.

DYNAMIC CUTTING   Cutting that places shots or sequences of shots in an order that implies a similarity of themes (also known as MONTAGE).

ESTABLISHING SHOT   The opening shot or scene that introduces the viewer to the production.

FADE (FADE IN or FADE OUT)   The gradual appearance or disappearance of the image from or into darkness on the screen.

FAVOUR   The shot is composed so that one subject, or character, is favoured, e.g., the favoured character may be in the foreground.

INCLUDE   A shot includes subjects who were not in the previous shot, e.g., INCLUDE POLICEWOMAN.

INSERT   A close shot of an object, usually inserted between shots of characters.

INTERCUT   Cutting back and forth between shots. After an intercut, you *resume* the shot.

OVER-SHOULDER SHOT   A shot of a character taken over the shoulder of another character.

POINT OF VIEW (POV) (or subjective camera angle)   The shot is taken from a character's point of view, as in TIM'S POV.

RESUME SHOT   A return to a view after an insert.

TWO SHOT   Shot of two characters, usually a medium shot.

Other

CONTINUITY   The smooth, uninterrupted and logical transition of a production.

EXTERIOR (EXT)   The scene or shot is filmed outside.

FAST MOTION (also known as accelerated motion)   The result of filming at a slower rate than the standard 24 frames per second, and then projecting the film at 24 frames per second. The movements are rapid and uneven. The technique is often used to depict humans as machine-like.

FILTER   A piece of glass or coloured plastic that is placed over the lens of the camera to distort the light that enters the camera, which, in turn, distorts the image and colour on the film. .

FRAME   Refers to one single picture or image, and to the dark line on a piece of film that separates the images.

FREEZE FRAME   A frame of the film is stopped or frozen, so it looks like a still picture.

INTERIOR (INT)   The scene takes place indoors, or on an indoor set.

JUMP CUT (in editing)   A transition between shots that is very abrupt. It is done by cutting out the middle part of a shot and then splicing the two ends of the film together.

MIT OUT SOUND (MOS)   Filming is done without any sound recording.

OFFSCREEN (OS)   Indicates an action or a sound taking place offscreen.

POST-PRODUCTION   The period of time after filming is finished when the editing is done.

ROUGH CUT   The complete footage of the film before the editing has taken place. It is like a rough draft of writing.

SEQUENCE   A section of film that tells a story in itself.

SHOT   The images that are filmed from the time the camera starts to the time it stops, with no cuts.

SLOW MOTION   The effect of filming faster than 24 frames per second and then projecting the film at 24 frames per second.

SOFT FOCUS   Filming is done with a piece of gauze or nylon over the lens to give a dreamy, soft quality to the images.

SPLIT SCREEN   The screen is divided, usually into halves, with a different action in each division. Often used to portray people talking on the telephone.

STOCK SHOTS   Film footage found in film libraries or stock houses of historical events or film that can be used in other productions. The footage is spliced into the film.

VOICE OVER (VO)   A narrator's voice is heard while the image is shown.

SCRIPT WRITING FOR TELEVISION

Scripts for television are written in various formats, depending on what the product is (e.g., commercials, newscasts, programs), whether it is being filmed or videotaped, and how many cameras are being used. Script writers usually identify a specific shot only when they feel it is necessary to establish something important (e.g., a mood, a scene, a fact). The director decides which camera angles and shots will be used.

Note that, in television scripts:

• The scenes are numbered. An intercut is numbered consecutively (e.g., scene 7) but a resume shot is given the original scene number (e.g., scene 6).

• The setting is in upper case (capital letters) at the beginning of each scene and indicates whether a scene is outside (EXT—exterior) or inside (INT—interior), the place, and the time of day.

• The description of what happens in the scene follows the setting and may also be written before and after the dialogue in a scene.

• The character's names are in upper case (capital letters).

• The dialogue is indented. The character's name is centred above this. Any directions to the actor or actress are in brackets and centred, and are on the line between the name of the character and the dialogue.

• Single spacing is used for scene directions and double spacing is used to separate scene headings, scene descriptions, and dialogue. Extra space is given between scenes.
For more information about writing scripts, see page 217 in the Reference Section.

The following script incorporates dialogue, short descriptions of the scenes, sound, and where necessary, directions to the actors. Camera directions have been handwritten. Some directors prefer to draw up a separate list of scenes.

"Blueberry Bicycle", <u>Spirit Bay</u>
Screenplay by Amy Jo Cooper
Story by Donna Young

2

EXT. FALLS. DAY.

2

Establishing shot—start on falls, PAN down and over. Reveal boys—they run into shot.

The cascading falls and the rushing water. The boys strip off their shirts and shoes and jump in. They swim and splash, totally carefree.

RABBIT
Hey, Tonka.

Reverse L (angle) from water.

CV Rabbit ⎱ from
CV Elton ⎰ bank.

RABBIT gives TONKA a splash which stuns him for a minute. TONKA recovers, laughing, and tries to splash RABBIT back. ELTON splashes RABBIT from behind. They wrestle in the water a bit.

CU Tonka, same L.

SOUND: the roaring falls, the splashing of water and underneath, barely perceptible, a low rumble which carries over to

3.
Various shots— truck moves from left to right in frame (keep tight to make more ominous!)

EXT. ROAD. DAY.

3

A very large, very fast, lumber truck comes tearing down the road.

SOUND: The loud rumble of the truck which becomes the roar of

4

EXT. FALLS. DAY.

4

MCV Elton— Rabbit surfaces into shot. Pull back.

ELTON is swimming on his back. RABBIT sur faces from a dive. He shakes the water from his head.

RABBIT
Hey, you look like a whale like that.

ELTON gets himself vertical again.

ELTON
(defensive about his weight)
I do not.
(then angry)
Get off it, string bean!

CU's of boys

Waterfight. RABBIT dives under the surface and swims towards the rocks. He gets out of the water and starts climbing the rocks.

↙ up slightly on Rabbit as he climbs Elton's POV

RABBIT
Watch this, eh?

5   EXT.   BICYCLES ON ROAD. DAY.

The bicycles lay innocently, unaware of their fate.

5 MS from across the road (same shot position in scenes 8, 11, 13.)

6   EXT.   FALLS. DAY.

RABBIT is almost at the top of the rocks.

6 ↙ up Rabbit (Elton in shot.) Elton's POV — Rabbit's POV ↙ down to Elton.

ELTON
Are you going to do a trick, or what?

SOUND: with ELTON, the waterfall; with RABBIT, the truck, gradually increasing.

A slow rumbling is beginning to develop in the air – softly at first, but loudly enough to cause RABBIT to look.

INTERCUT: *— LS (truck coming from right in frame.)*

7   RABBIT'S POV

The bikes on the road and the truck, down the road but fast approaching.

7

RESUME SHOT: FALLS

6

6

ELTON, not getting a response, tries again.

ELTON
That doesn't look like such a big trick
to me, man.

CU Elton
Elton's POV
(Rabbit's back.)

RABBIT, not concerned with ELTON, surveys
the situation from his perspective. He
puts two and two together and comes up with

RABBIT
Oh no.

ELTON
What?

TONKA
(imitating)
What?

CAMERA — Elton's
POV PAN DOWN
with Rabbit

RABBIT is already in action, heading
towards the bikes.

RABBIT
Get moving.

As quickly as his bulk will allow him,
ELTON moves, but stops, thinks twice, then
goes back and gets TONKA.

same as Scene 5

8
EXT. BICYCLES ON ROAD. DAY.   8

The bikes, awaiting their impending doom.

SOUND: the roar of the truck, louder and
louder.

MCU (same shot
in Scene 12)

9
EXT. INSIDE TRUCK. DAY.   9

The DRIVER of the truck is singing along
with the radio. He looks out the window.

INTERCUT:

10

DRIVER'S POV

MLS—travelling

10

The two boys, at a distance, running towards the road. They are waving frantically.

9

same as above

RESUME SHOT: TRUCK

9

The DRIVER waves back, smiling, friendly.

11

*Camera is same
position as in
5 and 9.*

*LS — boys running
toward road.*

EXT. BICYCLES ON ROAD. DAY.

11

The boys call madly as they race towards
the road in their efforts to flag down the
truck.

RABBIT
(waving with all his might)
Hey!

ELTON
Hey, stop.

SOUND: the truck, almost deafening,
drowning the boys' shouts.

12

same as in 9

EXT. INSIDE TRUCK. DAY.

12

The DRIVER, happily singing along with the
radio, waving and smiling. He bumps over
something on the road. His face registers
mild concern which, however, does not last
long.

13

*MS as in 5
LS with boys, of
truck disappearing*

*CU—∠ down
broken bikes.*

EXT. BICYCLES ON ROAD. DAY.

13

The boys reach the road, but they are too
late. The truck has gone and the dust has
begun to settle on what was, just a short
time before, their bicycles. The boys
stand stunned as they survey the mangled
mess.

RESPONSES

1. Discuss the sample shooting instructions that appear on the previous script. Suggest ways you might have shot the scene differently, and to what effect.

2. Over a period of a month's TV viewing, note as many examples of these techniques as you can, and indicate the effects they have created.

3. a) In groups, write a television script for one of the following situations, make up your own scene content, or continue the script you have just read. Your scene should be two or three minutes long. Before you begin writing, choose the type of program you are writing for (e.g., sitcom, crime drama).

• A teenager argues with a parent about his or her need to stay out late to attend a house party after a school dance. The conflict is resolved when a neighbour calls to say there will be parents in the house during the party.

• Two thieves are forced to abandon their goal of cracking a safe in a department store when they mistake the sound of footsteps inside the building for police. They discover the footsteps belong to members of a rival gang.

b) Mark camera directions on your script.

c) Choose the best scripts of the class. In groups, dramatize the scenes and, if you have access to the equipment, videotape them.

d) Compare the scripts with the scenes you enacted or taped. Discuss what directions were most effective and why. Which directions would you change? Give your reasons.

4. If you have access to the equipment, make an instructional video that demonstrates some of the camera techniques you have learned, e.g., close-ups, pan shots, over-shoulder shots, tilt, soft focus, crane shots. You could have a narrator describe each shot as it is shown.

TV AND OUR PERCEPTIONS OF THE WORLD

The world of television is very different from everyday reality—on TV, male characters are mostly young professionals, women are usually young and attractive, and life is often very violent or very glamourous. While network programmers insist television is harmless fantasy, social scientists claim the fantasy is not harmless because it presents a distorted view of the world.

Arabs— TV's Villains of Choice

by Jack G. Shaheen

One of the most serious criticisms aimed at television is that it presents stereotyped views of minorities. Since most of the television watched by Canadians is imported from the United States, we are largely subjected to the American view of American stereotypes. For example, following the energy crisis of 1973, Arabs became convenient scapegoats for the economic hardships experienced by North Americans. The following article excerpt illustrates how television shows have reflected a negative view of Arabs.

Turn to any channel, to any show from *Alice* to *Hart to Hart*. Billionaires, bombers, and belly dancers are virtually the only TV images of Arabs that Americans ever see. . . .

Extensive interviews with television executives suggest that they permit Arab stereotypes because they have run out of other villains. Hollywood films preserve traditional stereotypes, and television follows Hollywood's lead.

Some might argue that television has stereotyped most ethnic groups, not just Arabs. But through organized pressure, many of these images have been replaced. The popular comedy *Benson* featured a black as the savvy, sophisticated aide to a governor. *Chico and the Man* featured a Hispanic in a leading role as a tough, lovable, Los Angeles Chicano. And Captain Frank Furillo of *Hill Street Blues* is the Italian-American Eliot Ness, just the right blend of law-and-order cop and compassionate civil servant. Arabs have not received the same

second look as these groups.

Grotesque Arab images often appear in TV dramas. In one episode of *Charlie's Angels*, Arab terrorists attempt to murder an Arab delegation as well as scores of innocent Americans.

In *The Powers of Matthew Star*, "Mr. Moustafa" tries to purchase the services of kidnapped American geniuses.

In *Hart to Hart*, Arab dignitaries try to assassinate their king.

In *Small & Frye*, the detectives jeer: "You can tell the man's an Arab. He stole the bedsheets from the Aladdin Hotel."

In *Callahan*, an ABC pilot program, a mythical oil-rich Arab nation's symbol—a dagger—is stolen. If the dagger isn't found, the Arabs will "shut off" America's oil supply. . . .

Television comedy, too, has its share of anti-Arab barbs: Bob Hope, for example, in his 1982 *Pink Panther/ Thanksgiving Special*, said, "Not everyone in Beverly Hills has a turkey. The Arabs sacrifice a goat."

When Mork prepares a Moroccan meal for Mindy in a *Mork and Mindy* episode, he insists they eat with their fingers. First they wash their hands in dishwashing liquid. "Feet next," chuckles Mork. Silverware is a no-no because "all the silverware in Morocco is used to break out of prisons." Mindy gags on the food. Mork sighs, "It's so

> *"I don't have any other explanation for stereotyping other than it's easy," says Harve Bennet, producer of "The Bionic Woman"* . . .

hard to get fresh camel lips in Boulder."

"The great enemy of truth is very often not the lie—deliberate, continued, and dishonest—but the myth—persistent, persuasive, and unrealistic," said President John F. Kennedy. Here are a few of the myths that TV writers employ about Arabs:

Arabs are buying up America. In reality, European nations and Canada account for 80 percent of foreign investment in the United States, according to U.S. government reports. Direct investment by OPEC countries amounts to less than one half of 1 percent of all foreign investments. Arabs buy less than 1 percent of the American agricultural land sold annually.

Arabs are fabulously wealthy. The average gross national product of per capita income in the Arab world, notes the U.S. Department of Commerce, is about $1000 a year, or one eighth the per capita gross national product of the United States. . . .

OPEC's members are all Arab. Only seven of the thirteen member nations of the Organization of Petroleum Exporting Countries are Arab. Of the five largest oil-producing nations, only one, Saudi Arabia, is Arab.

Iranians are Arabs. Iranians are Persians. They are not Semites, as Arabs are. . . . They do not speak Arabic, but Farsi, an Indo-European tongue that shares several characteristics with Western European languages.

All Palestinians are terrorists. The Palestinian population is made up of more than four million peace-loving people who, like the once-scattered Jews, believe they have a historical right to a homeland. Explains an Israeli official: "Since 1948, out of approximately 450 000 Israeli Arabs, only about 400 have joined 'terrorist' groups." . . .

"I think the Arab stereotype is attractive to a number of people," says James Baerg, director of program practices for ABC-TV. "It is an easy thing to do. It is the thing that is going to be most readily accepted by a large number of the audience. It is the same thing as throwing in violence when an episode is slow."

"I don't have any other explanation for stereotyping other than it's easy," says Harve Bennet, producer of *The Bionic Woman* and *The*

Six Million Dollar Man. "Let me put it to you this way. Do you know how to play charades? Television is one great charade. You don't go for the meat of the material. You do a pantomime of a guy in a burnoose. It's sign language. It saves the writer the ultimate discomfort of having to think."

He also notes that the television medium itself often forces the writer to give subjects and characters only cursory treatment. "Sometimes, unthinkingly and under deadline pressure in a medium that has no lead time, everyone tends to think in quick solutions."

Some television officials say it would help if more Arabs worked in television. Scriptwriter Irving Pearlberg thinks Arabs should form a television-monitoring group similar to ones other minorities have. "Any minority group that has achieved anything [in broadcasting] has done it through organized pressure," says Pearlberg. . . .

But whom to pressure? "Go to the top, to the networks," advises Pearlberg, "because whatever pressure they exert goes downward and would affect everything. You should get to a point where a broadcast standards division of any network will say, . . . 'We will not accept anything that can be construed as anti-Arab.' If that can be done, I think the battle is half won."

As TV comedian Milton Berle said in 1951, "There is no room for prejudice in our profession."

—CHANNELS,
MARCH/APRIL 1984

Networks Read Those Cards and Letters *By Sally Steenland*

We've all heard of the celebrated cases of television shows — *Cagney and Lacey...Designing Women* — that were saved from cancellation by thousands of viewers who wrote in to urge the networks to keep them on the air. What most viewers don't know, however, is the sophisticated nature of the system that exists to file, computer-code, itemize, report on (and even read) letters from viewers. Letters provide sought-after feed-back from viewers that can make a difference in how issues are covered, how shows develop, what characters are introduced — or how they change.

What did you think, for example, about a program's treatment of a controversial topic such as abortion? Or the portrayal of women on a new dramatic series? Or the portrayal of a racial or cultural group on a series? What about a movie-of-the-week that you would watch if it were a regular series? The networks want to know.

Network executives say their awareness of trouble spots in programs is prompted by viewer mail. If they haven't received letters of complaint from women or Hispanics or steelworkers, for example, they assume these groups are content with what they see each week on the screen. Producers of shows tell of reading viewer mail to learn about audience reaction to characters....

It's important to write letters of praise as well as ones of criticism. Some pointers: Be sure to include a legible name and return address. Write an individualized letter. Letters that are mass-generated have less clout. And be concise. Keep network addresses handy; better yet, preaddress postcards to each network and keep them on top of the TV. Arrange to watch TV and write personal letters together as part of a group meeting.... By all means, let network and cable stations know when you're pleased about something—and why. Quality programming needs all the support it can get.

Television can seem to be the ultimate in one-way communication. But you *can* talk back — regularly, articulately, effectively. Write a letter today.

—Media and Values, Summer/Fall, 1987

RESPONSES

1. Discuss the meaning of "stereotype" and think of some examples of stereotypes you have encountered. As a class, write a definition of the word.

2. The author lists five myths about Arabs that the media have promoted. What do you think the effect of these myths is on the average person's attitudes towards new Canadians from an Arab nation? Towards an Arabian dignitary on a state visit?

3. Discuss the statement by Harve Bennett, producer of *The Bionic Woman* and *The Six Million Dollar Man*. "I don't have any explanation for stereotyping other than it's easy." If you could talk with him, what would you tell him about the causes and effects of TV stereotyping?

4. Does the stereotyped view of Arabs that Jack Shaheen described still exist today? Have other ethnic groups been successful at using organized pressure to remove stereotyped images from television shows? A 1980 study of Canadian cultural groups on prime-time English television revealed that 90 percent of the characters shown on entertainment programs were white North Americans. Complete your own study of cultural groups on television. Working in groups, examine the portrayal of different cultural groups over a three-day period. Record your findings in your media logs. Include all types of programs as well as commercials. Be sure to note the context in which a member of a cultural minority appears. For example, is the character a hero or villain, winner or loser? Is he or she employed or unemployed? Does he or she appear with other members of the cultural group? Summarize your conclusions, noting any characteristics you found common to the stereotypes you viewed. Present your conclusions to the class.

5. In groups, make suggestions that TV producers might consider for overcoming the problem of stereotyping in their programs.

6. Think of some old movies and re-runs of old TV shows that portray stereotypes. Do you think they should still be shown on TV? Have a class discussion.

TV as a Shaper of Culture

by Christopher Reed

Dr. Gerbner's studies cover light viewers (those who watch up to two hours a day) and heavy viewers (four hours and above). Commercial TV's need for a vast audience pulls its content and its viewers toward mainstream blandness. Thus, heavy viewers tended to regard themselves as "average," "middle class," and politically "moderate" despite their actual status or opinions, Dr. Gerbner found.

In fact, these "moderates" were usually well to the right of what would normally be regarded as centrist on such social matters as race, minorities, personal rights, freedom of expression, and law and order. This reflects TV's portrayal of the world as dangerous and nasty through its dramatization of crime and violence and obsession with disasters and mayhem.

Dr. Gerbner believes this stems from commercial TV's "mass mobilization of consumption." As a temple devoted to the glorification of instant gratification via its advertising, TV is bound to encourage fast and simple solutions to material desires. The world on the small

Some of the stereotyped images shown on TV programs seem easy to identify, but commercial television can distort reality in other ways. Programs and commercials contain hidden messages that viewers may or may not be aware of.

Professor George Gerbner has been studying TV for 20 years. He has done extensive research on the implications of television content on North American society. Because so many U.S. shows are broadcast in other countries—some critics call this cultural imperialism—Gerbner's findings are probably applicable to most of the industrialized world. Is TV just a harmless fantasy? Think about this question as you read this excerpt from an article about Prof. Gerbner.

screen, and those who people it, are far from reality. Average viewers see 300 screen characters a week in prime time. They are portrayed in apparent realism, but bear little relation to their real-life counterparts or to the viewers' actual world. Watchers see 30 police officers, seven lawyers, three judges, 12 nurses and 10 doctors a week, but only one engineer or scientist. Service or manual workers comprise 10 percent of the screen cast but are 65 percent of the real world. Men outnumber women on TV three to one.

The popular male age range is from 25 to 55, but for women 25 to 35. People under 18 are a third, and those over 65 a fifth of their actual presence in the U.S. population.

Violence is seen six times an hour in peak time, of which two incidents per evening are fatalities (so that in 10 years a heavy viewer will

have seen about 7000 screen deaths). Women and the elderly, although actually under-represented in comparison with reality, are disproportionately the victims. Young white males occur most often in violent scenes, but are least likely to be victims—the opposite of the real world where they are the most likely—after young black males—to be injured or killed.

Since this is TV's version of mainstream reality, no wonder heavy viewers believe they are moderates and no wonder their opinions are conservative. TV violence contributes to apprehension and increased support of right-wing ''law and order'' campaigns.

Aggravating the anxiety is the medium's preoccupation with crime—among the week's 300 characters are 23 criminals and crime is at least 10 times more frequent on the screen than in life. Nor are children spared: during their weekend daytime programs, the ''kidvid ghetto'' as advertisers call it, there are 18 violent acts an hour.

A curious side effect of the violence is the role of medicine. Screen violence rarely causes pain or suffering and never seems to need medical attention. On the average, only 6 to 7 percent of major characters require treatment.

Nevertheless, the doctors are beyond reproach: fewer than 4 percent are shown as evil—half the percentage shown in other professions. Doctors are also characterized as fairer, more sociable, and warmer than other characters and are rated as more intelligent, more rational, and more stable and fair than the (female) nurses. The MD "symbolizes power, authority and knowledge and possesses an almost uncanny ability to dominate and control the lives of others."

If this helps to explain the demigod status of physicians, the daytime soap operas must contribute to what strikes many foreigners as rampant U.S. hypochondria.

Nearly half of all soap opera characters are involved in health-related occurrences. Half the pregnancies end in miscarriage and 16 percent in the mother's death. Health is the most frequently discussed topic. The second most common location in the soaps is a doctor's surgery.

This preoccupation with health could have something to do with the TV characters' reckless attitude toward it. On most shows, seatbelts are rarely used and few safety precautions are taken at work. Eating, drinking, or talking about food occur nine times an hour in peak time, yet characters almost always remain sober—and slim.

TV may explain why Americans eat and drink in public so much— gobbling and gulping junk food and sticky drinks while going up in elevators, driving cars, or shopping. TV people eat on the run all the time (one commercial shows two men eating pizzas while practising basketball) and scenes of families sitting down to a balanced dinner hardly ever appear in the shows. Dr. Gerbner links this constant snacking with an attempt to resolve frustration, a point echoed by U.S. dieticians, who constantly warn the overweight millions against compulsive eating.

Junk food is much advertised on TV, of course, but Dr. Gerbner believes the programs are "worse" than the commercials.

As the advertising criterion for TV's content is cost per 1000 viewers, rather than pure income from commercials, TV shows may be put

Eating, drinking, or talking about food occur nine times an hour in peak time . . .

together with little concern for quality or accuracy in the infinite quest for the impossible: a show costing nothing but seen by everyone.

"We are only now discovering our environment of symbols and messages," says Dr. Gerbner, "rather than in the conventional sense of our surroundings—and only now realizing that, as with other things, these are also mass-produced. We should alert our citizens to this. . . . Perhaps what we need most now is a prime-time program alerting viewers to the hidden political messages behind the messages they know about."

Simpler might be a warning like the one now carried on cigarette packets, to precede a soap opera or prime-time drama: "This show may turn you into a neurotic right-winger."

—*THE GLOBE AND MAIL*, TORONTO, MAY 14, 1985

RESPONSES

1. Explain the following statement of Christopher Reed: "Commercial TV's need for a vast audience pulls its content and its viewers towards mainstream blandness." How does the statement relate to the article by Paul Klein, "Why You Watch What You Watch When You Watch" (p. 67)? Do you agree with this assessment of prime-time shows? Explain.

2. What is Professor Gerbner's explanation for heavy viewers' right-wing outlook? If possible, talk to a heavy viewer to discover his or her opinions on issues such as capital punishment, crime, racial discrimination, and equal opportunity a) in real life experiences and b) as portrayed on television. Summarize your findings and present them to your group or class.

3. a) Have each member of your group watch a different prime-time program and its commercials to verify the statement, "Eating, drinking, or talking about food occur nine times an hour in peak time."
b) Discuss Gerbner's belief that television programs are "worse" than commercials for encouraging viewers to snack. Start by discussing in your group whether you or members of your household have ever been consciously influenced to eat certain foods by what you have seen on TV.

4. a) Working in groups, examine the content of one night's prime-time television commercials and programs. Compile the results in a chart in your media log. Include information in categories such as the following: the relative ages of men and women; the situations in which children, teenagers, or the elderly appear; the professions that are represented; the age and sex of victims of crime. Note the problems the characters face and how their problems are resolved. Present your findings to the class and discuss what they reveal.
b) Use the results of your survey to present a parody of the "reality" of a typical television show. You might want to refer to "Meet Me Tonight in TV Dreamland" in the Advertising chapter (p. 282) for a sample parody. You may find it helpful to assign the responsibilities for scripting and presenting the show (and commercials) to different groups in the class. If the equipment is available, you may wish to tape your presentation. See the Reference Section for tips on script writing and videotaping.

5. Do you agree with the statement, "The world on the small screen, and those who people it, are far from reality."? Give examples to support your opinion.

6. Write a short essay on one of the following topics:
a) the "demi-god status" of doctors or athletes
b) television's obsession with health problems
c) the connection between television and poor eating habits
Share your essay with others.

7. Imagine you are a reporter from another planet. Use the information you have collected from the surveys you have done in this chapter to write a short article about life on Earth. Describe the photographs or illustrations that would accompany your article.

How do television shows entertain us? According to author Morris Wolfe, it is not just the subject matter of commercial television programs that keeps audiences interested. Wolfe says that TV shows keep audiences' attention by "jolting" them. "Jolts" include violent acts, rapid cutting, high decibels in the soundtrack, and sudden movements. As you read the following excerpt, think about how many jpm's (jolts per minute) you like to experience in your television viewing.

The First Law of Commercial Television

by Morris Wolfe

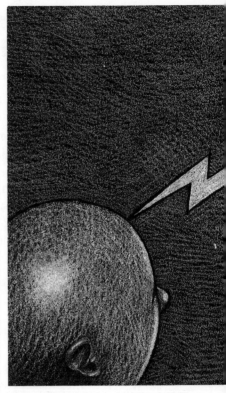

Given the number of jolts our viewing of U.S. television has conditioned us to expect, it's easy for Canadians to fall into the trap of trying to imitate the American style. American programmers discovered some time ago that most of us have short attention spans and that those attention spans can be easily manipulated. They realized that if a long time goes by without a jolt of verbal or physical or emotional violence on the screen, or if the picture doesn't change quickly enough as a result of a jolt of rapid editing or camera movement, or movement by people or objects within the frame, or if the soundtrack doesn't have enough decibels, viewers will switch to a channel and programme that gives them more of those things. That's how almost all the top American shows get their audiences. They obey the First Law of Commercial Television: *Thou shalt give them enough jolts per minute (jpm's) or thou shalt lose them.*

Let me illustrate what I mean by describing the jpm content of an episode of an American programme . . . *Charlie's Angels*. This particular episode had three murders and seven attempted murders (including one in a bed that blew up and another resulting from an exploding tennis ball); one accidental death (in a plane crash); two serious injuries (one in a fall from the top of an oil storage tank); seven acts of miscellaneous violence (including the release of poison gas);

and five crimes—illegal entries, etc.—committed by the Angels themselves in the cause of justice. This list doesn't include other kinds of jolts—such as car chases and rapid editing—to say nothing of the sexual jolts for men provided by the Angels' jiggles and innuendo. . . .

Now we have *Miami Vice*, a new kind of show, the rock video police programme. It uses rock selections by popular performers—such as the Rolling Stones—and combines them with tightly edited visual material. The result is television not unlike the videos one sees on *MuchMusic*. (The programme is simulcast on FM radio in a number of American cities.) And, as with rock videos, plot doesn't (and isn't supposed to) make sense. All that matters is the tension built up in the viewer through the beat of the music and the editing. The programme plays with the viewer's nervous system. . . .

Sesame Street is another example of a popular American programme with high jpm content. The programme, which is seen by more than 75 percent of North America's two-to-five-year-olds, became a hit as soon as it began in 1969. . . . *Sesame Street* was unabashedly modelled on the staccato, fragmented style of a cluster of television commercials. "All art," Walter Pater wrote in the late nineteenth century, "constantly aspires toward the condition of music." In the late twentieth century, however, all television increasingly aspires to the condition of the TV commercial. *Sesame Street* consists of an average of forty-five items per hour—commercials for the letter Y, for the number 3, etc. The shortest items are five seconds long, the longest just over three minutes.

The programme is so popular that it can now be said, as it was of the old British Empire, that the sun never sets on *Sesame Street*. It's probably the most widely viewed (and celebrated) programme in the world. It's seen in almost sixty countries—in Brazil, in Indonesia, in Japan, in Pago Pago and in Zambia. Poland, Yugoslavia, and Romania show it, even mainland China has a version. . . . The children in McLuhan's global village are all watching *Sesame Street*.

But *Sesame Street* has its detractors. Mexican writer Guillermo Tenorio, for example, has criticized *Plaza Sesamo* as an "imperialist intrusion" into the social, educational and political life of countries where it's shown. In Brit-

Undesirable characters are crushed under the weight of huge objects; letters get smashed or kicked . . .

ain, the BBC has refused to show *Sesame Street*. The BBC's head of children's programming asked "Do we really have to import commercial hard-sell techniques into Britain because . . . American children will not watch anything quiet or thoughtful?" Concern has been expressed in New Zealand about how loud and aggressive the Muppets are.

Others have criticized the programme's "violence," which they see as typically American. Undesirable characters are crushed under the weight of huge objects; letters get smashed or kicked off the screen. . . .

I spent many pleasant hours watching *Sesame Street* with my children when they were young. Now I sometimes still watch it alone. There's no doubt about the programme's entertainment value—each item is as beautifully crafted as the best-made commercials. But I do have doubts about its educational value. *Sesame Street*, after all, was originally intended to prepare children to read—to teach them "reading readiness." Research has shown that not just underprivileged children (for whom the show was originally intended) but all two-to-five-year-olds who watch *Sesame Street* know the names of the letters of the alphabet and the numbers from 1 to 20 better than those who don't watch the programme. Given *Sesame Street's* constant repetition of that information, it would be astonishing if they didn't. The result is that more children enter school these days with the alphabet more firmly fixed in their heads than ever before.

But knowing the alphabet doesn't make one literate, any more than knowing the names of tools makes one a carpenter. I find it hard to believe that *Sesame Street* prepares children to read. Books, after all, have static printed pages and a very slow pace. *Sesame Street* has

Philip Michael Thomas and Don Johnson of *Miami Vice*—the "rock video police programme."

neither. I would argue that what the programme teaches is not a love of books, but a love of high jpm television. One doesn't graduate from *Sesame Street* to reading Victorian novels. On the contrary, I suspect one graduates to watching high jpm programmes like . . . rock videos. . . .

None of what I've said is meant to suggest that high jpm television programmes impair viewer intelligence. What I am suggesting is that a steady diet of nothing *but* high jpm television tends to condition viewers' nervous systems to respond only to a certain kind of stimulation. Their boredom thresholds are frequently so low that TV viewers find it difficult to enjoy anything that isn't fast-paced.

I have other reservations about *Sesame Street*, especially about some of the invisible lessons it teaches. The programme is sexist; 75 percent of the cartoon and Muppet characters are male. Other invisible lessons include the notion that learning is an activity grown-ups initiate and control and that children are passive participants in; that one never goes off on tangents; and—now that stores everywhere carry a stock of *Sesame Street* products—that everyone has something to sell. . . .

—*JOLTS: THE TV WASTELAND AND THE CANADIAN OASIS*, 1985

RESPONSES

1. If your class has access to a television, watch a TV program together, and count the jolts per minute, both in the program and in the commercials. To help you identify the jolts, remember the camera and audio techniques you studied earlier in this chapter.

2. In groups, write a script for a news announcer or sportscaster, using an exaggerated amount of jpm's. See page 88 for tips on script writing. You may wish to use an interview situation. If the equipment is available, make a video with sound effects. Present your scene or video to the class.

3. Morris Wolfe says that Canadians might try to imitate the high jpm style of American programming. Working in groups, select one scene each from an American and a Canadian drama—for example, *L.A. Law* and *Street Legal*. (A scene is usually about five to seven minutes long.) Count the jolts per minute in each sample. Do the same with segments from American and Canadian current affairs programs such as *60 Minutes* and *the fifth estate* or with American and Canadian newscasts. Do you notice any difference in the number of jolts? What purpose do the jolts serve in each case? Write a brief essay summarizing your findings and share it with others.

4. Refer to the script you wrote after examining television techniques (p. 84). How many jolts did you include in your script and camera directions or use in your videotape? Why did you use the jolts when you wrote the scene?

5. Professor Gerbner suggests that television has a number of hidden messages (see p. 101). What are the hidden messages in *Sesame Street*, according to Morris Wolfe? Do you agree or disagree with Wolfe's assessment of them? Why?

6. Do Wolfe's observations about *Sesame Street* apply to other TV shows for children? In groups, watch a variety of programs for young viewers. Try to watch both American and Canadian shows. Count the jolts per minute for each show. Present your findings to the class.

7. Wolfe says American TV programmers think that most audiences have short attention spans and are easily manipulated. Write a letter to an imaginary programmer stating your response to this idea.

Neil Postman, an American educator, has written several books that criticize the role television plays in our lives. In this excerpt, he examines the extent to which television and entertainment have affected us.

The Age of Show Business

by Neil Postman

I have heard (but not verified) that some years ago the Lapps postponed for several days their annual and, one supposes, essential migratory journey so they could find out who shot J.R. . . .

To say that television is entertaining is merely banal. Such a fact is hardly threatening to a culture, not even worth writing a book about. It may even be a reason for rejoicing. Life, as we like to say, is not a highway strewn with flowers. The sight of a few blossoms here and there may make our journey a trifle more endurable. The Lapps undoubtedly thought so. We may surmise that the 90 million Americans who watch television every night also think so. But what I am claiming here is not that television is entertaining but that it has made entertainment itself the natural format for the representation of all experience. Our television set keeps us in constant communion with the world, but it does so with a face whose smiling countenance is unalterable. The problem is not that television presents us with entertaining subject matter but that all subject matter is presented as entertaining, which is another issue altogether. . . .

Film, records, and radio (now that it is an adjunct of the music industry) are, of course, equally devoted to entertaining the culture, and their effects in altering the style of American discourse are not insignificant. But television is different because it encompasses all forms of discourse. No one goes to a movie to find out about government policy or the latest scientific advances. No one buys a record to find about the baseball scores or the weather or the latest murder. No one turns on radio anymore for soap operas or a presidential address (if a television set is at hand). But everyone goes to television for all these things and more, which is why television resonates so powerfully throughout the culture. Television is our culture's principal mode of knowing about itself. Therefore—and this is the critical point—how television stages the world becomes the model for

> *As the details of her achievements were being recounted, many people left their seats and surged toward the stage.*

how the world is properly to be staged. It is not merely that on the television screen entertainment is the metaphor for all discourse. It is that off the screen the same metaphor prevails. As typography once dictated the style of conducting politics, religion, business, education, law, and other important social matters, television now takes command. In courtrooms, classrooms, operating rooms, board rooms, churches, and even airplanes, Americans no longer talk to each other, they entertain each other. They do not exchange ideas; they exchange images. They do not argue with propositions; they argue with good looks, celebrities and commercials. For the message of television as metaphor is not only that all the world is a stage but that the stage is located in Las Vegas, Nevada. . . .

At the commencement exercises at Yale University in 1983, several honorary degrees were awarded, including one to Mother Teresa. As she and other humanitarians and

scholars, each in turn, received their awards, the audience applauded appropriately but with a slight hint of reserve and impatience, for it wished to give its heart to the final recipient who waited shyly in the wings. As the details of her achievements were being recounted, many people left their seats and surged toward the stage to be closer to the great woman. And when the name Meryl Streep was announced, the audience unleashed a sonic boom of affection to wake the New Haven dead. . . .

Prior to the 1984 presidential elections, two candidates [Ronald Reagan and Walter Mondale] con-

fronted each other on television in what were called "debates." . . . The men were less concerned with giving arguments than with "giving off" impressions, which is what television does best. Post-debate commentary largely avoided any evaluation of the candidates' ideas, since there were none to evaluate. Instead, the debates were conceived as boxing matches, the relevant question being, Who KO'd whom? The answer was determined by the "style" of the men—how they looked, fixed their gaze, smiled, and delivered one-liners. In the second debate, President Reagan got off a swell one-liner when asked a question about his age. The following day, several newspapers indicated that Ron had KO'd Fritz with his joke. Thus, the leader of the free world is chosen by the people in the Age of Television.

What all of this means is that our culture has moved toward a new way of conducting its business, especially its important business. The nature of its discourse is changing as the demarcation line between what is show business and what is not becomes harder to see with each passing day. . . .

—*AMUSING OURSELVES TO DEATH:*
PUBLIC DISCOURSE IN THE AGE OF
SHOW BUSINESS, 1985

RESPONSES

1. Identify some of the areas of life that have been particularly affected by the "show biz metaphor"—the concern to entertain first and foremost. What negative influence might this have? Suggest possible solutions.

2. Discuss why you agree or disagree with Neil Postman's statement that "how television stages the world becomes the model for how the world is properly to be staged."

3. Compare Postman's article with Morris Wolfe's material on jolts per minute (p. 104). How are the ideas of these two authors compatible?

4. What was your reaction to the author's description of the commencement exercises at Yale University? Do you think this kind of behaviour is typical? If the lead singer from the current top rock group had been waiting in the wings, would your class have acted the same way? Write a brief description of that scenario.

5. Postman suggests that abstract subjects such as philosophy, religion, and science do not translate well into the entertainment format of television. He says that the subtle qualities of these subjects can't be portrayed visually but we are deluded into thinking we see it all.
   a) Make a list of current programs on both American and Canadian networks that focus on topics like this. Some examples of these programs are *The Nature of Things*, *Man Alive*, and *Nova*. After viewing a cross-section of these programs, discuss whether you agree or disagree with Postman's opinion.
   b) In groups, write proposals (one to two pages long) for a television show on an abstract subject such as moral dilemmas or the nature of religious belief. Have someone from another group take on the role of Neil Postman. Convince "Postman" that your show would both entertain and educate viewers.

CANADIAN TELEVISION

Canadian programming on TV plays an important role in defining and reflecting the Canadian cultural identity. Just how that should be done is an issue that has been debated for years. How effectively it has been done, and is being done today, is an issue that has often provoked sharp criticism of the Canadian television industry.

What is the problem with Canadian television? Are Canadian shows more boring than American shows? Or is there just not enough Canadian programming?

Morris Wolfe argues that Canadian shows *are* less exciting because they contain fewer audience-grabbing jolts than American shows. But it is also true that there are, quite simply, more American shows on TV. Seventy-five percent of television programs available in the evenings on Canadian TV are American, according to an article by A.W. Johnson, president of the Canadian Broadcasting League. "Out of 220 hours of TV programming available each week, only 60 are Canadian, with the balance being American."

It is far cheaper for Canadians to buy American programs than to make their own. Johnson says that "making up the deficit could cost upward of $1 billion." Should something be done about the deficit? Even if we do spend more money on Canadian programming, how can we be sure Canadians will watch these programs?

RESPONSES

1. Suppose that the $1 billion was available to make programs for Canadian viewers. In groups, make a list of shows that you think would attract the viewers currently watching American programming. Give your shows titles and present a brief description of each show. Suggest ideas for theme music and think of whom you might cast in your shows. Explain how your shows would be distinctively Canadian.

2. Do you think Canada should have equal time on Canadian screens? Write to or interview people who are part of Canadian cultural industries and ask their views.

3. Debate the following. "Resolved: That broadcasting significant Canadian content is essential to Canada's national dream if we are to enter the 1990s with a sense of accomplishment."

On Top of the News in Prime Time

Not all the criticism aimed at Canadian television shows is negative. For example, the CBC news program *The Journal* has earned a large audience in Canada, and is highly respected around the world. It has provided us with a view of our own country and a distinctly Canadian view of current affairs. As you read the following excerpt, consider what makes *The Journal* different from and superior to many current affairs programs.

by Martin Knelman

Can reruns of *Dallas* and *Three's Company* do what the War of 1812 failed to do—destroy Canada's will for national survival and deliver it into the hands of the Americans? That's only a slight simplification of the view of nationalists north of the border when they argue that English-speaking Canada is being colonized by cable television. The state-owned Canadian Broadcasting Corporation has always had the mandate of holding the country together, reflecting its scattered regions to one another, but CBC television, tarnished by commercials and imported American entertainment series, hasn't enjoyed the same respect as its higher-minded rival, CBC radio.

Now, however, CBC-TV has something to crow about. Its five-nights-a-week, prime-time information hour—a 22-minute newscast called *The National*, followed by a daring 38-minute current affairs program, *The Journal*—has turned out to be a surprising hit. Going head-to-head with popular entertainment shows, the package has doubled the CBC's audience in the critical 10-to-11 p.m. time slot, creating a formidable journalistic institution in less than four years and giving the CBC a strong new identity and sense of purpose just when it was most sorely needed. It also gives Canada the first hopeful sign in more than a decade that it has a fighting chance to resist American domination of its airwaves. Mark Starowicz, *The Journal's* executive producer, talks only half-jokingly of his mission to "stop the Americans at the border." . . .

It was a rare stroke of boldness for the CBC in early 1982 when the network moved its flagship newscast, *The National*, back one hour from 11 p.m. to 10 p.m. and coupled it with the all-new *Journal*. The tandem not only took viewers away from the U.S.-produced series on other channels, but also drew some 500 000 Canadians who previously hadn't been watching any television at that hour.

The Journal wins 22 to 25 percent of viewers, remarkably large shares for Canada, where much of the urban population can choose among a dozen or more Canadian and U.S. channels. Over the course of a week, one third of all English-speaking adult Canadians watch the program.

Already *The Journal's* influence extends beyond Canada because it has become the world's largest producer of television documentaries, exporting many to foreign broadcasters. "*The Journal's* international reporting is superior to

anything I've ever seen on any North American network," says Les Crystal, executive producer of PBS's *MacNeil/Lehrer NewsHour*, which uses more than 20 *Journal* documentaries a year from such places as Lebanon, Pakistan, Chile, and Ethiopia. Crystal, a former president of NBC News, ranks *The Journal* "among the best in the world."

In a way, the program is the CBC's attempt to revive its great days of current affairs programming. In the 1950s, when Canadian viewers had fewer choices on the dial, CBC television had a huge audience. Current affairs programs were the CBC's greatest achievements between 1962 when the network went on the air and 1966, when the abrasive *This Hour Has Seven Days* (a precursor of *60 Minutes*) was killed off by CBC manage-

"The Journal" wins 22 to 25% of viewers, remarkably large shares for Canada . . .

ment. That the CBC took the risk, 16 years later, of launching *The Journal* was largely due to the policies of CBC vice president Peter Herrndorf, who later left the network.

Behind the CBC's decision to launch *The Journal* lay the notion that if it could create one prime-time hour that revealed the country to itself and saw the rest of the world from a uniquely Canadian viewpoint, the network would be on the way to justifying its existence and continued tax support. But even before the show got on the air,

Opposite page: Canadian television journalist Barbara Frum

jealousy toward the program was rampant among CBC employees, partly because it was getting so much attention. *The Journal's* cocky style presented an irresistible target, and the people who ran it were regarded as brash upstarts. . . .

Starowicz had to put together the people, format, and technology that would get *The Journal* on the air. He assembled a staff of 136, most

> **From the start the producers decided to shoot with electronic newsgathering (ENG) equipment . . .**

of whom work in the program's crowded Toronto headquarters, and was allocated an annual budget of $14 million. . . .

From the start the producers decided to shoot with electronic newsgathering (ENG) equipment rather than film cameras. ENG is highly mobile and there's no waiting for film to be processed. The ENG image looks crisper and more modern than a film image and has the look of live coverage.

The Journal also turned to technology to get interviews without bringing guests to studios or resorting to expensive, extremely cumbersome live television relays. Starowicz and his team solved the problem by reviving the flexible and economic "double-ender" interview technique developed in television's creatively explosive early days by CBS's [Columbia Broadcasting System] *See It Now*. In a *Journal* double-ender, interviewer

and guest can't see one another. They converse by audio lines while a crew videotapes the guest. Later the pictures go by satellite to Toronto, where, through the magic of electronic editing, the guest's face appears on a screen in the studio. . . .

The program has given the CBC a nightly national platform and a chance to cover world events without the pressure faced by American networks. Its cool, detached tone and air of calm neutrality seem definitively Canadian. It has become so much a part of Canada's psychic landscape, it's hard to remember that only [some] years ago it didn't exist. When you check into a hotel, switch on the TV, and catch that boom-boom theme music, followed by the let's-get-down-to-business facial expression of Barbara Frum—that's how you know you're in Canada.

Buoyed by this success, Mark Starowicz harbors fantasies of even greater triumphs. *Journal* documentaries, already shown in 20 countries outside of Canada, are already offering an alternative, more dispassionate slant on world affairs than the one offered by the American news media. So why couldn't *The Journal* be beamed by satellite to every corner of the planet where there is an English-language audience ready for information without any American bias? Starowicz may no longer be content with stopping the American fans from crossing the border—he may turn out to be a closet imperialist.

—*CHANNELS*, SEPTEMBER/OCTOBER 1985

RESPONSES

1. Watch as many editions of *The Journal* as you can in one week. What do you think makes *The Journal* such a distinctive program? Discuss any items that you think offered high entertainment value.

2. How is the success of programs such as *The Journal* heavily dependent on the quality of the interviews? Discuss your ideas, using examples from interviews you have watched and/or heard.

3. Why did the executive producer of *The Journal* decide to use the double-ender interview? After watching one or more of them on *The Journal*, discuss your response to this technique.

4. To what extent do you think *The Journal* offers a distinctively Canadian perspective? Give reasons for your answer. How important is it that a Canadian viewpoint of the news be presented to Canadians? To other countries?

ISSUES FOR FURTHER STUDY

Re-read what you wrote about your view of television at the beginning of this chapter. Has your opinion changed?

This chapter has helped you investigate the factors that influence television and how, in turn, the medium influences viewers. Has an increased awareness of how television works caused any changes in your viewing habits? Has it affected your enjoyment of television? If so, explain how it has.

As you watch and examine television and as you work on the following research questions, continue to evaluate your attitude towards TV and its influence in your life.

1. Is it true that television has a negative influence on society? Or does TV just have an image problem? If television programming is bad, who is responsible for changing it—members of the television industry or the audience? Write an essay or newspaper editorial about the influence of television on our lives. Or, if you wish, create an advertisement or commercial warning about the dangers of television or explaining its benefits.

2. *Being There*, a novel by Jerzy Kosinski, is about a man whose whole world revolves around TV and who eventually becomes a TV celebrity himself. Read the book or see the 1979 film version. What is Kosinski saying about the effects of TV on our lives? Explain why you agree or disagree with him.

3. Some people are so worried about the influence of television in their lives that they choose to decrease the amount of TV they watch or stop watching TV completely. How does this affect them? If you know any such people, interview them to find out what is different and what is the same in their lives since they made their decision. If you cannot interview people directly, find newspaper and magazine articles about people who watch little or no TV. Compare the reasons for their decisions and the consequences.

4. Commerical television depends on advertisers' money to survive, but two technological developments may be affecting how much attention audiences pay to commercials. Viewers with remote controls find it easier to flip to other channels during commercials. People who use videocassette recorders to tape shows for later viewing can "fast-forward" through commercial breaks to avoid them. Do some research to discover how extensive these practices are among audiences and how they they might affect commercial television. Pay-TV and public or government funding provide some revenue to the television industry, but are there alternatives for private stations and networks?

5. If television blurs the line between reality and fantasy, how might this alter the audience's perception of how significant an event or issue is? Do some research into how television presents important issues and how that might affect our view of them. Choose a topic from current events or examine television's influence in one of the following areas:

• making celebrities of people connected with crime

• the proceedings in the House of Commons

• how political figures present themselves, in office and/or during an election campaign.

6. Some TV mini-series and made-for-TV movies are based on novels or plays. Choose a show you have seen that was based on something you have read and, in an essay, compare your reactions to both. What changes were made in the adaptation?

7. Research the "early days" of television in Canada and write a report on your findings. You could look for the following: When was the first broadcast made, and from where? What were the popular shows and who were the celebrities? What did people think of TV? How much did a TV cost? Was there any advertising? You might want to interview people who would remember those early years.

8. In groups, brainstorm to develop a list of positive aspects of television. Write an essay, poem, short story, or script that features some of these aspects. You might want to describe what life without television would be like.

CHAPTER 3

Film

"Thumbs-up." "Stunning!" "Powerful and awesome." "Enthralling!" "A unique and unforgettable film." "A comic masterpiece!" "Engrossing and provocative." "Gripping." "A blockbuster." "Brilliant and terrifying." "It's a must-see." "One of the best films of the year." While we know these glowing words are part of the language of film promotion, there are many films that are worthy of such praise. It is certainly a powerful medium. It is also a very expensive one. For example, *E.T. The Extra-Terrestrial* has earned approximately $700 million in theatres worldwide. Television actor Bruce Willis was offered an estimated $5 million to star in a movie in 1988. In the U.S., the average cost to make and release a film in 1984 was $14.4 million, and in order to break even, the number of tickets needed to be sold was 15 million.

Like television, films send us messages about cultures, trends, role-models, social issues and concerns. As with television, we have to ask ourselves if films reflect society or help shape it, and how.

REACTING TO FILM

"I believe that films should have power, the power of good and the power of darkness, so you can get some thrills and shake things up. And if you back off from that stuff, you're shooting right down into lukewarm junk."

—DAVID LYNCH, FILM DIRECTOR

"The evaluation process is one of reacting and trying to order that reaction. Then what you try to do is analyze the emotion and find out what created that."

—JAY SCOTT, FILM CRITIC

Films cause audiences to have emotional reactions. One media educator described movies as "emotion pictures" and the Russian filmmaker Sergei Eisenstein said "A film without emotional feeling is scarcely worth consideration." Many film-goers have said that they go to the movies to get away from reality, to be transported to another place. Such is the power of films—their combination of visual imagery, portrayal of character, dialogue, music, and sound effects allow for very effective communication of meaning, resulting in the audience's emotional reactions.

How do filmmakers get us to react? How do they hold our attention for 90 minutes or more, or why do some films fail to do so? How do filmmakers create meaning in their films? Understanding films is much more than understanding plot. Watching films involves perceiving symbols; noticing technical aspects of production such as lighting, set design, camera action, and composition; assessing the acting; and listening to the music and sound effects. Analyzing all these aspects of film allows you to understand why people find films "powerful," "evocative," "gripping," and "stunning."

If you have ever watched the Genies or the Academy Awards, you will know that films fall into, and are judged according to, different categories. **Feature films**, for example, are either fictional or based on fact, over an hour in length, present performers in leading roles, and are made for release in commercial movie theatres. They usually appear in 35mm format, which means the actual celluloid film that runs through the projector is 35 millimetres wide. Some feature films now appear in 70mm format, and are shown on wide screens. **Short subject films**, or shorts, are just that—brief films about a subject; for example, animated films, educational films, or documentaries.

Documentary films give a factual account of a subject, are non-fiction, made in real locations and feature non-performers, and are often made with hand-held cameras. The focus in this chapter is on feature films.

AT THE MOVIES: A SURVEY

To determine the importance of film-going in your life, and to see how much of a film "buff" you are, complete the following survey in your media log.

1. a) Approximately how many films do you see per month in a movie theatre? on television (including pay TV)? on videocassette?
   b) What is the total per month? Per year?

2. Do you usually watch films alone or with friends or family?

3. List your ten all-time favourite films in order of preference, with 1 as your top film. For your top two films, explain why you liked them.

4. List your main reasons for seeing films.

5. List your favourite types of films; for example, comedy, adventure, horror, romance, science fiction, other.

6. Name five feature film directors and at least one film for each director.

7. List five of your favourite film actors and actresses. Explain why you find the top two on your list appealing.

8. List the Canadian feature films you have seen in the past few years.

9. List five films you disliked and give reasons for your opinion.

10. What recent trends in films do you like? dislike? Why?

11. What values do you think were represented in three or four of your favourite films?

12. List three of the most popular films of the last year. Why do you think these films were so popular?

In groups, share the results of your surveys. What were the leading films, and types of films? Who were the favourite actors and actresses? Discuss the film-going habits of your class, their likes and dislikes, and any other patterns that the surveys revealed.

v̌

"Motion Pictures"

DISCUSSING FILM

Because the film medium evokes strong and varied emotional reactions, when discussing films in class, you and your classmates should go through a process that will enable you to order your reactions, as Jay Scott suggests. To do this, consider the following strategies:

• If you have the chance to see a film in a group, try to have a short break immediately following the viewing, to give everyone time to gather their thoughts before beginning your discussion.

• Share your perceptions and feelings about the film but, as in your brainstorming sessions, do not judge others' views as right or wrong. No one should be considered an expert; however, collectively, you will have a considerable amount of expertise.

• To begin your discussion you could do an "image scan" of the film. Each of you could comment on one or more powerful scenes or images and decide what makes them so memorable. Discuss how these images or scenes can tell us something about the goals of the filmmaker.

• After a variety of images are shared, you could make some statements about the themes and the purposes of the cinematic techniques. (If you have access to the film on videocassette at home, you can study some of the important scenes again.) The following questions may help your discussion: Is this film like others you have seen? How does it reflect current social trends? What would your parents like or dislike about this film? If the film was a box office success, how do you account for its popularity?

A STUDY OF GENRES

One of the pleasures of the film medium is the wide variety it offers. Most of us have some favourite types of film; for example, horror films, westerns, or science fiction films. These film types are called "genres." (Some producers prefer the term "formula.") Genre refers to a category or form of film in which the subject matter, themes, and/or techniques are similar to other films of its type. We can recognize a genre film because the characters, stories, and situations are familiar. The conventions and codes are recognizable and expected. For example, in a western, the villain usually wears dark clothes. In beach party movies, we know that the hero will suffer a few setbacks before he "wins over" the girl and we know they will eventually sing to each other at a bonfire on the beach.

FROM BEACH MOVIES TO B-MOVIES

The following is a list of some film genres, a brief explanation of each, and an example of two past films of the genre. For each one, try to think of one or two recent films that would fit the genre.

B-Films Films made on low budgets, with inferior, or B-grade production values and skills. *Crime Doctor* (1943) and *Frankenstein Meets the Wolf Man* (1943).

Comedy Covers a wide range of films. The following are three types of comedy films, or three sub-genres:

1. Black Comedy Popular during the early '60s, films of this genre treated macabre subjects such as war, nuclear threats, and murder humourously. *Dr. Strangelove, or How I Learned to Stop Worrying and Love the Bomb* (1964); *M*A*S*H* (1970).
2. Screwball Comedy Zany comedies typified by a conflict between the male and female protagonists, frenetic action, fast-paced dialogue, and exaggerated characters. *Bringing Up Baby* (1938); *It Happened One Night* (1934).
3. Slapstick Comedy Films in which the humour is based on the hero's physical or social blunders. Charlie Chaplin and Buster Keaton were the stars of the genre. *The General* (1927); *The Gold Rush* (1925).

Disaster Films Usually tell the story of a group of people, each with a personal problem, who are together when disaster, usually natural, strikes. *The Poseidon Adventure* (1972); *Earthquake* (1974).

Epics Film spectacles, usually based on a historical event, characterized by huge casts and elaborate sets. *Gone With the Wind* (1939); *Lawrence of Arabia* (1962).

Experimental Films Usually non-commercial, produced independently rather than by a large production company, and often express the film-maker's view in unique, sometimes bizarre ways. *The Grandmother* (1970); *Snow* (1969).

Film Noir (literally, black film)   Popular in the '40s, usually crime thrillers, typified by dark, urban settings, violence, and cynicism. *The Maltese Falcon* (1941); *Citizen Kane* (1941).

Horror Films   Thrillers which frighten the audience, are often about ordinary people caught up in extraordinary events, and feature the supernatural, monsters, mad scientists, mutants of nature. *Frankenstein* (1931); *The Omen* (1976).

Science Fiction Films   Films about scientific fantasies, often depicting fear of the unknown. Typified by elaborate sets and special effects. *Invasion of the Body Snatchers* (1956); *2001: A Space Odyssey* (1968).

Westerns (also known as horse operas)   Usually depict a conflict between good and evil in the "wild" west, and feature simple, stock characters, sweeping landscapes, frontier towns, and gunfights. *High Noon* (1952); *A Fistful of Dollars* (1964).

This list of genres is not all-inclusive. There are many other categories of films, such as romances (*Roxanne*, 1987), chase films (*The French Connection*, 1971), spy or detective films (the James Bond films), musicals (*Fame*, 1980), space operas (the *Star Wars* trilogy). As a class, think of some other film genres to add to this list, and offer some examples of films of those genres.

Some filmmakers depend heavily on the audience's knowledge of films and genres when they create films that are parodies of a type. Mel Brooks' *Blazing Saddles* (1974) is a parody of several westerns and his *High Anxiety* (1977) sends up the films of Alfred Hitchcock. Woody Allen's *Love and Death* (1975) parodies epics and Russian literature. Think of some other films that are parodies of genres.

Study the film stills shown here. Name the genre that each film seems to represent. How did you make your decision?

RECENT GENRES

If filmmakers follow the codes and forms of a genre closely, the meaning of the film can be limited. To make their films memorable, some filmmakers try to use the genre form creatively. Many filmmakers have played with our expectations of film genres by combining characteristics of several genres or using them in new ways.

David Edelstein, a critic for the New York paper *The Village Voice*, noted in "The Joys of Genre" that there were four formulas that have recently dominated the box office. He also pointed out that there were a few films that he described as genre busters—films which do not rigidly follow the expectations of the genre or formula and hence offer something fresh and unexpected. The following is a summary of his four formulas and examples of films that can qualify as genre busters.

The go for it Movie   Dealing mainly with the underdog, this film trend started with *Rocky*. "The go for it movie works in big, dumb, black-and-white, win-or-lose strokes. . . . There is frequent use of rock music to boost the audience into an I-can-do-anything frame of mind." Examples include: *Top Gun*; *Iron Eagle*; *The Karate Kid*. Choice for a genre buster: *The Colour of Money*.

The Teen Flick   Films made for teenage audiences. Many of these films have limited social or artistic value. Choice for a genre buster: *The Outsiders*.

The Magic Spielberg Kingdom   In spite of the incredible popularity of these films: *Jaws*; *Close Encounters of the Third Kind*; *E.T. The Extra-Terrestrial*; *The Colour Purple*, and the defence of some of them by reputable critics (see Pauline Kael's review of *E.T.* in "The Pure and the Impure," p. 141), David Edelstein comments, "Spielberg doesn't trust his audience to make any decisions, and by spelling everything out, he rids his films of all tension—the kind between the conventions of a genre and the life being photographed." Choice for a genre buster: *Gremlins*.

The Fish Out of Water   The idea is simple; in these films the comedy depends on the contrast between the conventional world of the hero and the different one that he or she is placed in. "Freshness is its mode of operation: through the eyes of a fish out of water, the familiar becomes strange and new. The larger purpose is to make us question the assumptions that connect us to our culture, and to suggest that, if we need to, we can transcend it." Examples include: *Splash*; *Back to the Future*; *Witness*; *Crocodile Dundee*. Choice for a genre buster: *Lost in America*.

RESPONSES

1. Clip some ads for films from the entertainment section of a newspaper.
a) Categorize them according to the appropriate genres. Do any films fit in more than one genre? Explain.
b) How did the ad help to convey the characteristics of the genres? Consider the illustrations, copy, and quotes from the critics.

2. In groups, brainstorm to create a story outline for one or more of the following genres, or genres of your choice: science fiction, horror, disaster, spy, western. Share your outline with other groups. If more than one group has chosen the same genre, note any similarities in your outlines and discuss why you think the similarities appeared.

3. Many genre films feature stock characters, or characters that are common to most films of the genre; for example, the "sidekick" of a western hero. In groups, choose a genre, establish a setting, identify some stock characters, and write the dialogue for a scene. You could use clichés, or phrases that you have heard many times in films of the type; for example "So you think you're a tough guy, eh?" from the detective genre. Choose people from your group to play the roles, and present the scene to the other groups. You could also have representatives of several genres stay "in character" and improvise a scene in which they are all together at a party.

4. For a class seminar and/or an essay, choose one genre and try to see several current films of that genre or watch them on videocassette. In order to discover the significance of the trend, you may want to apply some of the principles of the media outlined in the opening of this text as well as some of the ideas in the chapter on popular culture.

5. Discuss David Edelstein's categories for recent films and suggest some of your own categories. Also discuss his category of genre busters and think of some other films which would fit this category.

6. In groups, brainstorm ideas for a "Go for it" or a "Fish out of Water" film. Try writing a scene for a film script.

John Hughes: The Teen Film Director as Auteur

One genre that has been around for a long time but has recently become very popular is the teen film. Ever since Marlon Brando played the surly, dynamic leader of a motorcycle gang in *The Wild One* (1953), and James Dean played the troubled teen in *Rebel Without a Cause* (1955), there have been many films about adolescence. A current and prominent filmmaker in this genre is John Hughes. The following is an excerpt from an essay written by a grade twelve student from Etobicoke, Ontario, about Hughes and his work.

by Theressa Puchta

The trouble with teen films is that a large proportion of them are pretty bad; this is primarily because they are written by men in their 40s or 50s or even 60s—they're far removed from their own teenage experiences, and they don't really know or care about the way teenagers are today; they just want to exploit them. As a result, there have been only a handful of genuinely good teen films, and an even smaller number of directors who can transform the genre—or even become skillful at it. The most notable of these is John Hughes.

When you mention the name "John Hughes" to someone out on the street, he or she will immediately think of *Sixteen Candles* or *The Breakfast Club* or *Ferris Bueller's Day Off*—films that have helped give the teen film genre some much-needed respect. Hughes' name has become synonymous with teen films; thus, it is fitting that he is the genre's lone auteur.

What is an auteur? In the film sense, auteur usually refers to the director of a film; the director is the

one who in most cases stamps his [or her] personality onto a film. . . . The two main characteristics of films by auteurs are a) consistency of theme and b) the personal style of the director (usually it is one or the other). . . . Pauline Kael [a film critic] has called for an alternative definition of auteur—the director who also writes his or her own scripts. There is a third type of auteur, that of the screenwriter who imposes his or her personality so strongly on the scripts that it is difficult for a director to transcend it, for example, the films of Paddy Chayefsky.

John Hughes qualifies as an auteur on two counts of the word; he is an auteur in the traditional sense . . . and he is also an auteur in the way Kael would have it. The characteristics and themes in Hughes' films have almost become clichés by now; we know them all by heart. There's the suburban (usually near Chicago) settings, the vague social concerns, the various high school cliques (as in *Pretty in Pink*), the missing or uncaring parents (a characteristic of most—if not all—teen films), the characters wearing the latest fashions, the Top 40 soundtrack music. Most of all, there's the humour, easier to take than in most other teen films—which leads to the feature that has been mentioned most often in the context of Hughes' films—the dialogue, which has often been described by a number of critics as "realistic." . . . Humour and wit have always made most of Hughes' films enjoyable (even *The*

Breakfast Club, which is ostensibly a drama, has a number of zingers). Coupled with a certain spirit and élan, they have proven to be a winning combination at the box office.

How has Hughes arrived at where he is? If you looked at his background, he'd seem an unlikely choice for the "Boswell of the teen set" as one critic described him. . . . He was a quiet kid raised in a genuine slice of sleepy suburbia— Grosse Point, Michigan. After dropping out of college, he worked in the advertising world for a while, then decided that what he really wanted to be was a writer. To this end, he contributed regularly to *National Lampoon* for several years. Eventually he adapted a story he wrote for the *Lampoon* into *National Lampoon's Vacation*, his first film script. He then wrote *Mr. Mom*, which eventually led to his first directing assignment, *Sixteen Candles*.

Hughes started writing movies for teens because he felt that they were not being served well by other members of his generation (he is a baby boomer) and because stories for teens were often told from an adult point of view, seldom from a teen's. He sought to change that. As a result, the characteristic of Hughes' films that has been commented on the most has been the dialogue, which has often been described as "realistic" and "hip—just the way teens talk." Well, not quite. Though Hughes' dialogue is realistic, funny, and literate—certainly several notches above the drivel

Opposite page: A scene from *Pretty in Pink* starring Molly Ringwald and Jon Cryer.

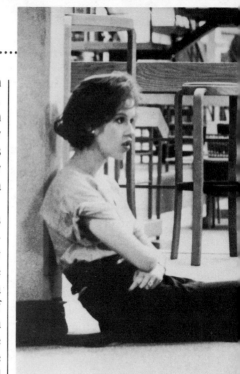

usually spoken by people in teen films—it's sometimes a bit too rich. When Judd Nelson wisecracks in *The Breakfast Club*, "Does Barry Manilow know you're stealing his wardrobe?" it is a good and funny line. But I really can't imagine a typical teen uttering it.

One point Hughes definitely has in his favour is the absence of gratuitous sex—indeed, virtually any nudity—in his films. One of the things that has given teen films a bad name is the exploitation of (usually female) teens, usually as a source of titillation to teenage boys. . . . Hughes . . . doesn't see the point of putting lots of sex and

A scene from *The Breakfast Club* starring, left to right: Molly Ringwald, Anthony Michael Hall, Emilio Estevez, Ally Sheedy and Judd Nelson.

nudity in his films. . . . As Hughes himself has said, "Most of my characters are romantic rather than sexual. I think that's an essential difference in my pictures. I think they are more accurate in portraying young people as romantic, as wanting a relationship, an understanding, with a member of the opposite sex rather than physical sex."

Females and the family always get a better treatment in Hughes' films than in other teen films. Hughes has stated he wrote *Sixteen Candles* expressly from the female point of view . . . because females often get the short shrift in this male-dominated genre (i.e., they are usually little more than sex objects). That movie also showers quite a bit of attention on the family; the plot concerns Samantha (Molly Ringwald) whose 16th birthday, as it turns out, falls close to the same

day as her sister's wedding, so it's virtually forgotten. One the whole, Hughes does treat the parents somewhat better than other teen film writers and directors; for instance, Harry Dean Stanton, as Ringwald's jobless dad, is a very sympathetic character in *Pretty in Pink*.

I'm not trying to say that Hughes treats the parents—and other authority figures—nicely in all his films. In fact, some would say that one of Hughes' biggest weaknesses as a filmmaker is that he panders too much to teenagers, i.e., you don't see too many parents in his films. . . . The protagonists in *The Breakfast Club* confess to each other the same sentiment . . . they hate their parents. The two geeks in *Weird Science*, after creating their ideal enchantress, throw a wild party during which the grandparents of one of the guys gets put into what seems like cold storage in a pantry

(they are actually made catatonic by the girl).

Matthew Broderick, at the beginning of *Ferris Bueller's Day Off*, looks into the camera and gives us tips on how to deceive parents. . . . Most of the adults in *Ferris Bueller* are complete buffoons . . . but none more so than Mr. Rooney, the high-school principal. . . . Hughes may not really care for the adults in his films that much, but he cares about his young actors deeply. In a number of cases, he uses them regularly, basically in the same roles. Molly Ringwald, the leading lady of many of Hughes' films, usually plays a princess in preppy gladrags (though her character in *Pretty in Pink* was from the wrong side of the tracks), and Anthony Michael Hall has basically played, with variations, the same character (the geek) in all three of his Hughes films. . . . One of the few adults Hughes has really been sympathetic to in his films has been Annie Potts, as Ringwald's thirty-ish best friend in *Pretty in Pink*, but even there the sympathy probably came because she seemed more like an overgrown teenager. . . .

Now Hughes has indicated he may be ready to do more adult films; his two most recent films, *Planes, Trains and Automobiles* (1987) and *She's Having a Baby* (1988) are examples. However, he says he won't leave the world of teen films entirely behind, which will no doubt make his fans happy. Maybe he will be able to do something new with the teen film form in the next few years . . . enlighten as well as entertain teens. If he turned it into something more personal, then that would be the mark of a true auteur, which, I'm sure, is what Hughes wants to be.

—1987

RESPONSES

1. Summarize Theressa Puchta's description of the merits and limitations of John Hughes' films. If you have not seen any of his films, try to see one on video. Explain why you agree or disagree with the author.

2. Theressa Puchta points out that many filmmakers exploit teenagers. Do you agree with her comment that most filmmakers of the genre are middle-aged males? What do you think would qualify as exploitation in teen films? Give some examples.

3. Identify two of John Hughes' films that were box office "flops" and try to account for their failures. In terms of the craft of filmmaking and in satisfying the needs of the audience, what lessons might directors learn from these examples?

4. Respond to the critics of John Hughes, including Puchta, who claim that the director panders too much to teenagers or, as one critic put it, "He caters to teen narcissism—seeing mirror images of yourself—and tunnel vision, and butters them [teens] up by crudely trashing authority figures."

5. After identifying the teen film formula that John Hughes uses, brainstorm in groups and apply the formula to create some story outlines which could be made into films. Try to avoid the pitfalls so frequently associated with the teen film genre. You could then write a script for a scene based on your outline. See the Reference Section and page 88 in the Television chapter for tips on script writing.

6. Consider some other teen films, including those from previous decades. How do they follow or depart from the teen film genre?

7. Investigate further the role of the director and the meaning of "auteur." Choose a director who you think could be considered an auteur, read about him or her and/or try to view some of his or her films. Present a report on the director and his or her work.

FILM ADAPTATIONS

Films can be made from original screenplays or from scripts that are adaptations of existing works of literature, such as novels, biographies, plays, and short stories. For example, F. Scott Fitzgerald's novel *The Great Gatsby* was brought to the screen, *Who Has Seen the Wind?* was based on W.O. Mitchell's novel, and Tennessee Williams' *The Glass Menagerie* has been made (and re-made) into films. Think of some other examples of works of literature that have been brought to the screen.

The following is a poem by Raymond Souster. While you read it, think about it in terms of its potential for a film.

YONGE STREET SATURDAY NIGHT

Except when the theatre crowds engulf the sidewalks
at nine, at eleven-thirty,
this street is lonely, and a thousand lights
in a thousand store windows
wouldn't break her lips into a smile.

There are a few bums out,
there are lovers with hands held tightly,
there are also the drunk ones
but they are princes among men, and are few.

And there are some like us,
just walking, making both feet move out ahead of us,
a little bored, a little lost, a little angry,

walking as though we were honestly going somewhere,
walking as if there was really something to see
at Adelaide or maybe on King,
something, no matter how little
that will give us some fair return
on our use of shoe-leather,

something perhaps that will make us smile
with a strange new happiness,
a lost but recovered joy.

—*COLLECTED POEMS OF RAYMOND SOUSTER*, 1980

The Television chapter offers a sample script for television (p. 88) and the Reference Section gives some tips on writing scripts (p. 217). You could use these sources to help you in your script writing for film. Writing scripts helps develop skill in thinking in visual terms, and thus helps to understand film techniques.

RESPONSES

1. Adapt the poem to a brief script for a film. Compare your script with the scripts of your classmates.

2. Choose a poem that has a strong story line, or a short story (perhaps one you have studied in English class) or a popular song, and adapt it to a short film script. You can write a literal translation of the poem, story, or song or you can give it a more liberal interpretation. What are the effects of both methods?

3. Write a short film script of the following incident: a widow wakes one night to find a thief leaving with her expensive collection of jewellery.

4. In groups, brainstorm to create some ideas for short films and put the ideas in script form.

FILM TECHNIQUES

Much of the meaning of films is created by the **movement of the camera**; for example, the distance of the camera from the subject; the way the camera moves toward or away from the subject; the angle of the camera; the action of the camera, such as slow motion, fast motion, freeze frames, or fades.

Meaning also depends on the **framing and composition** of a shot; for example, the relationship of the subject to foreground and background or the interplay of shapes, colours, textures, and lines. Filmmakers in this respect are much like painters. The choice of what appears in a frame of film, and how it appears, is like an artist's choice of what to put in a painting and how to paint it.

Sound—whether sound effects or music—is very important to a film. Synchronous sound is sound that matches the image on the screen; for example, when characters speak on camera, we both see and hear them. Asynchronous sound is sound with no matching image. We do not see where the sound originates; for example, in some horror movies, we hear the heavy breathing and footsteps of what we imagine is a monster. While music soundtracks in films like *La Bamba* (1987) and *Dirty Dancing* (1987) are important for obvious reasons, the choice of music is very important in creating meaning in all films. Consider the famous soundtrack from *Jaws* (1975).

Editing is the process of joining or splicing pieces of film in ways to achieve continuity and give meaning to the whole film. The arrangement of these pieces of film is called juxtapositioning—placing items close together. When a series of juxtaposed shots is arranged to create a certain meaning, the process is called "montage." For example, a shot of a face with a longing expression, followed by a shot of a plentiful buffet table, indicates hunger. Follow that shot with one of a mansion, and then a slum, and you have a montage that makes a social statement. The point is that each separate image may have limited power, or effect, but juxtaposition of the images expands the meaning.

For more information on the terminology of film and camera techniques, see page 84 in the Television chapter.

Lighting can be very effective in creating atmosphere or symbols. Key lighting is the main source of light for the set. High-key lighting, which provides a uniform brightness and high illumination, is often used in comedies and musicals. Low-key lighting, which gives less illumination, leaves much of the setting in darkness and shadows, and is suitable for horror films, or film noir. Lighting can be:

flat: light comes from behind the subject and in front of the subject;
back: light comes from behind the subject and goes into the camera;
side: light comes from the right or left of the subject;
top: spot light from above focuses on the main subject of a shot.

Filmmakers also use filters, or pieces of glass or plastic which, when put over the lens of the camera, distort the light and colour to create different effects and moods.

1 Flat lighting

2 Back lighting

3 Side lighting

4 Top lighting

RESPONSES

1. Collect and discuss some examples of photographs and ads from a variety of magazines that demonstrate various camera distances and angles and their effects.

2. Watch some films or television shows, and find examples of different lighting, sound effects, synchronous and asynchronous sounds, and effective editing. In each case, show what purpose the technique achieves.

3. Comic books, especially the action-filled types such as *Superman* and *Marvel* comics, can help you practise your knowledge of film techniques. Comics use a visual shorthand; they are drawn to hold our attention, and to move the story forward in a dynamic and interesting way. In groups, choose one or two of these comics and turn them into short scripts.

4. In groups, choose one or two of the scripts you adapted, and film them. You could write camera directions on the script before you begin shooting. See page 89 in the Television chapter. You might want to assign different tasks to the members of your group; that is, one could direct, one could film, one could direct the lighting, and others could act.

5. Find some magazines that have many pictures, such as *Equinox*, *Life*, or *People*. In groups, arrange a number of pictures from the magazines to create a visual outline for a short film or a documentary. Try to create some montages.

6. In his book *Real to Reel*, David Coynik proposes a challenge for a film editor. The following four shots have not been arranged in any particular order. Arrange the shots to create different meanings. Compare your results with a classmate's.
   a) a medium shot of a group of soldiers, showing the worried looks on their faces
   b) a long shot of a huge ape-like monster trampling on a city
   c) a long shot of an explosion
   d) a medium shot of the same soldiers as in shot one, this time with calm expressions on their faces

FILM CRITICISM

In your class and group discussions of film, you have been developing the basic material and the critical attitude necessary for writing film reviews. You have been discussing subjects such as your overall impression of the film, theme, the quality of the acting, and the technical aspects—the basic ingredients of film reviews.

"Word of mouth" is one way of finding out what films we might like to see, and friends often serve as film-going advisers. But the power of professional film critics should never be underestimated; they have a great ability to influence the choices we make. Critics have often rescued some good films which would otherwise have been neglected. The term "sleeper" refers to a film that was made on a low budget and had little promotion, but became a success, often due to good reviews from the critics. Critics can also make films become fast failures.

Film reviews should be written in a persuasive and convincing style, and be lively enough to sustain readers' interest. Opinions expressed in film reviews should be qualified by references to specific scenes. As critic Jay Scott suggested (see p. 122), evaluating films means analyzing the emotion and then determining what created it.

The Reference Section offers some general tips on writing reviews of media products (p. 215), but the following is a list of suggestions specific to film. Film reviews generally include:

• A brief summary of the story.

• The names of the lead and supporting actors and actresses, and the names of the characters they play, e.g., Annie Hall (Diane Keaton). (When writing about the actor or actress, use his or her name; when writing about the character, use the character's name.)

• An assessment of the directing and the acting. Does the film flow smoothly?

• Mention of the scriptwriter, and whether the script is an adaptation or an original. Is it a good story? Are the lines good and believable?

• Comparison with other films by the director, or other films of the type.

• A note on the production aspects. Who was the producer? Was the film made on a high or low budget? Where was it filmed?

• Assessment of the technical aspects: lighting, special effects, soundtrack, and so on.

• An overall assessment of the film, including both good and bad points.

Pauline Kael is one of the most influential film critics in North America. Her reviews, which appear in *The New Yorker* magazine are regularly collected and published in book form. When you read the following review of *E.T. The Extra-Terrestrial*, try to find out how she approaches the craft of film reviewing.

The Pure and the Impure

by Pauline Kael

Steven Spielberg's *E.T. The Extra-Terrestrial* envelops you in the way that his *Close Encounters of the Third Kind* did. It's a dream of a movie—a bliss-out. This sci-fantasy has a healthy share of slapstick comedy, yet it's as pure as Carroll Ballard's *The Black Stallion*. Like Ballard, Spielberg respects the convention of children's stories, and because he does, he's able to create the atmosphere for a mythic experience. Essentially, *E.T.* is the story of a ten-year-old boy, Elliott, who feels fatherless and lost because his parents have separated, and who finds a miraculous friend—an alien, inadvertently left on Earth by a visiting spaceship.

If the film seems like a continuation of *Close Encounters*, that's partly because it has the sensibility we came to know in that picture,

Director Steven Spielberg in action.

and partly because E.T. himself is more like a corporeal version of the celestial visitors at the end of it. Like *Close Encounters*, *E.T.* is bathed in warmth, and it seems to clear all the bad thoughts out of your head. It reminds you of the goofiest dreams you had as a kid, and rehabilitates them. Spielberg is right there in his films; you can feel his presence and his love of surprises. This phenomenal master craftsman plays high-tech games, but his presence is youthful—it has a just-emerged

quality. The Spielberg of *Close Encounters* was a singer with a supple, sweet voice. It couldn't be heard in his last film, the impersonal *Raiders of the Lost Ark*, and we may have been afraid that he'd lost it, but now he has it back, and he's singing more melodiously than we could have hoped for. He's like a boy soprano lilting with joy all through *E.T.*, and we're borne along by his voice.

In Spielberg's movies, parents love their children, and children love their siblings. And suburban living, with its comfortable, uniform houses, is seen as a child's paradise—an environment in which children are protected and their imaginations can flourish. There's a luminous, magical view of Elliott's hilly neighborhood in the early-evening light on Hallowe'en, with the kids in their costumes fanning out over the neatly groomed wind-

ing streets as each little group moves from one house to another for trick-or-treat, and E.T., swathed in a sheet and wearing red slippers over his webbed feet, waddles along between Elliott and his teenage brother, Michael—each of them keeping a firm, protective grip on a gray-green four-digit hand. E.T. isn't just Elliott's friend; he's also Elliott's pet—the film catches the essence of the bond between lonely children and their pets. The sequence may call up memories of the trick-or-treat night in Vincente Minelli's *Meet Me in St. Louis*, but it's more central here. All the imagery in the film is linked to Hallowe'en, with the spaceship itself as a jack-o'-lantern in the sky, and the child-size space visitors, who have come to gather specimens of Earth's flora, wrapped in cloaks with hoods and looking much like trick-or-treaters. (The pumpkin spaceship is silent, though when you see it you may hear in your head the five-note theme of the mother ship in *Close Encounters*, and the music that John Williams has written is dulcet and hushed—it allows for the full score that the movie gets going in your imagination.)

E.T. probably has the best-worked-out script that Spielberg has yet shot, and since it seems an emanation of his childlike, playful side and his love of toys, it would be natural to assume that he wrote it. But maybe it seems such a clear expression of his spirit because its actual writer, Melissa Mathison, could see what he needed more deeply than he could hold himself, and could devise a complete structure that would hold his feelings in balance. Mathison was one of the scenarists for *The Black Stallion* and is a co-writer of *The Escape Artist*; it probably isn't a coincidence that all of these films have young boy heroes who miss their fathers. Writers may be typecast, like actors; having written one movie about a boy, Mathison may have been thought of for another, and yet another. In *E.T.*, she has made Elliott dreamy and a little withdrawn but practical and intelligent. And very probably she intuited the necessity for Elliott, too, to be bereft —especially since Spielberg himself had experienced the separation of his parents. Mathison has a feeling for the emotional sources of fantasy, and although her dialogue isn't always inspired, sometimes it is, and she has an ear for how kids talk. Henry Thomas, who plays Elliott, and Kelly Reno in *The Black Stallion*, and Griffin O'Neal as the boy magician in *The Escape Artist* are not Hollywood-movie kids; they all have an unusual—a magical— reserve. They're all in thrall to their fantasies, and the movies take us inside those fantasies while showing us how they help the boys grow up. Elliott (his name begins with an "E" and ends with a "T") is a dutiful, too sober boy who never takes off his invisible thinking cap; the telepathic communication he develops with E.T. eases his cautious, locked-up worries, and he begins to act on impulses. When E.T. has his first beer and loses his inhibitions, Elliott, at school, gets tipsy, and in biology class when each student is required to chloroform a frog and then dissect it he perceives his frog's resemblance to E.T. and sets it free. (His classmates follow suit.) The means by which Elliott manages to kiss a pretty girl who towers over him by at least a head is a

The slapstick helps to domesticate the feeling of enchantment and, at the same time, strengthens it.

perfectly executed piece of slapstick.

It's no small feat to fuse science fiction and mythology. *E.T.* holds together the way some of George MacDonald's fairy tales (*At the Back of the North Wind*, *The Princess and the Goblin*, *The Princess and Curdie*) do. It's emotionally rounded and complete. The neighborhood kids whose help Elliott needs all come through for him. Even his little sister, Gertie (Drew Barrymore), is determined to keep the secret that E.T. is hidden in Elliott's room. And when Elliott's harried mother (Dee Wallace) rushes around in her kitchen and fails to see E.T.— fails to see him even when she knocks him over—the slapstick helps to domesticate the feeling of enchantment and, at the same time, strengthens it. Adults—as we all know from the children's stories of our own childhoods, or from the books we've read to our children— are too busy and too preoccupied to see the magic that's right there in

front of them. Spielberg's mellow, silly jokes reinforce the fantasy structure. One of them—Elliott on his bicycle dropping what looks like M&Ms to make a trail—seems to come right out of a child's mind. (Viewers with keen eyes may perceive that the candies are actually Reese's Pieces.) Among the costumed children radiating out on Hallowe'en is a tiny Yoda, and the audience laughs in recognition that, yes, this film is part of the fantasy world to which Yoda (the wise gnome of *The Empire Strikes Back*) belongs. And when E.T.—a goblin costumed as a ghost—sees the child dressed as Yoda and turns as if to join him it's funny because it's so unaccountably right.

Henry Thomas (who was the older of Sissy Spacek's two small sons in *Raggedy Man*) has a beautiful brainy head with a thick crop of hair; his touching serio-comic solemnity draws us into the mood of the picture. When one of the neighborhood kids makes

> *The visual energy and graphic strength in his work have always been based on his storyboarding the material . . .*

a fanciful remark about E.T., Elliott reprimands him, rapping out, "This is reality." Dee Wallace as the mother, Peter Coyote as a scientist who from childhood has dreamed the dream that Elliott has realized, and the other adult actors are the supporting cast. Henry Thomas and E.T. (who was designed by one of the authentic wizards of Hollywood, Carlo Rambaldi) are the

stars, and Drew Barrymore and Robert Macnaughton, as the teenager Michael, are the featured players. Elliott and his brother and sister are all low-key humorists. When Michael first sees E.T., he does a double take that's like a momentary paralysis. Elliott has an honestly puzzled tone when he asks Michael, "How do you explain school to a higher intelligence?" Little Gertie adapts to E.T. very quickly—he may have the skin of a dried fig and a potbelly that just misses the floor, but she talks to him as if he were one of her dolls.

Spielberg changed his usual way of working when he made *E.T.*, and you can feel the difference. The visual energy and graphic strength in his work have always been based on his storyboarding the material—that is, sketching the camera angles in advance, so that the graphic plan was laid out. That way, he knew basically what he was after in each shot and how the shots would fit together; his characteristic brilliantly jagged cutting was largely thought out from the start. On *E.T.*—perhaps because the story is more delicate and he'd be working with child actors for much of the time—he decided to trust his intuition, and the film has a few fuzzy spots but a gentler, more fluid texture. It's less emphatic than his other films; he doesn't use his usual widescreen format—he isn't out to overpower you. The more reticent shape makes the story seem simpler—plausible. The light always has an apparent source, even when it gives the scenes an other-worldy glow. And from the opening in the dense, vernal woodland that adjoins Elliott's suburb (it's where we first hear E.T.'s frightened sounds), the film has the soft, mysterious inexorability of a classic tale of enchantment. The little shed in back of the house where Elliott tosses in a ball and E.T. sends it back is part of a dreamscape.

The only discordant note is the periodic switch to overdynamic camera angles to show the NASA men and other members of the search party whose arrival frightened off the space visitors and who keep looking for the extraterrestrial left behind. These men are lined up in military-looking groups, and the camera shows us only their stalking or marching bodies—they're faceless, silent, and extremely threatening. Their flashlights in the dark woods could be lethal ray guns, and one of them has a bunch of keys hanging from his belt that keep jan-

gling ominously. The rationale is probably that we're meant to view the men as little E.T. would, or as Elliott would, but most of the time neither E.T. nor Elliott is around when they are. Later in the movie, in the sequences in a room that is used as a hospital, it's clear that when adults are being benevolent in adult terms they may still be experienced by children as enemies. But the frequent intrusive cuts to the uniformed men—in some shots they wear moon-travel gear and head masks—are meant to give us terror vibes. They're abstract figures of evil; even the American-flag insignia on their uniforms is sinister—in modern movie iconology that flag means "bad guys." And this movie doesn't need faceless men; it has its own terror. Maybe Spielberg didn't have enough faith in the fear that is integral to any magical idyll: that it can't last.

When the children get to know E.T., his sounds are almost the best part of the picture. His voice is ancient and otherworldly but friendly, humorous. And this scaly, wrinkled little man with huge, wide-apart, soulful eyes and a jack-in-the-box neck has been so fully created that he's a friend to us, too; when he speaks of his longing to go home the audience becomes as mournful as Elliott. Spielberg has earned the tears that some people in the audience—and not just children—shed. The tears are tokens of gratitude for the spell the picture has put on the audience. Genuinely entrancing movies are almost as rare as extraterrestrial visitors.

—*TAKING IT ALL IN*, 1984

RESPONSES

1. Explain how Pauline Kael's "The Pure and the Impure" has the characteristics of a well-written film review. See page 215 in the Reference Section for more information on reviews.

2. Give examples that show how Kael's attitude toward the film depends on the effectiveness of the film's technique and the quality of the script.

3. What evidence is there that Pauline Kael likes films and is very knowledgeable about them?

4. What purpose is served by the comparisons with other filmmakers and other films by Steven Spielberg?

5. Choose a film you have seen recently and write a review of it. You could use Kael's review as a model, and refer to page 215 in the Reference Section for more tips on writing reviews. Share your review with others in your class. How effective are your classmates' reviews in influencing your decision about seeing the films they have reviewed?

HAVE YOU SEEN ANY BAD FILMS LATELY?

The media frequently offer lists of best films of the month, or year, or even all-time bests, but they also keep lists of the worst films. Most of us at some time have warned friends about films we think should be avoided. Some films are so overwhelmingly bad that they have become notorious; their "badness" has made them famous, or has, at least, turned them into "cult classics." Many of these films are of the B-Film genre. What makes a film bad? Writer Michael Pressler offers the following tips on how to avoid films destined for the "worst films of the year" list:

- almost anything with a II in its title, and anything (except Shakespeare) with a III or larger number in the title

- any film with "feast," "transplant," "cheerleader," or "bloodbath" in its title

- anything with Sensurround, Aroma Rama, Emergo, 3-D, or anything hidden in the seats

- any film whose central character is a machine, a house pet, a plant, or a reptile

- any documentaries purporting to reveal the true facts about UFOs, abominable snowmen, reincarnation, or any part of the Old Testament

- any film set in a plane, bus, train, ship, or any other conveyance where people from all walks of life meet and share an experience which changes their lives forever

- any film destined to become a classic in our time

- any film set in a tempestuous period of history—for that matter, any film described as being tempestuous anywhere

- any films about teenagers who teach their parents how to dance

RESPONSES

1. List several films that you think fit into Michael Pressler's categories, and discuss your reasons for your choices. Compare your list with those of your classmates.

2. Explain how some of these films could fall into the "guilty pleasures" category; that is, films that critics found bad but you enjoyed, or were box office successes.

3. In groups, add some of your own recommendations for avoiding bad films. Provide some recent examples of films to make your case.

4. a) Do you agree or disagree that film sequels are rarely successful? Give reasons for your answer.
b) What difficulties are there in making a good film from a typical B-movie plot?

5. In groups, write a plot outline based on several ideas or plots found in bad films. Think of a title for the film, and have one or two people from your group design a movie poster to advertise it. Using proper script form, write a script for a scene of your film; if you have the equipment, you could film the scene. In the process, you will probably be creating a take-off or a parody of this kind of film. What did you learn about film formulas from this exercise?

THE CANADIAN FILM INDUSTRY

There are probably very few Canadians who have graduated from high school without seeing at least one film produced by the National Film Board of Canada. It was founded by John Grierson in 1939. Since that time, the NFB has produced some outstanding short films and documentaries, as well as feature films. Films produced by the NFB have won over 2000 awards at major international film festivals. Two of the most famous NFB productions, and ones which left deep impressions on most viewers, are *Not A Love Story*, an anti-pornography film, and *If You Love This Planet*, a film about nuclear war. Certainly the NFB has played a major role in Canadian film history. But many of the films it produced in the early days were short films, not features. For feature film entertainment, Canadians depended on the United States.

John Grierson, founder of the National Film Board of Canada

National
Film Board
of Canada

Office
national du film
du Canada

This Is Where We Came In

In the late '60s and the '70s, Canada experienced a surge of cultural awareness and a desire to resist American dominance of entertainment and cultural events. Martin Knelman, an author and film critic, wrote the following in his book about the Canadian film industry.

by Martin Knelman

People started putting on their own plays in converted churches and warehouses. Small publishing houses began popping up. Kids who had dreamed of going to Hollywood shot movies in their own neighbourhoods instead. Meanwhile, politicians actually began to believe what they'd been saying for years: that Canada couldn't survive politically and economically without a sense of cultural identity. By the early 1970s, we suddenly had among other things, a movie industry of our own—a problem-plagued, instant industry without any sense of its past or purpose, but nevertheless a movie industry.

Now we're at the second stage of development: we are becoming self-conscious and deciding what to do with what has finally started to happen. As Northrop Frye has observed, it has taken Canadians a long time to get imaginative control of their own space. Frye may be right in seeing this development as an accomplished fact in the traditional arts, but in mass culture it is just beginning to happen. To create a pop mythology requires not just talent and money, but something like an advertising person's self-promotional confidence—and that may be the definition of what Canada has never had.

How else can one explain that Canadians have been content to exist for most of the twentieth century without films of their own, while living next to a country whose movies have culturally colonized the world? Even now, the few good films produced in this country have to compete with American movies, not only for playdates in the theatres but also for the publicity that makes people want to see them—publicity that is most spectacularly generated through American television or American magazines. . . .

—*THIS IS WHERE WE CAME IN:*
THE CAREER AND
CHARACTER OF CANADIAN FILM,
1977

HOLLYWOOD NORTH?

The government founded the Canadian Film Development Corporation in 1967 to provide money for a movie industry, not just for shorts and documentaries, but for feature films. At first, it invested in a number of English and French films of value to Canadian culture, but later recognized a need for more commercial films. While the money was available for production, the means of distributing and showing the films was not. Producers often had to turn to American investors, who were eager for the tax shelter (if they invested their money in a project, they would not have to pay taxes on the money). Many films during this phase of our film history were imitations of Hollywood movies and were done with minimum awareness of Canadian culture or concerns. Locations were made to look American, second-rate American actors were usually used, and the results were often dismal failures. Some films were never even released.

Amid this American-dominated phase, a few films heralded a change in Canadian filmmaking. *Goin' Down the Road* (1970), a film about two young men from Nova Scotia who move to Toronto and become caught up by the big city, and *Mon Oncle Antoine* (1971), a coming-of-age story of a boy in small-town Quebec, told genuinely Canadian stories. The late '70s saw a series of hits for Canada: *The Apprenticeship of Duddy Kravitz* (1974); *Outrageous* (1977); *Why Shoot the Teacher?* (1977); and *Who Has Seen the Wind?* (1977). But the same problems existed: filmmaking is expensive, and because most of the distribution companies and theatre chains were controlled by American corporations, Canadian films were poorly promoted and often did not reach a large audience.

"Hollywood North" is the term often used to describe American involvement in the Canadian film industry. Recently, because the exchange rate of the dollar is favourable to Americans, many American productions are filmed in Canada. Montreal, Toronto, and Vancouver often double as American cities. While this practice gives American filmmakers cheaper production costs, Canadian technicians, production personnel, and some actors receive jobs and valuable experience.

By 1985, the Canadian film industry had experienced more changes. The CFDC became Telefilm Canada, and it stipulated that producers, in order to receive funds, had to have a Canadian distributor for their films. Marcel Masse, the Minister of Communications in 1985, explained:

"American films are greatly enjoyed and valued in Canada, but they do not and cannot express what we are and who we are. Only Canadians can do that. A country which cannot express its own identity is in danger of losing it. And a country that finally succeeds in this self-expression and then cannot distribute the results of its success faces cultural frustration."

There were more hits in the 1980s—*The Grey Fox* (1980); *90 Days* (1985); and *My American Cousin* (1985). In 1987, more Canadian films, such as *Loyalties* and *Dancing in the Dark*, scored both box office and critical success. *I've Heard the Mermaids Singing* (1987) was a hit at the Cannes Film Festival.

Films such as these give us hope that the Canadian film industry is at long last on the right track and suggest that if Canadian films do poorly at the box office, it is not because of their lack of quality. Perhaps the reasons for poor box office results are the same as they have always been: the high costs of making films and the problems of film promotion and distribution.

Top, left to right: *Goin' Down the Road, I've Heard the Mermaids Singing, The Grey Fox.* Bottom, left to right: *John and the Missus, The Apprenticeship of Duddy Kravitz, John and the Missus*

RESPONSES

1. In class, view some NFB shorts. You could borrow them from your local library. Or, if you have the equipment at home, rent videos of some of the Canadian films mentioned in this section, or others of your choice. Assess the films in terms of how they express Canadian identity and concerns and note any patterns or characteristics that make them uniquely Canadian.

2. Canadian film critic Peter Harcourt has noted that the American film industry "has colonized our imaginations, offering its product as if it were our own. Without ever being aware of it, we have been so conditioned to respond to the kinaesthetic excitements of fast-moving action, to the glamour of stars, and to the over-riding mythology of power, of big money, of the glamorous life, that when we don't find those qualities in our own films, we tend to think of them as inferior." By referring to some Canadian films you have seen, discuss Harcourt's observation.

3. Refer to Morris Wolfe's *Jolts: The TV Wasteland and the Canadian Oasis* in the Television chapter (p. 104). Explain how his assessment of the differences between Canadian and American TV programs do or do not apply to the film industry. Debate the following. "Resolved that: Canadians will always prefer American films to Canadian productions because they want the excitement and glamour that popular American films deliver."

4. Try adapting an American film to give it Canadian content. In groups, choose an American film that you have all seen and re-write one or two scenes, giving it a Canadian "look." Choose Canadian actors for the roles. Share your scenes with other groups and discuss the kinds of changes you made to reflect the Canadian character.

5. How important is it to you for Canadians to be able to see our identity, special concerns, and interests on the screen? Write your answer in an essay or a letter. To whom would you send the letter if you wanted your concerns addressed?

6. Some critics say that Canadian films are often low-key, realistic treatments of unheroic characters who often end up as survivors, rather than depictions of John Wayne-style heroes. Using films you have seen as examples, support or refute this theory.

My American Cousin opens with a sulky young girl scrawling "Nothing ever happens" repeatedly in her diary. The 12-year-old who desperately wants to be 16 lives on a ranch in the panoramic Okanagan Valley in British Columbia. Sandy (Margaret Langrick) is bored with the view. But under a baking sun in the summer of 1959, the local scenery is enhanced by the sudden appearance of her Californian cousin, Butch (John Wildman), who shows up unannounced behind the wheel of a lipstick-red, shark-finned Cadillac convertible. Vancouver writer and director Sandy Wilson has filled the screen with bold 1950s stereotypes and created a funny, warm-hearted film that goes beyond nostalgia. Unlike so many Hollywood efforts to revive the 1950s, My American Cousin looks at male

Conjuring Up a Lost Age of Innocence

by Brian Johnson

The Canadian film *My American Cousin* (1985), made by Sandy Wilson, had a wide audience. It grossed $900 000 in Canada and ran for 34 weeks in Vancouver, according to *Cinema Canada* magazine. After its successful theatrical run, it appeared on video and also had several showings on television. As you read the following review, note any elements in the film which highlight Canadian concerns.

adolescence from a female perspective. And its ironies are exaggerated by the sobering distance of the Canadian hinterland.

As Sandy's visiting cousin, Wildman creates an effective caricature of a brash American boy who is too good-looking for his own good. A self-styled James Dean, Butch is in love with his image and his car, although neither belongs to him. He wears a white T-shirt on his muscular torso with a pack of Camels tucked in the sleeve. The Okanagan girls have never seen anything like him beyond a movie theatre, and he soon becomes the object of their giggling adulation.

Sandy's father (Richard Donat) gives him a job picking cherries, but Butch has little patience for manual labor. He is more interested in testing the local morals. Dodging Sandy's precocious advances, he pursues her older friends. The sex never goes beyond cautious petting, and the violence produces no more than a cut lip and a bent bumper. But seen through Sandy's eyes, Butch's joyriding exploits are full of danger and romance.

In the end, not much happens—certainly not enough to fulfil the usual plot requirements of a Hollywood feature. But that is partly what makes *My American Cousin* so

John Wildman as Butch and Margaret Langrick as Sandy. Opposite page: Director Sandy Wilson on the set.

believable. Wilson has preserved the authenticity of her story by relying on personal instinct. To shoot the film she returned to her childhood home, the 642-acre Paradise Ranch overlooking Lake Okanagan. To play her younger self, she chose a former neighbor with no previous acting experience. The spunky 13-year-old Langrick brings a level of wit and candor to her role that no amount of craft could contrive.

Sandy dominates the film, not just as its main character but as an insouciant observer who is still looking at adolescence from the outside. Living proof that girls grow up faster than boys, Sandy judges Butch to be "conceited and immature" but decides to like him anyway. She is as astute in her preteen naiveté as he is short-sighted in his American chauvinism, and the exchanges between them are rich with cultural nuances. As he tries to punch some life into the car radio, she tells him: "They only play rock'n'roll on Saturday afternoons." Butch boasts: "In the States we got rock'n'roll all day long."

My American Cousin conjures up a lost age of Canadian innocence, that uncertain time when the Red Ensign and the Union Jack fluttered side by side while America transformed the world with cars and TV sets. On the one hand, the film tells a simple story about a young girl who is alternately entranced and amused by the worldly posturing of an older boy. It is also a vivid portrayal of a country that had yet to discover the adult pleasures of cultural nationalism. Representing Canada's Victorian past are Sandy's strict but forgiving parents: Jane Mortifee is convincing as her mother, but Donat overplays his role as her father with a stilted performance—the only serious discord in a film that is otherwise beautifully executed. Richard Leiterman's photography captures the pristine look of 1950s Canada with breathtaking clarity. And the scenery of the Okanagan forms an almost surreal backdrop for Butch's indigo jeans and red Cadillac.

My American Cousin . . . deserves to be seen on the big screen. The freshness and power of its visual images help forge the magical connection between the director and her childhood memories. And the result serves as vivid evidence that independent film-making is gradually coming of age in Canada.

MACLEAN'S, NOVEMBER 4, 1985

RESPONSES

1. If you have seen the film, share your reactions to the film with your classmates and compare your opinion with that of Brian Johnson.

2. Using your knowledge of film reviews, evaluate Johnson's review.

3. Explain why you agree or disagree with the idea that it is important to have young people see a film that the critic claims "conjures up a lost age of Canadian innocence." What are some of the differences in having the film's events told from a girl's point of view rather than a boy's?

4. In the film, Sandy and her friends are in awe of her American cousin partly because of what the United States represented in 1959: its wealth, and especially its alluring popular culture. Do you think the film could have the same theme if it took place in the '80s? If a similar film were to be made today, what changes in the content and style would you make?

5. Think of some other coming-of-age films, and write a review of one of them.

6. Research the history of the film industry in Canada. You could focus your research on one aspect of Canadian film, such as the NFB; Quebec film history; or a single period in Canadian film history. The Inquiry Model in the Reference Section (p. 211) might help you develop a thesis.

HOLLYWOOD SINCE 1975: SOME FAST CUTS

The decade between 1975 and 1985 was a very important one in American film history. It was a decade of blockbuster hits and major publicity campaigns, of new technologies and special effects—all of which attracted huge audiences. In the mid '70s, such trends as the buddy film (*Butch Cassidy and the Sundance Kid*, 1969), the vigilante film (*Death Wish*, 1974), and the disaster film (*Towering Inferno*, 1974) began to disappear. In their place came slapstick comedies, space operas, slasher films, remakes, and youth films.

Steven Spielberg's *Jaws* (1975) is an example of the new kind of filmmaking. Unlike the previous disaster films, *Jaws* was optimistic. It featured a man who was able to defeat not only a deadly shark but also the local immoral politicians. Fuelled by a massive publicity campaign (so convincing that some people imagined they saw sharks in the water near their summer cottages), the film became the fourth biggest box office success in film history. Spielberg was among the new young filmmakers dubbed "the movie brats." He, Martin Scorcese (*Taxi Driver*, 1976), Brian de Palma (*Carrie*, 1977), Francis Ford Coppola (*The Godfather*, 1971), all had grown up on a steady diet of the classic films of the '40s and '50s. Realizing that the age of classic cinema was over, many of these filmmakers worked playfully with cinematic styles by including in their works references to old plots, reworking traditional film genres or, as in the case of Mel Brooks (*Young Frankenstein*, 1975), using the genre for comic send-ups or parodies. Eventually, some filmmakers simply recycled material from the past, e.g., the new versions of *Superman*, *Popeye*, and *Tarzan*.

Trends in film are often closely related to trends in television. In 1975, ABC (American Broadcasting Corporation) commissioned a survey that indicated viewers wanted a return to traditional values. On television, the heavy-action police shows (*Cannon*, *Kojak*, *Police Story*) were shelved, and the family hour took their place; sitcoms and superheroes became popular. Among the ten top-rated programs, the shows of producer Norman Lear ranked high (*All in the Family*, *Maude*, *The Jeffersons*). Characterized by a frank treatment of contemporary social issues—from racial prejudice to abortion—Lear's success has not been equalled since. The social commentary of Norman Lear was soon replaced, in 1977, by programs such as *Happy Days*, *Laverne and Shirley*

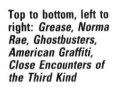

Top to bottom, left to right: *Grease, Norma Rae, Ghostbusters, American Graffiti, Close Encounters of the Third Kind*

(both influenced by the film *American Graffiti*) *Charlie's Angels*, *Three's Company*, and *The Love Boat*.

Sylvester Stallone as *Rocky* (1976) presented a new kind of film hero—a hero of the working class. Stallone, who declared that movies were about making the audience feel good about itself, presented film-goers with the image of realizing the impossible dream.

In 1977, George Lucas' *Star Wars* became a megahit—the biggest box office hit up to that time. Lucas showed Hollywood how to borrow from many elements, both current and traditional: westerns, war films, fairy tales, cartoons, myth, science-fiction films, and classics such as *The Wizard of Oz*. *Star Wars*, with its militaristic themes and space age technology was also a universal story about the quest of its hero (Luke Skywalker) for self-knowledge. Spielberg, also in 1977, released *Close Encounters of the Third Kind*, which combined the science-fiction ele-

ments of *Star Wars* and the "feeling strong" mood of *Rocky*. And in 1982 came the biggest box office hit ever, *E.T. The Extra-Terrestrial*.

Saturday Night Fever (1977), starring John Travolta as the street-smart dance-wise hero, began another major trend. With disco all the rage, and a sound track album as a publicity boost, the film anticipated the success of later dance-musical films—*Grease* (1978), *Fame* (1980), *Flashdance* (1983), *Purple Rain* (1986), and *Dirty Dancing* (1987). With more and more young people making up the film-going audience (60 percent attending movies were under 25), a huge youth market opened up. In 1978, *Saturday Night Fever* was followed by two films pitched to a young audience: *Grease* and *Animal House*. These films preceded both the exploitative but commercially successful films for young audiences such as *Porky's* (1982), and the more realistic teen portrayals found in the work of filmmaker John Hughes—*Breakfast Club* (1985), and *Pretty in Pink* (1986).

From *Animal House* to the more thoughtful work of Woody Allen, comedy has often resulted in a box office bonanza. In 1980, half of the top ten money-making films were comedies: *The Jerk*, *Airplane!*, *Smokey and the Bandit II*, *Private Benjamin*, and *The Blues Brothers*.

Ghostbusters (1984), the highest-grossing comedy of its day, was a sign of the times—it was suited to the Ronald Reagan-dominated Amer-

ican attitudes, which embraced big business and social conservatism. Under this influence, films with the hero acting as a one-person army who "settles the score" on behalf of America appeared: *The Terminator* (1984), *Invasion USA* (1985), *Missing in Action* (1984), and *Rambo: First Blood Part II* (1985). Hollywood was also beginning to examine the meaning of Americans' experience in the Vietnam War and audiences were confronted with the moral and political dilemmas surrounding it: *Coming Home* (1978), *The Deer Hunter* (1978), *Apocalypse Now* (1979). The theme continued with *Platoon* (1987) and *Good Morning Vietnam* (1987).

In the late '70s and early '80s, a number of horror films appeared. Some of them were anti-feminist slasher films—*Hallowe'en* (1978), *Friday the 13th* (1980), *Prom Night* (1979)—but others such as *Alien* (1979), Spielberg's *Poltergeist* (1982) and *Gremlins* (1985) had many redeeming qualities in terms of theme and artistic impression.

The films described here are only the films of the big Hollywood studios. But there has been ample proof that independent filmmakers can make it on their own. Films such as *Reds* (1981), *Return of the Secaucus Seven* (1980), *Norma Rae* (1979), and *Under Fire* (1983) are examples.

What has remained constant in many American films since the mid-'70s is their self-reflexiveness, or the self-conscious tendency to refer to other films—their styles, dialogue, settings, and twists in plot. For a generation of filmmakers raised on television, also a self-reflexive medium, this trend was probably inevitable. Equally predictable is the recycling or exploitation of popular culture trends. For example, the police shows that were shelved in the mid-'70s reappeared in new forms in the mid-'80s, e.g., *Hill Street Blues* and *Miami Vice*.

The film industry is currently experiencing major challenges from several sources.

1. The youth audience is declining and, as a result, filmmakers are looking for material which will satisfy the need of more mature audiences.

2. There have been huge business mergers among the big studios, often affecting the creative and economic climate necessary for good films.

3. With the rise of the VCR (it is predicted that by 1990 over three quarters of Canadian households will own one), people are buying or renting tapes, and even taping films from network television or from pay television.

4. Pay television is now producing its own films and competing with films shown in theatres or rented in video stores. All of these factors have led to more fragmented audiences and to a decentralized movie industry. How well the movie industry copes will define the role of movies in the popular culture of the 1990s.
—ADAPTED FROM

"TEN YEARS THAT SHOOK THE WORLD" BY JIM HOBERMAN. *AMERICAN FILM*. 1985

RESPONSES

1. Identify some other trends in Hollywood movies since 1985. Predict trends which you believe will occur in the next few years. What current trends may come to an end? Discuss which trends, both past and present, you like and dislike, and why.

2. What are some of the connections between the trends in television and the trends in films? In groups, research the TV shows that were popular during a particular year or two and compare them with the films that appeared in the same years. Each group could study a different year or two years.

3. *Star Wars*, *Jaws*, *Close Encounters of the Third Kind*, *E.T. The Extra-Terrestrial*, and *Ghostbusters* were all block-buster hits. What was the basis of their appeal? What other films or TV shows have these films inspired? What other major films in recent years have inspired sequels or served as a catalyst for new trends?

4. As outlined in the concluding paragraph, the film industry is facing several important challenges. Research one or more of these challenges and present a report to the class.

5. The "Star Wars" defense systems or Clint Eastwood's famous expression in his Dirty Harry movies, "Go ahead. Make my day," are examples of how our language and thought has been influenced by the movies. Discuss the idea that movies have assumed a role as a metaphor for our culture, using examples from as many popular films as possible.

6. From *Casablanca* (1942) to *The Rocky Horror Picture Show* (1971), audiences have shown strong loyalty to certain films which are given extended runs, and are often seen several times by their adoring fans. By choosing one or more examples, research the phenomenon of cult films.

7. Do a study of some films from a non-North American country. Or, choose a non-North American film currently available in videocassette and write a review of it to present to the class. Discuss what you like and dislike about foreign films. What are the advantages of seeing films from other countries?

ISSUES FOR FURTHER STUDY

From what you have learned in this chapter, going to the movies may now mean more than settling into the seats with your popcorn and being transported from the "real world" for a couple of hours. Discussing films, practising your filmmaking techniques, writing scripts, analyzing film methods, and assessing films in the form of reviews can help you become a critical viewer. Now when you watch films, perhaps you will be more aware of the ways in which they can evoke emotional reactions. The following questions allow you to expand your knowledge of film and film techniques.

1. Refer to the story outlines and scripts you wrote for films earlier in the chapter, or create a new outline, and simulate the process of making it into a box office hit. Choose some current popular or "bankable" stars for the roles. Think of a title for your film, and design the poster. Discuss the marketing of the film, choose when you think it should be released, and plan a multi-media promotional campaign. You could think of some advertising gimmicks, such as merchandising of clothing and other consumer products, write the copy for the TV and radio commercials, and plan a sneak preview night.

2. Research the roles of the various film personnel you see listed on film credits; for example, producer, director, cinematographer, best boy, gaffer, and editor.

3. Evaluate the success of literature adaptations for film by examining two or more novels, short stories, or plays which were made into films. Try to assess the success of the films, without judging them on the basis of how faithful they were to the original. What technical methods were used to convey elements such as setting, characterization, plot, foreshadowing, and symbolism? The following are a few examples from which to choose (or think of your own adaptation): *A Separate Peace*, *To Kill a Mockingbird*, *Lord of the Flies*, *The Outsiders*, *Tex*, *Shane*, *A Streetcar Named Desire*.

4. Research various special effects (SPFX) that are used in filmmaking. Do a report on the kinds of special effects there are, how they are done, and refer to some films that demonstrate some of these effects.

5. Feature films are an important source of contemporary insight into life's meaning. By taking a thematic approach to film, you have an opportunity to see a variety of films, do some comparative studies, and consider some important issues. Choose a theme from the following list, or a theme of your choice, and see how it has been treated by the film medium. The following are just a few themes and films (all of them are available on videocassette) to help you. Note both the similarities and the differences in the cinematic treatment of the themes.

Heroes *Superman*; *African Queen*; *Casablanca*; *Rocky*; *Star Wars*; *The Terry Fox Story*; *The Mission.*

The Quest *Citizen Kane*; *The Great Gatsby*; *Who Has Seen the Wind?*; *E.T. The Extra-Terrestrial*; *Mon Oncle Antoine.*

Images of Youth *The Breakfast Club*; *Pretty in Pink*; *Ordinary People*; *Breaking Away*; *A Separate Peace*; *Fame*; *My Bodyguard*; *The Outsiders.*

War *Gallipoli*; *Slaughterhouse Five*; *The Wars*; *Patton*; *Das Boot*; *Good Morning Vietnam.*

Comedy *Annie Hall*; *Young Frankenstein*; *Monty Python and the Holy Grail*; *Animal Crackers*; *Modern Times*; *The Goldrush*; *Ghostbusters*; *Crocodile Dundee.*

Images of Women *My Brilliant Career*; *Norma Rae*; *Coal Miner's Daughter*; *Julia*; *Tess*; *Marie.*

Implications of the Media *King of Comedy*; *Network*; *Being There*; *Broadcast News.*

6. Watch a few films—feature or shorts—and analyze them in terms of their technical aspects. Describe the lighting, sound, camera work, editing, and composition. You may wish to refer to the Television chapter's Glossary of Terms (p. 84). Describe how the techniques used in the film enhanced meaning.

7. Have a class film festival. Present what you feel is your best film, or scene. You may want to involve classes, or the whole school. After the screenings, you could have an awards ceremony, like the Genies, or the Academy Awards, and present awards for Best Film, Best Director, Best Screenplay, Best Actor, Best Actress, Best Lighting, and any other category you choose.

Edward Muybridge experimented with photographs and motion in the late 1800s. He photographed a galloping horse using 24 cameras activated by trip wires. The series of photographs, and the device he invented to make them seem to move, is an early "motion picture." Flip through the pages of this chapter to see this horse in "action."

CHAPTER 4

Sound and Music

I f you think about it, people rarely experience truly quiet moments. Sounds are everywhere—pleasant sounds and annoying sounds, natural sounds and electronic sounds. Although hearing is one of our five senses, we seem to know very little about how sound functions in our lives, what meaning it has, and how we interact with our acoustic environment.

Many of us like the company of sound, and turn to music to provide that company. We seem to like music so much, in fact, that the recording industry is the biggest of the entertainment industries. In turn, popular, or pop, music is the biggest segment of the recording industry. There are, and always have been, controversies surrounding pop music: the power of the lyrics and the messages they contain; fans' emulation or copying of the performers and the values they represent; the messages of music videos; and the role of women are a few of the issues. Perhaps these controversies exist because of the sheer magnitude of the industry.

Despite any negative influences, many people simply like to listen to the music. For many people there is a certain incomparable pleasure in removing the cellophane from a new album, compact disc or tape, placing it gently on the turntable or in the tape player, "cranking up" the volume and listening—to the sound.

SOUNDSCAPES

While most of us are familiar with the landscapes that surround us, being aware of "soundscapes" can be just as important. The term was coined by Canadian composer and music educator, R. Murray Schafer.

Schafer has researched and studied the social and artistic aspects of sound environments. He believes that the acoustic environment of a society reflects the social conditions and trends that produce it. Investigating the soundscapes of rural settings, small towns, urban areas, or the soundscapes of periods in history is a way of learning about those environments. Schafer terms a characteristic of our electronic age as "schizophonia," the splitting of sounds from their sources. Examples of this are the telephone, radio, and record player.

In 1969, Schafer initiated a World Soundscape Project to raise people's awareness of sound, and to keep track of the changes in the sounds of our environment. He also pursued the idea of designing soundscapes to offset noise pollution. Basic to Schafer's ideas is his concept that noise is "unwanted sounds, or sounds that we have learned to ignore". In order to distinguish the sounds we like from the sounds we dislike, we have to listen critically to our acoustic environment.

RESPONSES

1. List some of your favourite and least favourite sounds. Compare your list with others in your class. Are there students whose favourite sounds are disliked by other students? How do you account for the idea that some people's noise is other people's sound?

2. In your media log, keep a record of the sounds of your household and your immediate neighbourhood for one or two days. Compare your soundscapes with those of your classmates.

3. What sounds do you think dominated the soundscape in cities and towns before the Industrial Revolution? Compare those sounds with the typical sounds of a contemporary urban soundscape.

4. Explain why you agree or disagree with Murray Schafer's definition of noise as "sounds we have learned to ignore." Apply this definition to your soundscapes. What sounds would you put in the category of noise?

MAKING SOUND COLLAGES

A collage is a picture made from an arrangement of items of different textures, colours, styles, and shapes. To learn about the meaning different sounds and combinations of sounds can make, and the emotions that can be evoked, try making a sound collage. In groups, record a variety of sounds: spoken word, sounds of nature, sounds of technology, and music. The following are some suggestions for planning your collages.

• You could have a brainstorming session to decide on a dominant theme and mood for your collage and suggest sounds that you think would best express the theme.

• You may find it helpful to write a script for your sound collage, indicating the selections, the length of the selection, and any special instructions, such as "fade in music." See the glossary of terms (p. 84) in the Television chapter for the correct terminology.

• You should rehearse your sound collage and make any necessary revisions in your script before you tape it.

• You could use original commentary or dialogue, or readings from various works.

• You could use records or tapes of sound effects that may be available in your library.

• You could use sound effects and music as the background to the spoken word segments, or as separate components.

• If your school or someone in your class has a microphone mixer, or mixing board, perhaps you could use it to make your collage. A mixer is a machine used in sound recording to blend and vary the intensity of sounds from various sources. You can hook up microphones, record players, and audiocassette and reel to reel tape recorders directly to the mixer. The number of sources depends on the number of channels the mixer has; they range from 2 – 4 – 6 – 8 – 16 – 24.

CAN THERE BE NO SILENCE?

An informal study of your acoustic surroundings will reveal that we are rarely without sound, and that we are rarely without music. For example, many businesses and services fill your ear with music when you are put on hold on the telephone. The jarring sound of an alarm clock has been replaced with the more soothing sounds of clock radios. "Institutional sound" is the term for the music we often hear in elevators, shopping malls, and dentists' offices; it has also become known commercially as "muzak." This music is usually constant, but not very noticeable, and usually instrumental.

The following excerpt is from a book by Gary Gumpert, a professor of Communication Arts and Sciences. As you read it, think about institutional sound and the questions it raises about individuality, freedom of choice, and social conditioning.

Institutional Sound

by Gary Gumpert

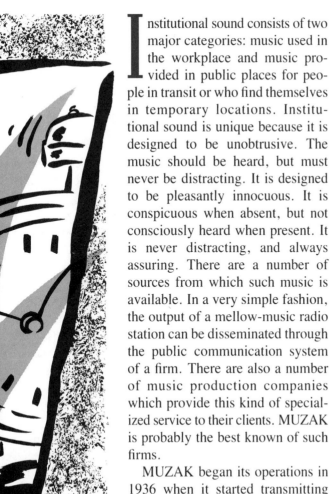

I nstitutional sound consists of two major categories: music used in the workplace and music provided in public places for people in transit or who find themselves in temporary locations. Institutional sound is unique because it is designed to be unobtrusive. The music should be heard, but must never be distracting. It is designed to be pleasantly innocuous. It is conspicuous when absent, but not consciously heard when present. It is never distracting, and always assuring. There are a number of sources from which such music is available. In a very simple fashion, the output of a mellow-music radio station can be disseminated through the public communication system of a firm. There are also a number of music production companies which provide this kind of specialized service to their clients. MUZAK is probably the best known of such firms.

MUZAK began its operations in 1936 when it started transmitting music via telephone lines to hotels and restaurants. In 1980 the company was transmitting its programming to a daily listening audience claimed to be around 80 million people via a communication satellite. A spokesperson for MUZAK pointed out that the basic concept is to provide music which is part of the total environment. "We take a musical selection and re-arrange it, and re-record it with different instrumentations and different styles so that it does not intrude. You can work with it and can converse with it without interrupting your concentration." Music supplies an aural environment and is part of the decor which characterizes a business establishment. Sound used in this way has three basic (not mutually exclusive) functions: to establish the appropriate mood and decor; to cut down on noise and distractions; and to increase productivity. However, the use of music to establish environment is indicative of a general attitude toward silence. Obviously, uncontrolled noise can be distracting, counterproductive, and even psychologically and physically harmful. But the presence of silence is seen as an equal, perhaps even greater menace. The spokesperson for MUZAK stated, "We maintain that most people are uneasy with an absence of sound. We feel an empty space requires some kind of pleasant sound. Music is one of the more pleasant sounds."

It is also pointed out that some noises are accentuated and startling if they occur within relatively silent environments. But there are few places which are truly silent, except those created by twentieth-century technology. Part of the problem was created by modern office buildings which seal out all extraneous noise, creating a relatively silent environment which is unnatural and annoying. A need for a substitute auditory environment has been created. . . . Relative silence can present a threat. For example, when you go into an empty public area that is usually full of activity, you feel a little bit uneasy. What is more haunting than standing on the stage of an empty theatre or being in a large office space late at night? . . . The unexpected leaps out of silence. It is not part of the desired human experience to exist in silence. In those situations we produce our own human sounds to reassure ourselves. We accompany our fears with words muttered under the breath, a whistled or hummed tune, a nervous cough.

Silence ought not be confused with quiet. . . . Are there places where one expects to meet a quiet atmosphere, where the presence of music would be inappropriate? It is hard to think of such a place. The funeral parlor? No! One cannot bear the thought of death without pastel music filtering through the air. In a house of worship? Very seldom. The choir or the organ even provides background for prayer. Most people, and there are, of course, exceptions, sleep without music, but make sure that they fall asleep or awaken to the music of the clock radio. This culture has been programmed and

weaned on a musical environment. When there is an absence of voice and/or natural sound in an enclosed place, we feel disconnected, disoriented, and desire music to reestablish a complete environment.

On the other hand, the presence of noise is considered undesirable. The shrill sounds of sirens, the hammering of pneumatic drills, the clatter of typewriters, the hissing of steam, and the screeching of machinery can be harmful and is certainly counterproductive. It is, therefore, desirable to eliminate noise whenever possible. Many companies are aware of their noise problems and solve the situation in different ways. When the landscape concept of office design became popular in the late 1950s, when management began to remove office walls to create an open working space for employees, both benefits and problems occurred. The new arrangement was seen as a means to improve communications and the flow of paper. In addition, it offered different design possibilities. . . .

But the number of potential distractions also increased. Telephone conversations, calculators, typewriters, and general office noise have to be muffled as much as possible. . . . Ways of decreasing general background noise in such an office and at the same time providing an acoustical territory for each employee included using screens to redirect and absorb sound, treated ceilings, and masking devices. One such masking device is a white noise generator which produces a low, almost imperceptible, level of sound that masks other noises. While it is effective, the sound of the white noise generator, reportedly like an air conditioner, is constant and irritating with no variation in pitch or intensity. Therefore, many companies seeking some means of masking noise began to look for an alternative. One solution which MUZAK developed was a sound generator tuned to the ambience level of the particular environment. Selective frequencies match or combat the frequencies in a specific area and music is then superimposed over the masking frequencies. Apparently, the selective use of the sound generator achieves such acoustical privacy that a telephone conversation ten feet away is unintelligible. The sounds can be heard, but not understood. The intentions of the employer are positive in the sense that a better and efficient working climate is created for the employee. One wonders, however, if employees are informed when either white noise or sound generators are utilized. What are the employees' rights in regard to acoustical self-determination?

The economic welfare of the particular company and its productivity is paramount to its management. In that sense worker morale is a major factor since it is linked to economic success and failure. In order to combat monotony and offset boredom, and since individual radios (portable or the Walkman type) might present some chaotic problems, a very carefully arranged

selection of music can be provided in which each quarter hour is programmed. MUZAK calls this programming "Stimulus Progression." Very simply, it assumes that during the course of a working day an employee's attention, concentration, vigor, and enthusism will vary. For example, at 10:30 in the morning the worker is less alert than at the beginning of the shift or just before the lunch break. Therefore, that dip can be countered by a change of beat and/or orchestration at that point. The slump is countered with

> *While it is effective, the sound of the white noise generator is constant and irritating . . .*

an injection of up-beat musical energy. Productivity figures do indicate a positive change with this type of programming. There is to be found, for instance, a reduction of errors by typists and a decrease in the number of assembly line rejects. The MUZAK literature states:

Experiments performed by the Human Engineering Laboratory of the U.S. Army in Aberdeen Proving Ground, Maryland, found that programmed functional music improves human vigilance, mental alertness, working efficiency. This applies particularly to routine or repetitive assignments.

Among the companies that use both the masking device and muzak are the Xerox Corporation, United

Parcel Service, the Telephone Company of Connecticut, the Young and Rubicam advertising agency, and Nissan Motors in Japan. The system works because it supplies or creates an audio environment which some find pleasant, it decreases irksome noise, and it aids in raising the efficiency of the employees. There are, however, some questions to be asked.

Does the employee have a choice? Is the worker informed in the job interview that he or she will be subjected to muzak for the entire working day? Or is it to be considered merely part of the decor over which the employee has few rights, if any? What are the psychological effects of being bathed in music during an entire working day? Obviously, once the person has been hired, choice is eliminated and control of the musical environment is in the hands of the executive in charge. One of the badges of the executive's authority is the control of his or her own acoustical environment. However non-executives are subject to musical manipulation. . . .

—*TALKING TOMBSTONES AND OTHER TALES OF THE MEDIA AGE*, 1987

RESPONSES

1. What do you like and dislike about institutional music? According to Gary Gumpert what are its advantages and disadvantages?

2. How do you feel when you are in a space that is very quiet? Explain why you agree or disagree with the author's statement "When there is an absence of voice/and or natural sound in an enclosed place, we feel disconnected, disoriented, and desire music to re-establish a complete environment." You could write your answer in prose or poetry. Describe some examples from your personal experience.

3. What do you think are the psychological effects of constant exposure to institutional music or white noise? Interview some people about their workplace and the sounds to which they are exposed. If any of them work where muzak and/or white noise generators operate, find out how they feel about working in those conditions. See page 212 in the Reference Section for tips on conducting interviews.

4. According to the author, what ethical problems are created by the use of institutional sound? In groups, brainstorm to think of some other problems it might create.

5. Debate the following statement. "Resolved that: Institutional music has conditioned us to accept the need to fill the silent intervals of our day."

SOUND AND SPACE

We have probably all felt the discomfort of being crowded, or of having someone stand too close to us. There have been studies of people's sense of "personal space" or "social distance"—the space that people like to keep between themselves and others. Although the boundaries are not defined, and they may differ from person to person, we also have a sense of acoustical space. For example, when a person is standing centimetres away from you, your conversation would probably be in whispers. Shouting at someone while standing that close is an act of verbal aggression. R. Murray Schafer defines acoustical space as the volume of space in which a sound can be heard, so that a human's acoustical space would be the distance his or her voice carries. New technology, however, has changed this sense of acoustical space. Consider the person with the blaring portable cassette deck under his or her arm. That person has increased his or her acoustical power and space, and has invaded the space of others.

Gary Gumpert refers to our sense of acoustical space as a "wall of sound." But, he points out, these walls do not have to be marked by sound that everyone can hear. Listening to music privately is also a way of putting up a wall of sound. With the appearance of the personal stereo in the 1980s (commonly known as a "Walkman," the name used by its original developer, Sony Corporation), the experience of hearing manufactured sound has been significantly changed. Many people seem to have become permanently attached to their personal stereos. The following selection by Gary Gumpert is about our walls of sound, and personal stereos and their impact on our acoustic space.

Walls of Sound

by Gary Gumpert

Many of us surround and protect ourselves with walls of sound while we are engaged in public activity. A bicycle is adorned with a small radio. A picnic includes a portable radio in the spread. The distance between blankets on a crowded day at the beach is not only determined by personal space, but by zones of music. Dials are adjusted and speakers stationed in the right direction. And when we enter our cars and automatically turn on the radio we are assured that we are not alone and that we have protective company for as long as the journey lasts.

The wall of sound, that sense of acoustical space which surrounds each of us, is not always displayed by speakers blaring out sound. The wall of sound is often silent, non-public, not shared with others. In contrast with large portable stereophonic cassette units, the alternative of mini-portable stereophonic units has been developed for people who are mobile and wish to hear music privately. The spectator at the baseball game carries a mini-portable radio and an ear plug which provides the "play by play" broadcast. The jogger, the walker, the skier, and the roller skater can wear tiny headphones equipped with padded ear cushions. The office worker can listen to his or her own tunes without disturbing colleagues. The rest of the world can be shut out. "Walkman" (previously also called "Soundabout") was originally developed by the Sony Corporation in Japan for weary commuters who wanted relief from the boredom of their routine daily roundtrips. . . .

Richard Warren of *The Chicago-Sun Times* described the unit as "the final solution to the punk problem. Require all the kids with those blaring boxes [boom boxes] on the trains to trade them in for a Soundabout." In *The New York Times* Hans Fantel said that the unit was ideal "for commuters traveling by train, giving them the same chance to sweeten their daily trek as is enjoyed by automobile travelers riding to the tunes of their car stereo." . . .

While the speakers of a portable radio or cassette player create a wall

of amplified sound, earphones and earplugs create a silent wall, which separates the listener from those around him or her. The earphone mentality is based on privatization and isolation—on withdrawal from public sound and interaction. For some, like the roller skater or the music aficionado, excluding the extraneous helps them concentrate. For commuters, the motive is to create another sound environment, replacing the one which accompanies the mundane, routinized ritual, or to substitute pleasant sound for often harmful noise. Some jobs do not require thinking, because they have been absorbed into a routine of repetitive manual tasks. How many times have you commuted from home to work or school without remembering anything that occurred during the trip? People who drive are often not aware of the many manual operations they perform during the usual repetitive trip. Earphone listeners separate the sensory world transmitted into the cranium from the reality of mindless manual tasks. The sanitation or assembly line worker does not care to hear the sounds of the street or the factory; he or she prefers to escape them. The jogger is distracted from

the pain of running or avoids the monotony of a daily route. In such situations the original sound source is separated from its new use and environment. Energy is directed inward, the visual images induced by the sound not congruent with the task at hand. The music triggers memories and fantasies, while muscle and motor coordination operate in the routine world.

One example of substituting a sound environment occurs frequently in the experience of air travellers. The airlines recognize the danger of boredom in long-distance travel. The passenger who is kept busy forgets the ordeal of travel. One pays to be plugged into the multichannel sound system. If you are unable to sleep on a plane, if your neighbor seems morose and uncommunicative (or if you wish to be morose and uncommunicative), if there is nothing you wish to read, the flight [becomes] long, and the scenery does not change. The desire to wander down the aisle and visit the pilot grows stronger, but the urge is suppressed by the watchful crew. Strapped in the middle of a six-person row, there is nothing to do but concentrate on the vibrating engines which sound a bit strange and fantasize the plunge downward and the moment of impact. Strapped to an unhealthy auditory and visual experience, one surrenders to the substitute two-dollar sound environment, along with earplugs that offer the additional sensation of pain (first-class passengers have the benefit of mod-

ern padded earphones and are robbed of the additional sensory experience). . . .

Using earphones in public has another additional consequence, perhaps intentional at times, but often incidental in intent. The user is cut off from interaction with others. The airline passenger leaning back wearing earphones signals neighbors that conversation is not desired. The plugged-in commuter retreats into private sound. A colleague walks down the halls locked into an unknown world of music, precluding conversation with an unplugged scholar, which might have been equally stimulating and entertaining. The earphone/earplug prevents outside but often necessary sounds from entering awareness. One manufacturer has therefore produced a muting switch which temporarily turns down the volume when the conductor asks for a ticket or someone simply asks a question. The muting switch allows the questioner to reach you at half the decibel level. The person has your attention, but not all of it is granted. You maintain control of your sensory world.

The public earphone user creates a private world similar to that of the "box" user. Joyce Brothers considers the Walkman user more polite than the "boom box" culprit and suggests that the Walkman statement is "I am concerned about your reaction, but not all that concerned. I'm still in my own world." Is the user of the Walkman more considerate than the master of the "monster box"? Each moves in a portable acoustical bubble, and while the effect of the miniaturized unit is less political than the box (certainly an important distinction), each of the users displays some attempted mastery of his or her own movable turf. The earphones establish an acoustical territory which is not to be entered without permission and which restricts interaction with outsiders. The wall of sound is silent, but communicates quite clearly. The presence of a Walkman renders the outsider invisible—a strange and unsettling feeling. It is equally strange to witness a person gyrating and foot-tapping to an imperceptible beat. The suspicion of a possible mental disturbance vanishes with the sight of an earphone, and the alien walks and jogs to the beat of a different tape. . . .

—TALKING TOMBSTONES AND OTHER
TALES OF THE MEDIA AGE, 1987

RESPONSES

1. If you own a personal stereo, explain the satisfaction you get from it. If you do not like them, give your reasons.

2. Summarize in your own words the author's examination of the pros and cons of personal stereos.

3. Discuss the author's observation that, "The earphones establish an acoustical territory which is not to be entered without permission and which restricts interaction with others." What do you think are the advantages and disadvantages of such a situation? What do you do when you want to talk to someone who is physically close to you but, because of a personal stereo, or earphones, is acoustically somewhere else? In groups, discuss and then enact this situation, either from a script or through improvisation.

4. From your studies in the Film chapter, you may have learned that there is a dynamic interrelationship that develops between sound and the visual. One commentator remarked, "A Walkman not only fills you with sound, it turns the outside world into a film for which your Walkman's sound now becomes the sound track." Suggest several pieces of music that you think would be good accompaniment to various activities, or create a soundtrack for your daily life. For example, what music do you think would best accompany having a shower, travelling on a bus, canoeing, skating, riding horseback, or shopping? You might want to play pieces of the music you choose to the class, and have them guess what activity is taking place.

THE MUSIC INDUSTRY— A SOUND BUSINESS

A business that exists on the theory that, "It is not part of the desired human experience to exist in silence" is the music industry. The business of creating and selling music is a huge and very expensive one, whether it is the production of an album, the sale of promotional items at a concert, or buying advertising time from a music radio station.

If radio stations are successful, their listening audiences will buy tickets to a concert that the station might be co-sponsoring and promoting. If the performer at that concert is successful in "hooking" his or her audience, these fans will head to the record store to buy the performer's latest album. And if record companies and performers are lucky, the fans will also buy T-shirts and posters while at the store. Radio stations hope that these fans will tune in to hear this album, and others like it, when the fans are away from their record players. And if music videos work the way they are intended, viewers will head to the record store again to buy more albums. These are some of the reasons why the recording industry in North America makes over $5 billion per year.

How much rock groups make
(Concert ticket grosses by major touring rock acts. The number of cities most tours play has grown from 24 in 1965 to almost 80 last year.)

Year	Group	Gross
1965	The Beatles	$ 2 000 000
1979-80	Supertramp	50 000 000
1981	Rolling Stones	40 000 000
1983	David Bowie	50 000 000
1984	The Jacksons	70 000 000
1985	Bruce Springsteen	70 000 000
1987	U2	35 000 000
1987	Bon Jovi	28 400 000

—*Billboard Publications, Inc.*, 1988

• Pink Floyd's three nights at Exhibition Stadium in Toronto in 1987 was the top-grossing rock event in North America. They brought in more than $3 700 000.

• Michael Jackson's *Bad* video cost approximately $2 million to make.

• Bruce Springsteen's 1985 concert tour made $20 000 000 in merchandising sales (T-shirts, paraphernalia).

You and the Music: A Survey

To see how important the music industry is in your life, complete the following survey in your media log.

1. How much time per day do you spend listening to the radio? tapes? albums? compact discs?

2. How much money do you spend per month on tapes? albums? compact discs? music fan magazines? music paraphernalia (T-shirts, posters)?

3. How many concerts do you attend per year? How much money do you spend on them per year? List any recent concerts you have attended.

4. What kinds of music do you enjoy? What kinds do you dislike and why?

5. What is your favourite radio station? Your favourite disc jockey? Why do you like them?

6. What is your current favourite song? Your current favourite music video?

7. List your five all-time favourite bands and five all-time favourite solo artists.

8. Who are your favourite Canadian bands and solo artists?

9. List your five all-time favourite videos.

10. List your top ten albums.

Compile the results of the survey or compare your survey results with those of some classmates. Either alone or in groups, answer the following questions: Is your current favourite song near the top of the charts that appear in industry magazines such as *Billboard*, *Rock Express*, and *Variety*? How many of your favourite bands and solo artists appear near the top of the charts? How often is your current favourite video shown on TV? What do your answers tell you about the effect of popular trends in music on personal tastes? Total the amount of money you contribute to the music industry annually. Does this amount surprise you? Refer to the survey you did in the Television chapter (p. 61). How does your time spent watching TV compare with your time spent listening to music?

How do hits become hits? How do radio stations choose what to play? Why do you choose one station over another? The following article describes music programming on radio in the U.S. and the way that radio, like television, is dependent on ratings.

How Hits Are Made: Radio's Rating Game

by Rosalind Silver

FOR WEEK ENDING MARCH 19, 1988

Billboard HOT 100 SINGLES™

Compiled from a national sample of retail store and one-stop sales reports and radio playlists.

*ARTIST — LABEL & NUMBER/DISTRIBUTING LABEL

THIS WEEK	LAST WEEK	2 WKS AGO	WKS ON CHART	TITLE / PRODUCER (SONGWRITER)	ARTIST — LABEL & NUMBER
1	1	2	14	NEVER GONNA GIVE YOU UP / STOCK,AITKEN,WATERMAN (STOCK, AITKEN, WATERMAN) ★★ NO. 1 ★★ 2 weeks at No. One	RICK ASTLEY — RCA 5347
2	4	4	10	I GET WEAK / R.NOWELS (D. WARREN)	BELINDA CARLISLE — MCA 53242
3	2	1	10	FATHER FIGURE / G.MICHAEL (G. MICHAEL)	GEORGE MICHAEL — COLUMBIA 38-07682
(4)	7	9	7	MAN IN THE MIRROR / Q.JONES (G.GARRETT, T.G.BALLARD)	MICHAEL JACKSON — EPIC 34-07668/E.P.A.
(5)	5	8	9	ENDLESS SUMMER NIGHTS / H.GATICA (R.MARX)	RICHARD MARX — EMI-MANHATTAN 50113
6	3	3	14	SHE'S LIKE THE WIND / M.LLOYD (P.SWAYZE, S.WIDELITZ)	PATRICK SWAYZE (FEATURING WENDY FRASER) — RCA 5363
(7)	8	12	8	OUT OF THE BLUE / Z.ARR.D.GIBSON (D.GIBSON)	DEBBIE GIBSON — ATLANTIC 7-89129
8	6	7	10	JUST LIKE PARADISE / D.L.ROTH (D.L.ROTH, B.TUGGLE)	DAVID LEE ROTH — WARNER BROS. 7-28119
(9)	9	16	10	I WANT HER / K.SWEAT (K.SWEAT, T.RILEY)	KEITH SWEAT — VINTERTAINMENT 7-69431/ELEKTRA
(10)	12	22	6	GET OUTTA MY DREAMS, GET INTO MY CAR / R.J.LANGE (LANGE, B.OCEAN)	BILLY OCEAN — JIVE 1-9678/ARISTA
(11)	14	20	7	HYSTERIA / R.J.LANGE (CLARK, COLLEN, ELLIOTT, LANGE, SAVAGE)	DEF LEPPARD — MERCURY 870 004-7/POLYGRAM
(12)	16	24	9	ROCKET 2 U / B.NUNN (B.NUNN)	THE JETS — MCA 53254
(13)	17	23	9	(SITTIN' ON) THE DOCK OF THE BAY / J.CAIN (O.REDDING, S.CROPPER)	MICHAEL BOLTON — COLUMBIA 38-07680
(14)	19	26	8	GIRLFRIEND / L.A.REID,BABYFACE (L.A., BABYFACE)	PEBBLES — MCA 53185
15	15	19	10	BE STILL MY BEATING HEART / N.DORFSMAN,STING (STING)	STING — A&M 2992
(16)	22	28	6	DEVIL INSIDE / C.THOMAS (A.FARRISS, M.HUTCHENCE)	INXS — ATLANTIC 7-89144
17	11	10	18	I FOUND SOMEONE / M.BOLTON (M.BOLTON, M.MANGOLD)	CHER — GEFFEN 7-28191
(18)	23	33	8	SOME KIND OF LOVER / A.CYMONE,DAVID Z. (A.CYMONE, J.WATLEY)	JODY WATLEY — MCA 53235
(19)	28	38	4	WHERE DO BROKEN HEARTS GO / N.M.WALDEN (WILDHORN, JACKSON)	WHITNEY HOUSTON — ARISTA 1-9674
(20)	27	35	10	WISHING WELL / M.WARE,T.T.D'ARBY (T.T.D'ARBY, S.OLIVER) ★★★ POWER PICK/SALES ★★★	TERENCE TRENT D'ARBY — COLUMBIA 38-07675
(21)	24	32	7	CHECK IT OUT / J.MELLENCAMP,D.GEHMAN (J.MELLENCAMP)	JOHN COUGAR MELLENCAMP — MERCURY 870 126-7/POLYGRAM
22	10	6	18	CAN'T STAY AWAY FROM YOU / EMILIO AND THE JERKS (G.M.ESTEFAN)	GLORIA ESTEFAN & MIAMI SOUND MACHINE — EPIC 34-07641/E.P.A.
(23)	30	36	8	ANGEL / B.FAIRBAIRN (TYLER, CHILD)	AEROSMITH — GEFFEN 7-28249
(24)	25	31	7	WHEN WE WAS FAB / J.LYNNE,G.HARRISON (G.HARRISON, J.LYNNE)	GEORGE HARRISON — DARK HORSE 7-28131/WARNER BROS.
25	13	17	11	LOVE OVERBOARD / R.CALLOWAY,V.CALLOWAY (R.CALLOWAY)	GLADYS KNIGHT & THE PIPS — MCA 53210
(26)	32	37	7	ROCK OF LIFE / K.OLSEN,R.SPRINGFIELD (R.SPRINGFIELD)	RICK SPRINGFIELD — RCA 6853
27	21	13	17	PUMP UP THE VOLUME / M.YOUNG (S.YOUNG, M.YOUNG)	M/A/R/R/S — 4TH & B'WAY 7452
(28)	36	43	4	I SAW HIM STANDING THERE / G.E.TOBIN (J.LENNON, P.MCCARTNEY)	TIFFANY — MCA 53285
29	20	11	20	HUNGRY EYES (FROM "DIRTY DANCING") / E.CARMEN (F.PREVITE, J.DENICOLA)	ERIC CARMEN — RCA 5315
30	18	5	15	WHAT HAVE I DONE TO DESERVE THIS? / S.HAGUE (TENNANT, LOWE, WILLIS)	PET SHOP BOYS & DUSTY SPRINGFIELD — EMI-MANHATTAN 50107

The merchandising of music makes the industry a fairly closed shop with record producers, distributors, radio stations, and music stores making up a complex web of decision-makers—that effectively single out only a few records to be hits with the rest left to survive as they can.

Not too surprisingly, a situation develops where everyone catches everyone else. And all try to minimize potential errors by taking few risks.

"Radio is the jury, it's never wrong," says Thomas Noonan, associate publisher/director of charts at *Billboard* magazine where he manages its Hot 100 pop chart and its various spin-offs. *Billboard* and its competing but less prosperous sister-publication, *Cashbox*, maintain highly influential and closely watched charting systems that highlight the hottest records each week.

"Hot," of course, does not mean the best musically, but rather the "most bought" or "most played."

Since many stations only add new songs when they reach a certain point on the rating charts, there's a chicken and egg quality to the system. But a record's initial progress on the charts is based on airplay. Sales aren't a significant factor for several weeks.

Naturally, established artists possess an overwhelming advantage when crucial decisions regarding radio playlists are made.

Besides its own quality and/or perceived commercial viability, a new act must depend on luck, pluck, and getting the promotion department really behind it to break the system.

"Generally speaking, you don't break a new act in a major market," the *Billboard* editor says. "Usually, they have to be proven someplace else," frequently in a part of the country that knows the performer and responds to a particular sound.

Some suggest that this is why proven performers like Tina Turner and Stevie Wonder have made recent comebacks in the pop-music world. There's less risk involved in updating them than grooming—and selling—a new act.

Although there's general agreement that promotion is very important, as a former head of promotion for Columbia Records, Noonan emphasizes that there's no set formula for promoting a record, only techniques.

"Timing is important. There are summer records and winter records and records that fit the mood of a particular time. Obviously, a promoter doesn't listen to music the way a musician or fan does. "We like music; we have to. But we have commercial ears. And every song has to have its hook." The "hook" is the point of difference that can serve as its selling point when the promoters sell it to radio stations.

Although he feels that songs that deserve to make it generally do, Noonan is the first to admit that the numbers are "real rough—it's a crapshoot."

Of approximately 4000 RPM singles, about 2500 are pop, he estimates. "Of those, maybe 5 percent will become hits. And a station like KIIS-FM (Los Angeles' hot topranked Top-40 station) might add as few as four records a week of the 50 or so released. . . .

Steve Resnick of A&M Records agrees that "every record is different." Although he asserts that "we try to promote every record fairly," he agrees that distinguishing features simplify the job and "major acts are easier—they can be sold simply on the music."

"My biggest frustration comes when I believe in a record that I just can't get played," he says. And he agrees that the situation has become somewhat tighter during his 17 years in the business.

"Radio stations have to provide high ratings," he says, referring to the Arbitron rating system, which, similar to Nielsen ratings, ranks radio stations on the basis of the listening preference of a relatively small number of sample homes.

The ratings, as in TV, determine how much each station can charge for its advertising time. And with dozens of radio stations competing for listeners in each broadcast market, the pressure is on to keep listeners from switching the dial. "Radio programmers are afraid to program records unless they can be sure they're hits," notes Resnick.

Nationwide, some of those crucial programming decisions are made, or at least supplemented, by consulting firms that have sprung up to package a particular "image" for a station. Such firms offer services ranging from completely pre-taped programs that include disc-jockey patter and intercuts of local advertising, to consulting advice and suggested playlists that are systematically designed to make the station appeal to a target audience. . . . Where playlists or pre-taped programs are used the programming risk is transferred to the programmers at the consulting companies, who then, of course, must bear the responsibility if their recommendations don't lead to the expected market share.

According to Robert English, president of Broadcast Programming, a Seattle-based consultant that services 100 stations in 32 states, research is very important in making his company's programming decisions. He estimates that up to one third of the nation's 10 000 radio stations use some form of consultant service.

"We monitor the national trade magazines and the action of certain radio stations whose decision-making we're familiar with."

He agrees that the selection process tends to favor "established product." "It's tough being a new act. We do make sure that we're aware of music that's out by new artists, but almost always they have to make their mark before we recommend them.

"Of course, if a client station in Davenport was aware of an act that was hot there and they wanted to play it, that might make sense for them."

But stations are taking an unnecessary risk and maybe wasting their money if they deviate from the prescribed playlist, according to Marv Sibulkin, director of public relations for Drake-Chenault of Canoga Park, California, another well-known consulting firm.

Company co-founder Bill Drake initiated the formula "more music, less talk" that was instrumental in transforming older, disc jockey-oriented stations of the '50s and '60s into music-driven programs featuring minimal announcing.

The result, according to some music industry watchers, has been a decline in the number of local working disc jockeys responsive to local community interests, and an increase in the number of stations that depend on canned programs.

Plus, with the recent change in ownership rules by the [U.S.] Federal Communications Commission, more and more radio stations are owned by fewer and fewer media chains. For some chains, it's easier (read cheaper) to program once for all of its stations than for each local outlet.

"I often hear the same voice from city to city," says a frequent traveler. "The only thing local is weather and traffic."

Drake-Chenault's 300 U.S. client stations include 49 that are number one in their target market for their formats. Its clients have also included stations in such farflung locations as Japan, Australia, and the Caribbean, bringing mass marketing techniques and targeted sounds to other cultures.

Although company programmers watch the market closely, they also depend heavily on the kind of market research that's so important in other industries. Computer analysis of listeners' reactions to songs played in test marketing sessions are broken down by age, sex, and lifestyle demographics. "If we have a 35-year-old woman in a certain city who likes country music and there are three country stations in her city, we're going to know which one she likes," Sibulkin says.

"There are occasional surprises, but in general we're paid to know what's going to happen," he adds. "We know how to vary the playlist to avoid repetition but make sure the public hears plenty of the hottest songs. It's true that a song that's not in the Top-40 is going to have a hard time getting in.

"Radio programming has become harder than ever," says Rick Lemmo

of Drake-Chenault, who was program director for a Toledo, Ohio area station. "I don't remember that we ever added more than 4 – 5 songs a week. But new formats and MTV have opened up the market in other ways. You have to pay attention to what the listener wants.

"There's not much margin for error. These radio stations are dealing in big money and they live and die by their ratings."

—*MEDIA AND VALUES*, WINTER 1986

This playlist from Halifax radio station C100 features a week's top 30 hits and top 20 albums. Their ratings are listed under LW (Last Week) and TW (This Week).

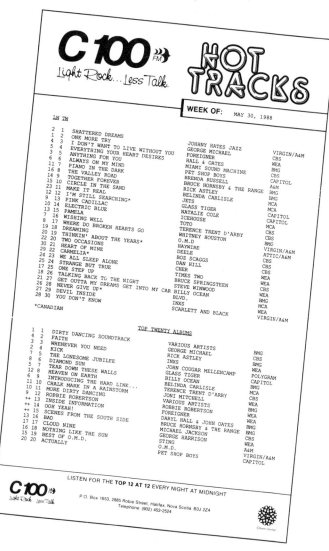

RESPONSES

1. The article describes American radio stations and consultants. Do some research to find out what systems exist in Canada. Try to find out how the station(s) in your area creates its playlist. Does the station use pre-taped programs, or suggested playlists from consultants? You might want to interview some people in the radio industry for their opinions.

2. The article points out that radio stations are aimed at target markets. In Canadian cities, the BBM (Bureau of Broadcast Measurement) surveys the popularity of stations and, on that basis, determines their advertising rates. Study the following chart describing station formats and their target audiences. Add any other formats you can think of to the list and identify the target group to which you, your friends, and members of your household belong. Discuss the formats of your local station(s).

Format/Description	Target Audience
Adult Contemporary	18 to 44 with high disposable income
Album-oriented Rock	25 to 49, especially males
Classical	30 to 60, males and females, affluent
Contemporary Hits/Top 40	10 to 35, especially females
Contemporary Hits	Baby Boomers of both sexes (to 44)
Contemporary Hits	World War II generation (to 54)
Country	18 to 44, especially middle-class males
Jazz	25 to 44, especially males
MOR (Middle of the Road)	35 up (music from '50s and '60s)
Oldies (Hit Parade)	45 up, especially women
Rhythm and Blues	18 to 35

3. In groups, choose one format from the previous chart, or a non-commercial station, such as CBC, or an all-news station, or a format of your choice. Pretend that you are the staff for the station, for 10 – 15 minutes of their broadcast time. Choose the songs you would play, the commercials you think would likely be played, and write or improvise the DJ monologue, and the weather and traffic reports. You might want to listen to a station that has the format you are copying in order to become familiar with their style and target markets. Present your radio show to the other groups either live or on tape.

4. If you have ever phoned in a somewhat obscure song request to a radio station, were you successful in having the song played? Have you ever had difficulty in finding an album in a record store? Discuss any such experiences in class. In what ways does the selection process of radio music favour "established product"?

5. Clip some album/song ratings charts from magazines such as *Rock Express*, *Billboard*, or *Variety*. Rearrange the listings, or add your own suggestions to create a new chart based solely on your taste. Compare your chart with others. How closely does your chart resemble the one from the magazine? To what extent does the Top-40 list affect your album-purchasing?

6. How might the knowledge of playlists, established product, ratings, and station "image" affect the way you listen to radio?

The Edge (left) and Bono (right) of Ireland's U2. Which target audiences listed on the opposite page do you think this band appeals to?

In 1985, Top-40 rock stations began to see trouble— they were losing listeners. An aging, and very large, baby boom audience demanded more "hits of yesterday," from the '60s and '70s. The teenage market became less important to advertisers. As a result, there were very few stations teens could call their own.

The Bubble Has Popped for Teen-Oriented Music

by Greg Quill

What happened to bubble-gum? What happened to teen music, teen pop stars, teen hysteria? What fills the musical gap in the late 1980s between Sharon, Lois and Bram and Bruce Springsteen, between nursery rhymes and U2? What are young teenagers listening to?

Not much. Radio, rationalizing that it's only reflecting the tastes of its largest and wealthiest audiences, is either old or gold, playing either sophisticated adult pop or pure nostalgia.

A few identifiable teen acts have squeezed through of late: 16-year-old California singer Tiffany, for example, with "I Think We're Alone Now" (a remake of Tommy James' old hit) and "Could Have Been,"

British singer George Michael with "Faith," and American movie star Patrick Swayze with "She's Like the Wind" from the *Dirty Dancing* soundtrack.

But teen stars are few and far between. Radio's preferred demographic is the 25 – 54-year-old age group, says Jeff Vidler, a consultant with Toronto-based Joint Communications, which advises and programs radio stations across North America.

"Baby boomers started changing radio three or four years ago, when the tail end of the age group hit 25. They'll attract attention to themselves until they're 75. And they'll always get what they want.

"Like it or not, the kids just don't have the numbers or the disposable income."

So like it or not, the kids aren't getting much of a break from either radio or the record industry these days. They certainly have precious little that's entirely their own, as their parents did: no Beatles or Monkees or Herman's Hermits or ABBA, no Archies or Elvis or Buddy Holly or Ricky Nelson, no Lesley Gore or Bobby Rydell or Frankie Avalon or Beach Boys.

And their dissatisfaction is reflected in the fall [1987] radio ratings published by the BBM Bureau of Measurement. One of the report's most disquieting features is a 16 percent drop in the total number of hours Canadian adolescents spend listening to radio. They're getting heavy metal mayhem or Sting's adult soul-jazz-pop stew or John Mellencamp's vision of a decaying America or teenage music their parents used to love. And they're tuning out. Powerful American radio consultant Lee Abrams, who virtually invented the post-adolescent Album-Oriented Rock (AOR) format that now dominates Canadian and U.S. airwaves, in an interview in an American *R&R* music industry tip sheet condemned programmers for "waltzing, just going through the motions.

"Five years from now when the libraries are cooked (when the nostalgia repertoire is completely used) and we're left with no current music image, we're going to be really stuck," he warned.

Radio has been "brainwashed into thinking 25-plus," Abrams added, "The real vacuum is in the 12 – 24 demographic (range). I'd love to own a station that owned (catered exclusively to) 12 – 24. Youth avails (prices of advertising spots for products in the adolescent market) are going through the roof."

Abrams' forecast is grim, both for radio and for the record industry that feeds it. But no one is tearing off in search of young music for a new generation.

"The future of the record business will always be with younger music," says Jeff Burns, artist and repertoire director at CBS Records Canada. "Record companies are generally eager to find it and exploit it, and we'd like to dictate to radio. But the truth is, radio at the moment isn't a significant contributor to the youth market."

For all that, Burns admits his company ruined a good thing by changing Toronto pop band Platinum Blonde's image and musical style to appeal to AOR radio tastes in the U.S. The group, whose first two albums—both unself-con-

sciously young and frothy—had combined sales of more than 1 million in Canada, toughened up and matured for its most recent effort, *Contact*.

"But growing up didn't work for them." Burns says. "We lost a ton of teens. We funked it up too much and we didn't get the sales." . . .

[Toronto's CFTR] program director says he has no shortage of teenage music to play, but admits there are very few teen stars in the making.

"Some cult bands that don't get

airplay on AM or FM radio—British bands like The Cure and Depeche Mode—seem to have a strong following among young teenagers, but I have no idea how," he says.

Maybe it's wrong to assume teen stars of the future will be as innocent as they've been in the past, says Lesley Soldat of MCA Records, which released the *Tiffany* album. "Indications are that when the radio pendulum swings back, it'll be dance music and metal pop that the young kids will listen to."

In any event, radio that aims itself at the 12 – 24 age group will likely clean up in the short term, she says. "AM-106 in Calgary and 1040-AM in Vancouver have proven lately that there's real money in teenagers, contrary to the prevailing opinion.

The secret is that they stay close to their audience, listen to their requests, promote local contests between young bands and interact with the kids on air."

Vidler, Abrams and other radio consultants foresee a swing back to younger music, too. "But the music will be hard rock for boys, like Whitesnake, and metal pop for girls, like Bon Jovi," Vidler says.

"The other component will be traditional dance pop, like George Michael.

"But for the next few years, record companies and radio will keep servicing the older group. Teenage stars? They'll pop up now and then, but not by the truckload."

—*THE TORONTO STAR*,
FEBRUARY 14, 1988

RESPONSES

1. Discuss your reaction to Greg Quill's article. Think of some "teen acts" and discuss your opinion of them.

2. Prepare a questionnaire and conduct a survey of some students from your school for their opinions of local radio stations. Compile the results. How do your findings compare with the information given in Greg Quill's article?

3. Write some brief biographies of current teen stars, or teen stars from the past. Or, write an essay comparing a current teen star with a star from the '60s or '70s. You could interview some people who remember those stars, or read about them in magazines from the time. How long did their fame last? How successful were they?

4. Write a letter to your local radio station offering suggestions for reaching a teen audience. Include advice on playlists, promotional material, and your likes and dislikes of disc jockey styles.

POP MUSIC AND ITS MESSAGES

Although there may be fewer venues for teen music, and fewer teen performers, pop music still belongs mainly to a young audience, and it still serves as an incredibly strong communicator—and shaper—of youth culture. The lyrics, the tunes, the performers' clothes and styles, the album covers, the concerts, the hype, and the videos are all part of a huge entertainment package that can have a profound effect on its audience. As students of media, we should recognize the elements, the patterns, and the messages of this package.

Benefit concerts have become powerful international events. "Tears Are Not Enough" was Canada's contribution to Live Aid, a benefit for Ethiopian famine relief.

While some pop lyrics are banal, illogical, obscene—or just unintelligible—some are poetic, thought-provoking, and inspiring, and they often reflect cultural or social concerns. In the '60s and '70s, when rock and pop stations were exclusively for youth, many songs became anthems for youth's social protest movements and rebellion. The following article excerpt describes the messages that *today's* pop lyrics send.

What Pop Lyrics Say to Us Today by Robert Palmer

Bruce Cockburn—a musician whose songs express his convictions on politics and human rights.

R ock is part of adult culture now, to an extent that would have been unthinkable as recently as a decade ago. It is no longer the exclusive reserve of young people sending messages to each other. But pop music has always reflected and responded to the currents of its own time, and today's pop music is no exception. What does it seem to be telling us about our own time? Part of the message is in the music itself—in the insistence of the beat, the shriek of heavily amplified guitars. But lyrics remain the most accurate barometer of what makes *these* times different from, for example, the 1960s and '70s.

Today's pop music is sending several dominant messages. Material values are on the ascendant, but idealism is by no means a spent force. Most pop songs are love songs, as always, but today's versions try to look at relationships without rose-colored glasses. Romantic notions are viewed with some suspicion; so are drugs. And important rock artists and rappers, while no longer anticipating radical change, are addressing issues, and challenging their listeners to confront actively the world around them. There have probably been more angry protest lyrics written and recorded in the last three or four years than in any comparable period of the '60s. . . .

In the '60s, stars like Bob Dylan and the Rolling Stones wrote and recorded outspoken lyrics that urged sweeping social change and an end to war and flirted with the rhetoric of revolution. . . . The music was the voice of a new generation and a constant reminder of the generation gap. The battle lines were drawn.

The rock lyricists of the '60s were fond of talking about "love." To the Beatles, "love" was transcendent, an irresistible force for good that could accomplish practically anything. . . . "All you need is love."

Love is still something one hears a great deal about in pop lyrics, but the contemporary version is more hard-headed and down-to-earth than the cosmic . . . love of the '60s. . . . "What's love got to do with it?" Tina Turner asked in her recent . . . hit of the same title. And Madonna . . . serves notice in her hit "Material Girl" (written by Peter Brown and Robert Rans) that she won't worry much about love as long as there's money in the bank. . . .

During the past decade, the hue and cry against rock lyrics that demeaned women seemed to have a broad and salutary effect. One didn't hear many songs of the sort the Rolling Stones and other '60s bands used to perform, songs like the Stones' "Under My Thumb." . . .

The title tune from Mick Jagger's new solo album, "She's the Boss," is sung like a taunt or a tease, but that doesn't disguise its message; Mr. Jagger seems to have experienced a shift in values since he wrote "Under My Thumb." . . .

Still, many of today's pop lyrics continue to celebrate male dominance. Aggressively macho rock has been making a comeback. Heavy metal rock, which appeals almost exclusively to white male teenagers and tends to treat women as either temptresses or chattel, is more popular than ever. Women like Tina Turner and Cyndi Lauper, who project a certain independence and strength, are helping to counter this trend, but sometimes one can't hear them very well over heavy metal's sexist thunder. . . .

Young people turned to rock, ex-pecting it to ask the right ques-tions and come up with answers.

Pop songs can do more than chart changing attitudes toward love and romance; they can address topical issues and appeal to our social conscience. In the '60s, Bob Dylan and other songwriters composed anthems that were sung by civil rights workers as they headed south, and by hundreds of thousands demonstrating for peace and equal rights. . . .

By the late '60s, the peace and civil rights movements were beginning to splinter. The assassinations of the Kennedys and Martin Luther King had robbed a generation of its heroes, the Vietnam war was escalating despite the protests, and at home violence was on the rise. Young people turned to rock, expecting it to ask the right questions and come up with answers, hoping that the music's most visionary artists could somehow make sense of things. But rock's most influential artists—Bob Dylan, the Beatles, the Rolling Stones—were finding that serving as the conscience of a generation exacted a heavy toll. Mr. Dylan, for one, felt the pressure becoming unbearable, and wrote about his predicament in songs like "All Along the Watchtower." . . .

The mainstream rock of the 1970s produced little in the way of socially relevant lyrics. But toward the end of that decade a change began to be felt. The rise of punk rock in Britain brought to the country's pop charts angry songs about unemployment and nuclear Armageddon. In America, the issue of nuclear energy and the threat of nuclear war enlisted the sympathies of many prominent rock musicians. But attempts by Graham Nash, John Hall, and other anti-nuclear activists to turn their concerns into anthems were too self-conscious; the songs were quickly forgotten.

Rap, the new pop idiom that exploded out of New York's black and Latin neighborhoods in the late '70s, seemed to concern itself mostly with hedonism and verbal strutting—at first. Then, in the early '80s, came "The Message," the dance-single by Grandmaster Flash and the Furious Five that provided listeners with an angry, eye-witness account of inner-city neighborhoods and people abandoned to rot, prey to crime, poverty, and disease. . . . But you can't give up, Run D.M.C. insisted to their young, predominately black and urban audience. You have to make something of yourself, rise above "the way it is."

Bruce Springsteen's recent songs have also been topical and deeply felt. They have also been the most popular music of his career. He is writing for and about the America of his dreams and the America he sees around him, and his lyrics are followed closely by a huge audience. . . . Mr. Springsteen's songs look at America and find both despair and hope. And like Chuck Berry and so many other rock and roll lyricists, past and present, he finds a source of strength and inspiration in rock itself. . . .

—*THE NEW YORK TIMES*, FEBRUARY 24, 1985

RESPONSES

1. Today's lyrics can roughly be categorized according to three dominant themes: love; social protest; the nature of rock itself. Using the songs on the current Top-40 list, categorize some of them according to their themes. In groups, listen to some of the songs and pay particular attention to the lyrics. How do the songs treat the theme? What recurring patterns do you notice in the lyrics? What values are being expressed? Do you agree with them? How do the lyrics influence your own values and beliefs?

2. Bruce Cockburn, Rush, U2, Australia's Midnight Oil, and Suzanne Vega are performers who often sing songs of social protest. Using their music, or that of other performers you think of as examples, discuss their effectiveness in conveying political and social concerns. Discuss your opinion of protest songs. What is the difference between art and propaganda? How do words and phrases, or slogans resemble political propaganda? You might want to refer to the section on propaganda and the language of violence in the Violence chapter (p. 308).

3. Choose a favourite pop lyric or a collection of lyrics and do a poetic analysis of it. Share your analysis with others.

4. Many films and some TV shows use songs to help depict a certain period of history; for example, consider the soundtrack for *Dirty Dancing*, *The Big Chill*, or *My American Cousin*. In groups, compile a list of songs that would best reflect the social climate and major events of the past year. You could create a "sound portrait" of the past year of your own lives, your school, or your city. You might want to play or perform some of the songs, read some of the lyrics, or accompany the music with pictures, slides, or skits.

5. There have been various attempts to ban controversial records. There have also been requests to have warning labels put on records that contain lyrics that some people consider offensive. Discuss the pros and cons of putting such labels on records. Write a letter supporting or refuting this idea or hold a debate.

TECHNOPOP

Recording has come a long way since the scratchy, tinny old 78 rpm (revolutions per minute) records. First there came high fidelity sound, then stereo sound, and now technology has given us digital recording and compact discs read by laser, and MIDI (Musical Instrument Digital Interface), which brings computers to music production.

Albums are usually recorded on tape, in studios. The various components of the song—vocals, vocal harmonies, guitar riffs, piano, drums, etc., are laid on separate tracks. The record producer, like a film director, usually directs the musicians and the sound engineers by suggesting, for example, a guitar solo here, more drums there, or less bass, or synthesized horns. The "mixing" process is something like the editing process in film: the many tracks are edited, spliced, blended, modulated, and then mixed down to two tracks.

". . .do you carry any LOW tech. . .?"

The combination of high-tech recording procedures and high-tech playback equipment has made many listeners come to appreciate—and expect—clean, crisp sound. But in the following article, music critic Mark Hunter notes some negative aspects of the impact of technology on the recording industry. He objects to "multitracking"—the procedure of putting instruments on separate tracks and then mixing them, rather than recording a band playing all together.

The Beat Goes Off: How Technology Has Gummed Up Rock's Grooves by Mark Hunter

I am fully aware that most rock fans, let alone most critics, couldn't care less about the technology involved in making records. But given the extraordinary extent to which rock music has penetrated our lives—a number-one pop hit could be defined as a song that nearly everyone in the world will hear at least once—one might well take an interest in how it was recorded, and how this in turn shapes the kind of music being made. The fact is that what might be called the *content* of rock—the songs, the sound—follows to a great extent from formulas imposed by recording techniques. And these formulas are giving us music that is murderously dull. . . .

The Beatles and the other great British bands arrived on the scene just ahead of a profound change in recording techniques—the move from monophonic taping, in which all the instruments used in a composition are recorded simultaneously on the entire width of the tape, to "multitracking," in which each instrument is recorded on a separate band of tape and then "mixed down" into the final product. . . .

In the monophonic era, recording a song meant gathering an ensemble in a room, putting out one or more microphones, and recording the music on one "take," live. If you didn't like the take, you did it over, period. . . .

The advantage of this method, in retrospect, . . . was that players could inspire one another to the kind of extra effort that comes only in ensemble work. If you have ever played in a good group, you know what those moments are like: suddenly, each musician seems to be hearing the music *before it is played*. . . .

The disadvantages of this method were considerable, however, and evident even at the time—in particular, the difficulty in getting a distinct sound color, or timbre, for each instrument, and in capturing a performance in which every musician and singer was at a peak. Producers went crazy when one verse on a take was poorly sung but the

A recording studio in Morin Heights, Quebec: Le Studio Andre Perry Inc.

rest were superb, because there was no way to cut out the bad and keep the good. . . .

All this changed with the invention of stereo machines with synchronized recording capabilities in the early sixties. Now an engineer could not only record the vocals and instruments on separate tracks, he or she could "punch in" a performer at a given moment on a recording. . . . Simply put, it was no longer necessary to record a song from beginning to end. "Synchronization" opened the way to true multitrack recording.

The pop album that most profoundly signaled this shift was the Beatles' *Sgt. Pepper's Lonely Hearts Club Band*, released in 1967. . . .

With multitracking, all the musicians involved in making a record no longer had to be present at the same time. . . . Once a bass line was on tape, the bass player could go home. Conversely, if one player

made a mistake, only his or her part needed to be rerecorded. . . . And the engineer could "treat" the sounds electronically during recording or mixing to alter their timbre. . . .

Multitracking also changed the dynamic flow of individual performances. All music achieves its effects through contrast; soft moments set up the tough ones, which in turn give way, relax. This follows naturally from performing a song in its entirety. . . . In the multitrack era, when a musician will cut an entire track and then go back to "correct" certain passages, often phrase by phrase, performances tend to settle at a single dynamic level. Vocalists in particular seem to lose a sense of overall dynamic flow. Listen to Madonna's "Material Girl": the final chorus sounds just like the first.

Along with this loss of dynamism there is, on an overwhelming number of records, an absence of rhythmic invention.

When multitracking made it possible to record the bass and drums separately, and to hear them distinctly even at high volumes, the role of rhythm musicians was deeply altered. Their sound was no longer far back in a percussive cloud, but could be moved right to the front of the mix—which works just fine in discos and dance clubs, where you listen mostly with your feet, but not at home in front of the stereo. . . . On one disc after another there is the "boom-BOOM" of a thudding bass drum followed by a snare enveloped in reverberation—a "handclap" effect. . . .

People like Clive Davis of Columbia Records believed in letting rock bands "do their own thing" in the studio. . . . However, aside from the fact that the entire ensemble is no longer needed to finish a record, multitracking has made bands more dependent on producers and engineers, who understand the new techniques better than most musicians do. Moreover . . . it takes far longer to make a record one sound at a time. In the studio, time is money, and in the multitrack era, time costs more money than ever. . . . With [so] much money at stake, most contracts now specify that the record company has the right to choose the producer; and . . . those producers tend to impose proven commercial styles on artists.

Multitrack technology long ago altered the terms of live performance as well as audience expectations. In the sixties, rock bands typically amplified each instrument individually. . . . The result was a charged, erratic, stormy sound. But when multitracking took hold, the rock public began to demand that live concerts sound as "clean" as studio recordings, and so stage amplification moved [to] complex live-mixing systems that could

Multitrack technology long ago altered the terms of live performance.

faithfully reproduce studio sound. These mixing systems sent the cost of concert production through the roof. And, in doing so, they drove a wedge between the thousands of local groups . . . and the better-heeled professional musicians who are the only ones who can afford the new equipment. . . .

It should not surprise us then, that we have "rock bands" today that are made up of as many machines—synthesizers and drum boxes—as young men and women, or that the audience for rock *watches* their favorites on TV. . . .

Close your eyes the next time you watch an MTV video, and you'll realize that the band could be anyone, which is to say *no one*. What rock video has confirmed is that rock music no longer requires an emotional—let alone physical—engagement on the part of its audience. It is merely something one watches, passively, without noticing its constituent elements. It is no longer worth *listening* to.

—*HARPER'S*, MAY 1987

RESPONSES

1. Discuss your reactions to Mark Hunter's article. If you have any musicians in your class, ask them to share some of their experiences.

2. Choose a cut from a record album or tape. Instead of hearing the song as a whole, listen to the various instruments singly, and make note of any "hooks" in the music, or pieces of music that are particularly memorable. Consider such things as the balance of the instruments, the dynamics and clarity of the sound, the use of drums and bass, special effects, and synthesizers. Then listen to a cut from an album from the '50s or early '60s and compare the sounds and quality of the recordings.

3. In groups, listen to some albums or tapes together. Some of you may be musicians or be familiar with the techniques of recording and sound mixing and could comment on those aspects of the album. You might invite a local musician or sound technician to your class who could discuss these techniques with you.

4. Locate three or four versions of the same song. Listen to them in groups, and discuss the different ways the songs have been produced.

5. In groups, discuss your opinions of new technology in recording. How do you feel about electronic music? What does the development of synthesizers mean for musicians? for concerts?

6. Research the radical shifts in musical style due to technological developments. Using as many examples as possible, share your findings with the class.

ALBUM AND CONCERT REVIEWS

Music magazines promote the industry by offering reviews, profiles of artists, and information on instruments and sound equipment.

As with film and television reviews, music reviews usually feature lively, strong, and descriptive writing, and they pack a great deal of information in a small space. They can also have a strong influence on the public. Sometimes we have only one cut by which to judge a new album, and a review can be a major factor in our decision to buy the album or leave it in the bin. A good review can also go a long way in establishing a new band or performer.

Concert reviews often serve as small consolation for those people who missed a concert they really wanted to see. The review usually captures the excitement and atmosphere of a good concert, and does not hesitate to criticize a poor performance.

The following are some sample reviews of a new band, a concert, and an album. While you read them, note the style of writing and the kind of information the reviews offer. You might want to refer to the section on writing reviews in the Reference Section (p. 215).

New Band Review

BLVD.
Looking Ahead
by Dave Watson

You'd expect a band associated with Bruce Allen Talent [Loverboy, Bryan Adams] to have a lot of commercial appeal, but that doesn't make Boulevard simply another radio band. Their self-titled debut album on MCA reveals a lot of intelligent touches, like an artsy Roxy Music-ish musical influence, a variety of song styles and well-rounded vocals (not just AOR screaming) that fit in the middle of the triangle made by Journey, the Alan Parsons Project and Air Supply—lots of range, pas-

sion and interplay with the other instruments.

The core of the group formed in 1984 in Calgary and moved to Vancouver in 1986. Randy Gould (guitar), Andrew Johns (keyboards), and Mark Holden (saxophone) then hooked up with talented vocalist David Forbes and bassist Randy Burgess. They're still looking for a drummer, having used a session musician on the album. All the members had been frustrated veterans of several club bands, and since they weren't getting any younger (they average in their mid-20s), they decided to head out on their own.

The folks at Bruce Allen's agency liked the band and signed them to a management deal, which led to a North American contract with MCA Records. According to Mark Holden, "They (MCA) had expressed a lot of interest in the group before, but when we hooked up with Bruce Allen Talent that seemed to be the final straw for the label to commit themselves." French-Canadian producer Pierre Bazinet (Luba) manned the boards for the recording.

Far From Over, Boulevard's first single, was released in February . . . as a lead off to the March album release. Meanwhile, the band has been writing material for a second album, because, according to Holden, "I've heard from so many people that once things start to happen it becomes very difficult to find the time to write."

—*ROCK EXPRESS*,
MARCH 1988

Concert Review

INXS
by John Robson

INXS "Kick-started" its 1988 tour . . . in grand fashion March 1 before a sold-out house. From the opening number, the title cut from the hit Atlantic album "Kick," the accelerator was mashed to the floor; stage patter was almost non-existent, and breaks for the audience to catch its collective breath were few. Virtually the entire audience stood on its seats for "Kick" and remained there for the rest of the two-hour, 25-song set.

Staging for the show was minimal, almost austere, and refreshingly video free, allowing lead singer Michael Hutchence plenty of room to work the boards. Combined with the largely black and white attire of the band members, the overall look was one of monochromatic power; color accents were sparingly provided by a well-crafted geometric lighting design.

The majority of attention was focused on Hutchence, but the show seemed most effective when he shared the spotlight with versatile guitarist/saxophonist Kirk Pengilly. On "Shine Like It Does," the first real tempo break, the rest of the band left them huddled together on stage right, Pengilly on amplified acoustic guitar and Hutchence contributing properly emotive vocals.

INXS stayed close to the album originals as it covered all of the "Kick" album and past favorites, including "What You Need," which elicited a strong crowd sing-along as it closed the regular set. "Need You Tonight," and "Never Tear Us Apart" were saved for encore delivery. . . .

—*BILLBOARD*, MARCH 19, 1988

Short Reviews

Idjah Hadidjah
by J.D. Considine

Idjah Hadidjah may not be a household name in America, but in Indonesia, Hadidjah is the Whitney Houston of jaipong, an indigenous pop-style that has taken the country by storm. And though it's not exactly hip-hop, the dreamy instrumental textures, achingly expressive vocals and burst of percussive power give it a beauty that matches the best of Arab, Indian or gamelan music.

—*MUSICIAN*, MARCH 1988

Album Review

Luba
Between the
Earth and Sky
by Keith Sharp

It seems almost every year a female artist emerges from the pack to set the music industry on its collective ear. Last year it was Whitney Houston—before that, Sade, Cyndi Lauper, Annie Lennox, and Pat Benatar took the honours. Add Luba's name to this illustrious list. An unknown south of the border, Luba has developed into Canada's prime female vocal asset during the past 12 months—and there's nothing on her new album to indicate a slowing of her rapid progress. With Narada Michael Walden producing the lead-off single, *How Many*, and equally talented Pierre Bazinet producing the balance, Luba has laid down an album that . . . can't stop from being an international hit. Blessed with a powerfully evocative voice and some meaty material to match, Luba has developed a more rhythmic direction this time out, allowing the arrangements to flesh out her songs and complement her voice. Aside from the more subdued tracks like *How Many* and the melodic sparkle of *Even in the Darkest Moments*, Luba knows how to pack a dance floor. The exuberance of songs like *Strength in Numbers*, *Back to Emotion*, and *Take It Like a Woman* provide a full-faced look at her varied attributes. The Walden moniker will hopefully do the trick in drawing attention to the new opus. Given that break, Luba will succeed—after all, it happens every year!

ROCK EXPRESS, JUNE 1986

RESPONSES

1. Discuss your opinion of these reviews. What kind of information is presented? Discuss their effectiveness in influencing your opinion of a performer, or your decision to buy an album.

2. Read a selection of record and concert reviews of albums you have heard and concerts you have attended. Compare your opinions of the albums and concerts with the opinions expressed in the reviews.

3. Who are the reviewers? What are their qualifications? How do they choose what to review? Appoint someone from the class to interview a music reviewer, or invite him or her to your class. Or, you could compose a class letter to a reviewer, asking for some information.

4. Refer to the survey you completed earlier in this chapter (p. 179). Write reviews for two of the albums you chose as your all-time favourites. Share your reviews with your classmates. How do their reviews affect you?

5. If you have been to a concert recently, write a review of it. If your school has a student newspaper, or radio, perhaps you could choose one or two of the best reviews and have them published in the paper or broadcast on the in-school radio system.

6. In groups, listen to some singles, and write short reviews of them without naming the song or the performer. Play the songs for other groups and let them read your reviews to see if they are able to match the review with the song. What did you learn from this exercise?

ISSUES FOR FURTHER STUDY

1. Rock concerts can be fascinating spectacles; they are usually very sensory, physical experiences. Discuss some concerts you have seen—their benefits and their limitations. Consider issues such as the reputation of the group and its rapport with an audience; the media hype surrounding the event; the theatrical techniques used to create a spectacle; the quality of the sound; and the response of the audience.

2. Prepare a detailed study of an individual artist or a group. Apply the key concepts of media to the career of the artist(s). Consider the development of style, the creation of image, the marketing tactics, and the success.

3. Imagine that you are involved in promoting a rising rock star. Establish the kind of image you wish the star to project and plan your promotion. Consider the use of rock videos, TV and radio commercials, interviews, posters and product endorsements. How will you organize a concert tour in order to have maximum impact?

4. a) Album covers present an opportunity to study a variety of art, photography, and graphic design. In groups, bring in a selection of albums and discuss their different artistic styles and their effectiveness in portraying the performers. Discuss which ones seemed best suited to the rock group represented. Which ones were least suited? How did the different artists reflect trends in popular culture? Find books or magazines that show the year's best and worst album covers and explain why you think they were chosen.
b) Create your own album cover for an imaginary band. Think of a name for the band, a name for the album, the album design or concept, and write the "liner notes" for the back of the album.

5. Investigate the challenges confronted by a performer or rock group who is just starting out. Find out about the costs of equipment, rental of rehearsal space, making a demo tape, costs for touring and promotion. What steps are necessary for the group to make a record that might be played on a local radio station?

6. What are the problems faced by Canadian pop performers who are hoping to make it internationally? Discuss your opinions of musicians such as Corey Hart, Bryan Adams, Anne Murray, Luba, Neil Young, Jane Siberry, Bruce Cockburn, Veronique Beliveau, Rock and Hyde, K.D. Lang, and Gordon Lightfoot.

7. Write an essay or present an oral report on a pop music type or style, e.g., punk, rap, new romantic, new wave. Consider the origins of the style, and its current status and influence. Evaluate the most representative musicians and albums produced and examples of successful concerts. Consult recent books or back issues of magazines such as *Rolling Stone*, *Spin*, *Rock Express*, *Musician*, *Canadian Musician*, and *Graffiti*, and interview any musicians and/or fans of the music.

8. Do further research on the recording studio or on the sound systems at concerts. Describe the roles of various personnel involved in these productions.

9. Before television, people were vastly entertained by the radio. Research the history of radio and the kinds of programs that were offered. Compare them to today's shows. Some libraries have audiotapes of these old programs. Or do a report on a non-commercial station, such as CBC. Describe the kinds of programs they offer.

10. Obtain some tapes or records of music from other countries. Listen to the music and describe the different kinds of instruments used. What kind of sounds do the various instruments emit, and what are the feelings they evoke? Some suggestions for study are gamelan music from Indonesia; aboriginal music from Australia; sitar music from India; bagpipes from Scotland.

11. Do a detailed analysis of one or more rock videos by commenting on the following: the clothing, moves, and poses of the performers; the settings used; the use of traditional symbolism as well as conventions drawn from other rock videos; editing techniques and camera work and the use of special effects; the connection of the lyrics to the visual. To what extent did this video effectively promote the image of the rock artist or group?

Reference Section

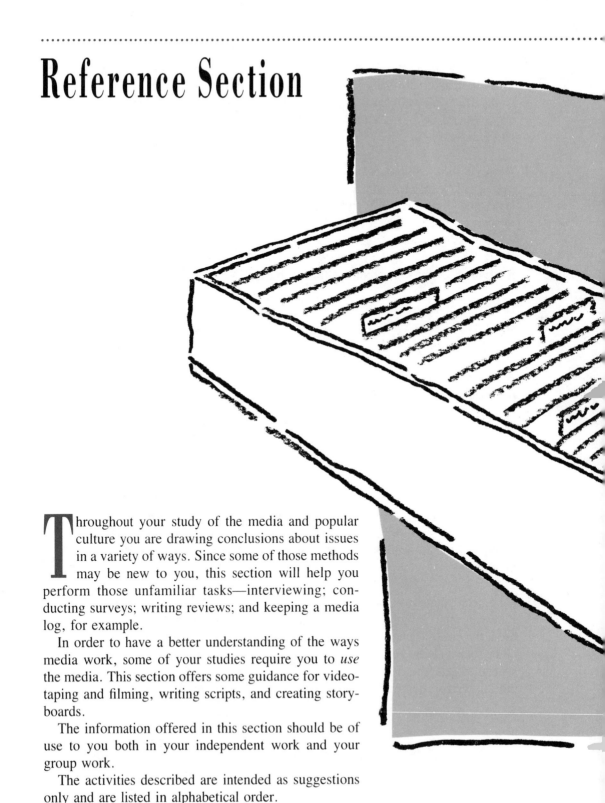

Throughout your study of the media and popular culture you are drawing conclusions about issues in a variety of ways. Since some of those methods may be new to you, this section will help you perform those unfamiliar tasks—interviewing; conducting surveys; writing reviews; and keeping a media log, for example.

In order to have a better understanding of the ways media work, some of your studies require you to *use* the media. This section offers some guidance for videotaping and filming, writing scripts, and creating storyboards.

The information offered in this section should be of use to you both in your independent work and your group work.

The activities described are intended as suggestions only and are listed in alphabetical order.

BRAINSTORMING

Brainstorming is a way of solving a problem or studying an issue by having the members of a group state every possible solution to the problem, or idea about the issue, that they can think of. Discussion of the ideas is postponed until the end of the brainstorming session.

The rationale for this strategy is based on the type of problem that arises from many class discussions about the media—the issues are often controversial, there will probably be conflicting opinions, and discussions may become heated. In these exchanges, we sometimes want only to confirm our present beliefs, and we remain unreceptive to new ones. What the text encourages you to do, however, is to understand how the media and popular culture function rather than simply state your likes and dislikes. Your obligation, above all, is to be open-minded and non-judgmental of others' ideas or opinions. Brainstorming should help you:

1. Become receptive to new ideas.

2. Develop some critical thinking strategies that will enable you to carry out research and inquiry. The following information will help you in your sessions.

• Brainstorming works best in small groups. You may want to sit in a circle, and have everyone state an idea—or even just a related word or phrase—in turn.

• Have someone record the ideas, or tape record the session.

• Set a time limit, and make every minute count.

• Criticism should not be allowed. The purpose of brainstorming is to have an unrestricted flow of ideas. Don't withhold—and don't criticize—ideas you think are too bizarre. Sometimes these ideas become the most useful. When your time is up, choose the best ideas. If your group has problems sorting out its ideas, you could categorize the ideas in three columns, called Yes, No, and Maybe, or Good, Bad, and Interesting. After pooling the most useful ideas from the various groups, the class could select the ideas or solutions which best suit the purpose.

At this point you may want to narrow down an idea or start some research—the inquiry model, described in this section, will help you.

FILMING AND VIDEOTAPING

The terms "filming" and "videotaping" are used interchangeably throughout this text, but they actually differ from each other. The kind of moving picture production you do will depend on the kind of equipment that is available to you.

You may have access to film cameras and/or video cameras. The main difference between the two is that video has no photographic emulsions and thus does not have to go through a developing process. Video cameras have a tube that converts images into electrical signals that are recorded on tape (much like audiotape). Unlike film, videos can be recorded and played back on a videotape recorder immediately. While video production is cheaper than film (the tape is cheaper and can be re-used), it cannot yet compete with the sharpness of film and its range of qualities of tone and light.

Film and video equipment is constantly being updated and improved, and there is a wide range of equipment available. For example, in film, you can work with 8mm, Super 8mm, 16mm, or 35mm, although the first two are becoming obsolete. Most amateur filming is done with video cameras. With both video and film, you can have various camera lenses, various speeds, automatic or manual focus, sound recording features, and so on. Before you begin your filming, make sure you understand the capabilities of the equipment you are using. Read any accompanying manuals and, if your school has an audio-visual technician, ask him or her for assistance. There are also many books on film and video production that can help you.

The following information offers general advice that is useful for both videotaping and filming. In conjunction with the technical terms and camera techniques listed in the Television and Film chapters, you should have enough information to begin experimenting with making motion pictures.

• Unless you are practising your techniques or shooting an interview, always work from a carefully prepared shooting script.

• Rehearse before the shoot begins, and make sure that everyone involved in the production knows exactly what is expected of them.

• Try to keep the production simple; if it is over-elaborate, it may also be confusing.

• Just before you begin to shoot, make sure your camera is loaded properly, focused, the speed and exposure settings are correct, and that your lighting is sufficient.

- Use a tripod if you have access to one, or try to keep the camera steady. Hold the camera with both hands, and with your elbows leaning against your body.

- Move the camera smoothly and deliberately.

- Compose your shots carefully, as when you take still photographs. Before you shoot, look through the viewfinder to "test" the shot. Make sure your subject is in the frame exactly where you want it to be.

- The establishing shot is very important. Viewers need to know where the action is taking place. For example, if you are shooting a canoeing scene, an opening pan shot of the surroundings will tell the viewer whether the locale is a river in the woods, a lake, a pond in a small town, or a river running through a city.

- If you are shooting unrehearsed action, be ready to follow the movement of the subject smoothly. Don't let the subject get out of the picture, and don't "chase" the subject with the camera.

- Keep the shots consistent and unconfusing. Don't make any sudden changes in perspective, and be aware of screen direction at all times. For example, if you're shooting someone roller skating from right to left and you cut away, make sure the positions are the same when you resume the shot.

- Maintain continuity. For example, if your subject has her hair in a ponytail in one shot, make sure her hair is the same for her next appearance in the sequence.

- Each shot should have a focus of interest. Try to keep the background simple and undistracting. Also, be aware of unexpected background inter-ference. For example, if a truck passes by in the background, both the sound and the image will be distracting when the film is shown. Listen carefully to all the sounds that are made during your filming.

- If you do not have access to special filters to put over the camera lens for various effects, try shooting through gauze, nylon stockings, a glass of water, a sheet of glass with cooking oil or petroleum jelly spread over it, or coloured plastic. Experiment to achieve different effects.

- A wagon, a skateboard, a chair on rollers, or a wheelchair can be used for a dolly, but make sure the surface you travel on is smooth.

- You can add titles to your production (the name of the production, the director, actors, producer, technicians, and so on) by writing them on a chalkboard, or a piece of paper, and shooting them.

INQUIRY MODEL

The inquiry model, shown here, could provide a framework for conducting your preliminary research and many of your class discussions on a topic. The model encourages you to direct your own learning and it suggests that asking the right question can often be more productive than offering quick answers. You may find that using the model roughly parallels conducting a scientific experiment, whereby you pose a question and a hypothesis, and, using the results of the experiment, determine if the hypothesis was correct. The following are some uses for the inquiry model in media classes:

- It allows for investigation in greater depth an idea or topic generated by your brainstorming sessions.

- It permits you to deal with some of the controversial issues and moral dilemmas media study presents. The inquiry model allows for emotional responses but helps you apply a disciplined, practical procedure for rational, in-depth research.

- It helps you establish a focussed point of view or thesis in your writing activities.

- It helps you acquire a point of view on a topic in the course of field research (surveys, interviews, library research).

---

1. Initial Experience:
▽ Exploratory ideas or activities are introduced.

---

2. Questions:
▽ Pose a question around which the study will develop.

---

3. Alternatives:
▽ Suggest a range of reasonable alternatives to answer the question. (Other alternatives may arise in the subsequent data-collection stage.)

4. Data Collection:
▽ Collect information on each alternative.

5. Synthesis:
▽ Arrive at a conclusion by deciding, on the basis of the data, which of the alternatives give(s) the best answer to the question.

6. Assessing the Conclusion:
▽ Decide whether the conclusion adequately answers the original question.

7. Expressing the Conclusion:
▽ Organize a clear expression and presentation of the conclusion. (Does not always have to be a written response.)

8. Evaluation:
▽ Assess the appropriateness of the conclusion and the way you expressed it. How well did it answer the original question?

INTERVIEWS AND SURVEYS

Interviews can be arranged in advance, with people in media businesses, and with people you know, or they can be done randomly at school or in your neighbourhood. The following are some suggestions for conducting productive interviews:

• If you schedule your interview in advance, be sure to give clear reasons for the interview, explain how long you expect it will take, and ask for permission to audio- or videotape the interview. If you conduct random interviews, also state your reasons and ask permission to tape them.

- Make sure you are prepared. Know the purpose for your interview, and write and organize your questions in advance. If you are audio- or video-taping the interview, make sure the equipment is working and ready to go before you begin. It is a good idea to make notes in addition to taping.

- Set a time limit, and let the person know when the interview is almost over, by saying "I just have two or three more questions."

- Try to make the person you are interviewing feel comfortable by making eye contact with him or her, listening carefully, and offering occasional responses. Your manner, gestures, and tone of voice can affect the quality of the interview.

- Try to keep the person "on track," but realize that what may seem to be a digression can often yield worthwhile information.

- Ask the person for examples or clarification if the answer was vague.

Questionnaires and surveys are designed for gathering a lot of information quickly and for compiling the information easily. The text has a number of questionnaires for you to answer, but you can also use them to survey other people. Or you could make up your own questionnaires. The challenge in writing them is to pose the questions clearly and precisely so the answers you get are brief and to the point. For example, don't ask, "What about sexual stereotyping on television?" Instead, ask, "Which commercials on television do you think portray sexual stereotyping?" The following are some tips for conducting surveys:

- Create a form that helps you organize and tabulate your information accurately and quickly. Ask all respondents the same questions in the same order.

- Test your questionnaire on a few people, evaluate the results, and revise the questionnaire if necessary.

- Ask permission to do the survey first, and state your purpose clearly.

- You may want to establish some categories for the people you interview, e.g., age, sex, whether the person is a student or a non-student, employed or unemployed.

- Keep the questionnaire brief—don't take up too much of the person's time (especially if the interview is a random one).

- Ask your questions as clearly and quickly as possible.

- Don't "lead" the person's response, that is, give any indication of the kind of answer you would *like* to hear. Remain impartial to the answers you receive; don't look surprised or shocked.

MEDIA LOG

The media log is like a workbook or notebook, but less formal. Since it will consist of both private writing and material to be shared with classmates and your teacher, you should use something that allows you to remove and re-insert pages—a binder, or an expandable file folder, for example. You may also want it to include space for storing audiocassettes. You may want to give your log a "media look"—design a cover or label that illustrates the media (you could use a computer for the design); include cartoons, quotes, and clippings; and create collages. The log can be your place to:

• Write notes on classroom activities such as discussions, group productions, talks by guest speakers, field trips.

• Jot down any thoughts, opinions, questions, ideas, quotes, stories, jokes related to media and popular culture that you might want to explore in more detail later.

• Keep your collection of articles and clippings, and your accompanying notes.

• Write immediate responses, in note or chart form, to your TV and film watching, magazine and newspaper reading, music listening, popular culture involvement, and any other monitoring you may do.

• Record your answers to surveys from the text.

• Write questions for interviews and record the results of the interviews.

• Keep your notes on any library or outside research you do.

• Keep notes on any event or issue whose media coverage you plan to follow over several weeks.

The material in your log should be mostly informal writing and immediate, brief responses to issues. You may wish to do your more formal projects and writing using this material. You might keep this finished work in another notebook, or in a separate section of your log. Keeping a media log throughout the year has many advantages:

• It allows you to think about and record your feelings related to aspects of the media that you may have taken for granted or never really thought about. Some people find it easier to formulate an opinion of something after they have written about it.

• It may raise questions for you to answer through formal research and the use of techniques such as the inquiry model.

- It helps develop critical thinking skills as well as the ability to write in a variety of forms.

- It serves as a record of your growth and development in media literacy. Your views of media and popular culture may change by the end of your studies.

RESEARCH

Much of your research will consist of carefully monitoring and observing media and popular culture and recording your observations in your log. From this starting point, you could use books for thorough, intensive research and magazines, journals, and newspapers for obtaining more current information. The following information may guide you in your research. Most large libraries have subject indexes for magazines and newspapers. In them, you will find titles of articles listed alphabetically by subject and author, and a reference to the magazine or newspaper that has the article. The following are some indexes:

- The *Canadian Periodical Index* lists articles by subject and author for 347 periodicals.

- The *Canadian News Index* lists articles from seven major daily Canadian newspapers, by subject.

- The *Reader's Guide to Periodical Literature* lists articles from many American and British magazines, by subject and author.

- If you need old issues of magazines for your research, some libraries will have them, often on microfilm. You can sometimes order back issues from the publisher, or you may find them in used book stores. Publishers sometimes produce retrospectives, such as *TV Guide: the First 25 Years*.

REVIEWS

For the purposes of this text, a review is a critical account of media products, such as a film, album, music video, radio program, commercial, or television show. Review writers give their opinions of the product's good and bad points. Most of the information for your reviews will come from the notes you make in your media log while watching or listening to these media. Usually, reviews include the following:

- Information such as the name of the item being reviewed, when it appeared, on what network or what record label it appeared, who the actors, artists, director, and other involved parties are.

- A very brief summary of the content. Try to avoid re-telling the whole story, or giving a detailed description of the content.

- The name of at least one major creative person involved. This could be the composer or producer of a song, or the writer or producer of a TV show or film.

- Identification of type of product. For example, if it is a TV show, name the type of program—sitcom, documentary, soap opera; if it is an album, indicate the type—comedy, rock, jazz, classical.

- An explanation of how this product compares with other products of its type. For example, if you are reviewing a science fiction film, explain how it compares with others of that genre.

- An assessment of the quality of the product. For example, evaluate the acting in a film, the writing in a TV show, the saxaphone-playing on an album.

- In television and film reviews, an opinion of the theme(s). This is a challenging part of a review, because you have to make a statement about the premise or philosophy of the product (with which you may or may not agree). A film or TV show's premise might be similar to one of the following:
  - love and compassion have great healing powers
  - a private investigator's intelligence and power solves crimes
  - Dad can usually give the best advice to resolve a family conflict
  - good triumphs over evil
  - might is right

SCRIPTS

A script is the text of a film, television show, play, or commercial. Media writers follow explicit format styles when they write scripts. Each medium has its own style or format, and there is often more than one acceptable format. You might follow the styles described in this text or, for more information, study some books about writing for the media.

Script writers include production directions in their scripts: directions to the actor, such as (LOOKS DOWN AND SMILES), cues to the camera operator, such as "CUT TO CLOSEUP OF HOUSE," and directions for sound, such as (MUSIC BUILDS). A shooting script is the final version of the script, complete with the script writer's instructions, director's instructions, camera angles, and any other directions for production. Since a typical script for a half-hour TV comedy consists of approximately 50

– 60 pages, you will probably be writing scenes, or parts of scenes. To make this terminology seem more familiar, think of a shot as the equivalent of a sentence in a book, a scene as the equivalent of a paragraph, and a sequence as the equivalent of a chapter.

In addition to the following information, see the sample television script on page 89 and the glossary of production terms on page 84 in the Television chapter to help you in your script writing.

SCRIPTS FOR TELEVISION SHOWS

TV scripts can be written in one of two formats: one-column and two-column. The two-column format, with the left column for video instructions and the right column for audio instructions, is compact, but the one-column format allows more space for director's comments. For an example of the one-column kind of script, see page 89 in the Television chapter. When writing scripts for visual production, the following tips may be useful:

- Remember that you are trying to tell a story in visual form.
- Establish and know your characters very well before you begin. Think about what they may have had for breakfast, or what they might wear today. The dialogue will seem more natural if you do this.
- Keep the ideas simple, the sentences short.
- Know the genre you are writing for—documentary, live television, or film, for example, and know how each genre may affect your writing.
- If you know your audience, keep them in mind when writing.
- If you are writing a scene for an existing show, keep in mind the sets used.

SCRIPTS FOR TELEVISION COMMERCIALS

TV commercials can have the same format as other TV scripts but, in addition, storyboards are used. See **Storyboards** in this section.

SCRIPTS FOR RADIO

The following is a sample script for a radio drama or documentary production. It could also be used for a radio commercial.

In radio scripts, notice that:

- Names of characters are in upper case (capital letters) and appear at the left side of the page.

6	SOUND:	DOCK SOUNDS, WAVES, SEAGULLS, CREAKING BOAT
7	NARRATOR:	Long before the rest of the crew is awake, Rob is up and on deck, checking and re-checking his cameras and diving gear. As lead cameraman for the film crew, he can afford no mistakes.
8	MUSIC:	OMINOUS MOTIF . . . BRING IN LOW. . . BUILD
9	NARRATOR:	(LOW... QUIETLY) Today *especially* is a day for no mistakes (PAUSE) Rob will be filming from inside the shark cage.

- Lines of dialogue, music, and sound cues are numbered along the left margin.

- Music and sound effects cues and descriptions are underlined and in upper case, and appear to the right of the characters' names and to the left of the dialogue, that is, they are not flush with the dialogue.

- Directions for reading the lines precede the lines and are in upper case and parentheses.

Two important things to remember when writing for radio are:

- You must supply the listeners with material that will prompt their imagination.

- Every sound you suggest should have a dramatic purpose.

STORYBOARDS

A storyboard is a series of drawings, like a comic strip, that indicates the composition and sequence of the shots of a film or video production. Roughly equivalent to a building contractor's blueprint, it is the link between the written word and the visual result. Used mostly for television commercials, storyboards can also be used for all television and film productions. The following are some tips for creating storyboards:

- They can be sketched roughly, with stick figures, or done in full colour and in great detail.

- Each frame represents a few seconds of screen time (a 60-second commercial should have at least ten frames).

- The frames should depict what is seen through the camera lens, not the floor plans or anything outside the lens frame.

- Each frame should include video and audio directions.

CLIENT: SHINE ON : 30 SECOND TELEVISION   "JENNY"

1.

GRANDAD:	Geeze, I don't know, Jenny. Sure you can fix it up?
JENNY :	It's no problem, honest, Grandad.

2.

GRANDAD:	You know, Jen, that carburetor needs some new bolts.
JENNY :	That's the distributor cap, Grandad.

3.

JENNY:	Well, that's that. Now all I've got to do is polish the chrome.
GRANDAD:	And I've got just the thing... Shine On.

4.

JENNY VO:	(WITH A SIGH) Okay, Grandad... I'll try it.
SFX:	SPRAYING SOUNDS

5.

GRANDAD:	I guess you wonder how I know so much about cars.
JENNY :	(WITH A CHUCKLE) Yeh, and I guess that's why I've taken such a shining to you all these years.

6.

ANNCR VO:	You'll take a real shining to Shine On.

CHAPTER 5

Journalism

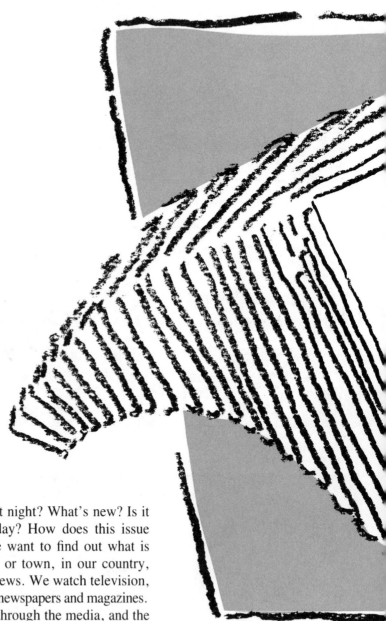

W ho won the game last night? What's new? Is it supposed to rain today? How does this issue affect me? When we want to find out what is going on in our city or town, in our country, in our world, we turn to the news. We watch television, we listen to the radio, we read newspapers and magazines.

But the news comes to us through the media, and the media can provide us only with images of reality. The reflection of "what is going on" is subject to the same factors that you have already discovered affect all media—factors such as time, technology, and money, and the people who deal with them.

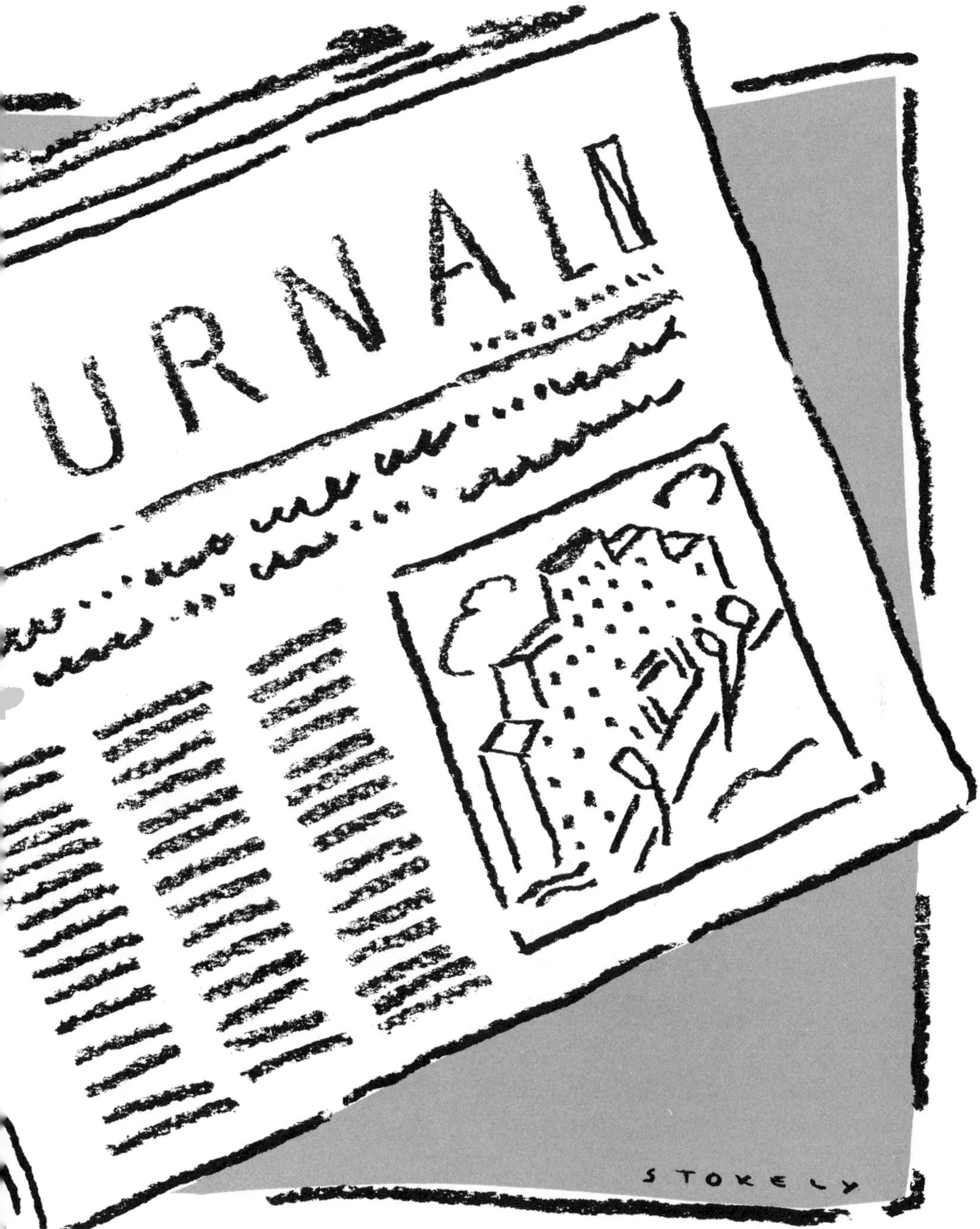
URNAL
STOKELY

NEWS AND JOURNALISM

It is important to clarify the difference between news and journalism. **News** has been defined as timely information of interest to many people, usually concerning events that have just occurred or are about to occur. The collecting, writing, editing, publishing, and broadcasting of news is **journalism**.

Journalism, in effect, shapes and defines the news. Its influence on how we view the world is considerable. For example, here are some quick facts on media use:

- The average Canadian spends 53 minutes a day reading the newspaper.

- Seventy-eight percent of all Canadians read magazines.

- There is at least one radio and one television set in almost every home in Canada.

- In 1983 there were 1420 radio stations and 1350 television stations in Canada.

- Eighty-nine percent of Canadian adults read at least one newspaper every week.

- There are 64 Canadian daily newspapers with a circulation of more than 15 000.

- The top ten paid-circulation magazines in Canada are listed below. Paid-circulation magazines are sold through subscriptions and at newsstands. Other magazines have controlled circulation, that is, they are sent free of charge to selected homes and/or offices. The circulation figures shown are the average paid circulations for six months ending December 31, 1985. Canadian magazines are marked with an asterisk (*).

Reader's Digest (Canadian English edition) 1 341 394
Chatelaine 1 098 580
TV Guide 802 982
National Geographic Magazine 757 150
Maclean's 649 079
Legion Magazine 556 300
Leisure Ways 529 036
Canadian Living 523 013
National Enquirer 412 872
Reader's Digest (Canadian French edition) 382 570

—AUDIT BUREAU OF CIRCULATION: CARD, AS PRINTED IN
THE CANADIAN WORLD ALMANAC AND BOOK OF FACTS, 1987

WHAT'S NEWS WITH YOU? A SURVEY

Before you begin to examine how journalism affects the news you receive, record your own responses to the news. Answer the following survey questions in your media log.

1. What is your most frequent source of news?
newspapers   magazines   television   radio   family and/or friends

2. What do you think is the best source of news? Why?

3. How much time do you spend per week doing each of the following?
reading the newspaper   watching the news on television
reading magazines   listening to the news on radio

4. How do your figures compare with time spent per week watching television, reading, and listening to the radio for entertainment only?

5. What newspaper(s) do you read? (Include local newspapers.) Do you read the entire paper? If not, what parts do you read?

6. List the magazines you read. Do you subscribe to any magazines? Which ones? How many of the magazines you read are Canadian?

7. What TV news show(s) do you watch? Do you watch the entire show? If not, what parts do you watch?

8. What radio news show(s) do you listen to? Do you listen to the entire show? If not, what parts do you listen to?

9. List your reasons for reading a) newspapers and b) magazines. Are your reasons for reading newspapers the same as for reading magazines?

10. Do you ever use one source of news to supplement the information you receive from another source? List some occasions on which you or members of your household have done this.

After you have completed this survey, discuss your answers with the class. What is the most frequent source of news in your class? What does your class think is the best source of news? What is the class average time spent per week reading newspapers and magazines, listening to radio news, and watching television news?

THE PEOPLE WHO OWN THE NEWS

News is big business, and the issue of who owns the business is an important one. Canada seems to be especially vulnerable to monopolies, in which the ownership of the media is limited to a small number of individuals or organizations. Concentration of ownership can lead to a community having only one newspaper, with no competition, or even to one person or group owning all the media in the community. This may limit perspectives of, or opinions about, the issues and events covered by the media. It may also lead to conflict of interest. For example, if the same group owns a newspaper and a television station in one community, the editors of the paper may be reluctant to print articles or editorials that criticize the TV station's sponsors or the way the TV news manager covered a story. Concentration of ownership of the media, however, does not always mean editorial dependence or sameness. The content of the publications or broadcasts are not necessarily dictated by the owner. No matter who owns the news media, news and information are the main products we seek from them.

The following deals with the ownership of the news media in Canada. As you examine it, try to decide on the advantages and disadvantages of concentration of ownership.

". . . Concentration engulfs Canadian daily newspaper publishing. Three chains control nine tenths of French-language daily newspaper circulation. Three other chains control two thirds of English-language circulation. Additional chains bring the circulation in English under concentrated ownership to three quarters of the total. In seven provinces—all but Ontario, Quebec, and Nova Scotia—two thirds or more of provincial circulation is controlled by a single chain. Often chain owners of daily newspapers also control community newspapers, broadcasting stations, periodicals, and major interests outside the media. We define a chain as the ownership of two or more daily newspapers in different urban communities by a single firm." . . .

—*REPORT BY THE ROYAL COMMISSION ON NEWSPAPERS*, 1981

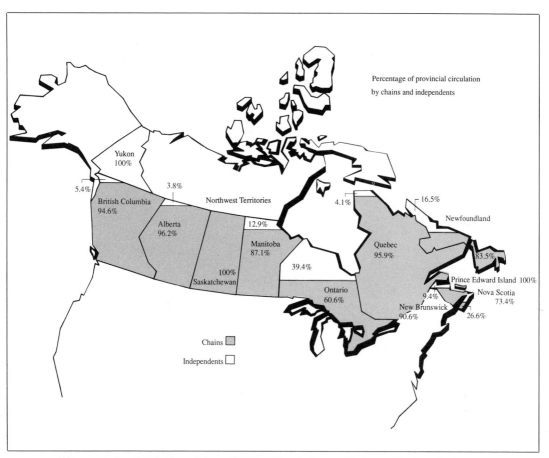

Who controls what in Canadian publishing: Circulation of Chains and Independents, broken down by province. Data from the _Royal Commission on Newspapers,_ 1981.

To give you an idea of the diversity and extent of the information and communication services of the major chains in Canada, study the following material.

According to its 1987 annual report, Thomson Newspapers Limited publishes 40 daily and 12 weekly newspapers in Canada, and 113 daily and 5 weekly newspapers in the United States, a total of 170 newspapers. The total daily circulation is 1 153 100 in Canada and 1 665 300 in the United States.

—*INFORMATION COURTESY OF THOMSON NEWSPAPERS LIMITED.*

Southam Inc.—Company Divisions, Products and Services

Southam Newspaper Group

Profile

Canada's largest daily newspaper group in terms of circulation. Average daily circulation in 1987 — 1 541 200. Established 1877 through half-interest in The Hamilton Spectator purchased by William Southam.

Newspapers

The Gazette, Montreal

The Ottawa Citizen

The Nugget, North Bay

The Hamilton Spectator

The Expositor, Brantford

The Sun Times, Owen Sound

The Windsor Star

The Sault Star

Medicine Hat News

The Edmonton Journal

Calgary Herald

The Province, Vancouver

The Vancouver Sun

The Prince George Citizen

The Kamloops Daily News

Financial Times of Canada, Toronto

Community newspapers:
Hamilton region, Durham and Markdale, Ont., and Winnipeg

Southam News bureaux

Ottawa (main bureau)	Calgary	Nicos
Halifax	Vancouver	Hara
Montreal	Washington	Zimb
Toronto	London	San
	Hong Kong	Cost
		Mos

Southam Syndicate

Ottawa, Toronto

Magazines

TV Times, Business Outlook

Newspaper advertising offic

Toronto, Montreal, Vancouver, representation in Ottawa

Marketing research service

Marketscope, Toronto

Distribution service

The Flyer Force:
Montreal, Ottawa, Hamilton, Winnipeg, Edmonton, Calga Vancouver

---

Southam Printing Limited

Profile

A leading North American printing company. Active in commercial web, consumer printed products, business forms and specialty printing market segments. Operates plants throughout Canada and in the United States.

Canada

Commercial web group

Canadian Publishers, Calgary, Winnipeg

Gazette Canadian Printing, Candiac, Que.

RBW Graphics, Owen Sound, Ont.

Southam Murray Printing, Toronto

Consumer printed products group

Agency Press, Vancouver

McLaren, Morris and Todd Limited, Mississauga, Ont.

Offset Print & Litho, Markham, Ont.

Business forms/specialty printing

Southam Paragon Graphics, Candiac, Dorval, Granby, Que.; Mississauga, Ont.; Regina, Sask.

Printing services

Empress Graphics Inc., Scarborough, Ont.

Network Studios Inc., Toronto, Mississauga, Ont.

United States

Dittler Brothers, Incorpor Atlanta, Georgia

Holladay-Tyler Printing C Glenn Dale, Maryland

LPS, Inc., Atlanta, Georgi

Moreno Press, Oakwood,

Coles Book Stores Limited

Profile

Canada's largest book retailer, with 189 stores in 90 cities and communities across the country.

Owns and operates World's Biggest Bookstore in Toronto.

Infomart

Profile

An electronic publishing company developing new products for the distribution of financial and general information to the business and professional marketplace.

Operates Informart Online, a full-text newspaper retrieval service pooling information resources of Southam newspapers and others in Canada and the U.S.

Profile

A leading provider of specialized information products and services in Canada and the U.S.

Canadian business publications

Automotive Marketer
Bath & Kitchen Marketer
Bodyshop
British Columbia Lumberman
Canadian Architect, The
Canadian Construction Record
Canadian Consulting Engineer
Canadian Doctor
Canadian Forest Industries
Canadian Industrial Equipment
  News

Heating, Plumbing & Air
  Conditioning
Housewares Canada
Human Resources Reporter
Jobber News
Journal of Commerce
L'Automobile
Laboratory Product News
Modern Medicine of Canada/
  Médicine Moderne du Canada
Motor Truck
Occupational Health & Safety

ıs Forestières
lth
e, Chauffage et
:isation
Paper Canada
Paper
ention Reporter
Station & Garage
gement
ı Building Guide
g Canada

Media holdings of daily newspaper owners March 1981

	Daily newspapers	Weekly newspapers	Radio	Tele-vision	Total
Thomson Newspapers	38	15	–	–	53
Southam	14	–	9	5	28
Sterling Newspapers	11	8	4	1	24
Irving family	3	1	1	1	6
Gesca	4	3	7	3	17
Bowes Publishers	3	7	–	–	10
Toronto Sun	3	2	–	–	5
Armadale	2	–	4	–	6
Northumberland Publishers	2	3	–	–	5
Quebecor	2	28	–	–	30
Uni Média	2	12	–	–	14
Torstar*	1	31	–	–	32
Kitchener-Waterloo *Record*	1	4	–	–	5
London *Free Press*	1	8	4	2	15
Red Deer *Advocate*	1	5	–	–	6
Robinson-Blackmore (St. John's *Daily News*)	1	10	–	–	11
St. Catharines *Standard*	1	4	1	–	6
Other daily weekly chains	9	14	–	–	23
Total	99	155	30	12	296

*Torstar holdings as at April 1981, following sale of its interest in Western Broadcasting.

Left: Data from the Southam Inc. 1987 *Annual Report*, courtesy of Southam Inc. Right: Data from the *Report by the Royal Commission on Newspapers*, 1981.

Should there be rules and legislation that would block companies from controlling too much of the media? Who would decide how much is too much? The following excerpt from a newspaper article is about the Irving family empire in New Brunswick, and it describes some government attempts to avoid a media monopoly in the Maritimes.

Lords of the Atlantic

by Alexander Bruce

For most of the 63 years that have passed since at age 25, Kenneth Colin Irving opened his first garage and gas station in Buctouche, the north coast village of his birth, he has utterly dominated the business life of New Brunswick. In the seaport of Saint John his name stands for the largest oil refinery in Canada, the first deep-water oil terminal in the Western Hemisphere, a shipyard and dry-dock, service stations, bus and transport companies, office towers, apartment buildings, television, radio and newspapers, convenience stores and laundromats.

Farther north, the name of Irving means millions of acres of choice timberland, pulp and paper plants, mines, smelting companies, trucking companies, and food operations. He controls about one tenth of the province's land, and employs one twelfth of its workers. He owns every English-language newspaper but one, and most radio and television stations. . . .

The unemployment rate [in New Brunswick] is 14.5 percent, compared to 12.8 percent for Nova Scotia and the 9.4 percent national average. Economic growth lags behind the national pace by at least one percentage point. There are few

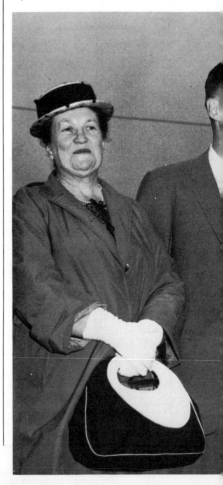

private sector investment opportunities and an underdeveloped financial and lending community, although there are plenty of federal and provincial incentive programs.

Mr. Irving does incomparably well partly because New Brunswickers admire him, partly because they fear him, and partly because local governments are often generous with him. Witness some examples from the history books.

In 1972 the federal combines investigation branch was, in the end, rebuffed in its bid to convict the Irving empire of monopolizing the provincial press. Irving companies were ordered to stand trial in the New Brunswick Supreme Court on four counts of contravening parts of the Combines Investigation Act. At the time, the group owned Saint John's *Telegraph-Journal* and *Evening Times-Globe*, the Moncton *Time-Transcript* and the Fredericton *Daily Gleaner*, among other newspapers around the province.

The trial judge found the companies guilty and fined them $150 000, stressing that "In my view, once a complete monopoly has been established, such as the evidence clearly discloses . . . detriment, in law, resulted," but the

Top left: K.C. Irving
Left: The Irving family in 1960 at an opening of an oil refinery in Saint John. Left to right: Mrs. Irving, son Arthur, K.C. Irving, sons James and John.

New Brunswick Court of Appeal reversed the conviction on the basis that the definition of the word monopoly was too broad to come under the jurisdiction of the act.

The appeals court statement said, in part: "The trial judge was using the word monopoly in the ordinary sense or dictionary meaning, not in the restricted (meaning) defined in the Combines Act. . . . If any presumption of detriment to the public arises out of the acquisition of a number of businesses by one individual, which (this court) does not accept, that inference is rebuttable."

In a 9-0 landmark decision, the

> *"He is a genius, an absolute genius," Saint John Mayor Elsie Wayne enthused about Mr. Irving.*

Supreme Court of Canada upheld the appeal court's ruling, establishing what many legal scholars consider a prime example of the inadequacy of Canadian combines legislation.

The Irving appetite for media companies grew unchecked. The empire picked up the monthly Atlantic Advocate and radio and television stations throughout the Maritimes. And last month the Canadian Radio-Television and Telecommunications Commission reversed its 1981 ruling preventing the conglomerate from buying any more broadcasting companies, granting it licences for new television stations in Saint John, Fredericton, Moncton, and Halifax. Presumably, the commission rea-

soned, the region is now better prepared for an Irving hegemony [leadership].

Mr. Irving and his three sons, James, Arthur, and John—who are now in charge of the daily operations—seem impervious to criticism that they control too much for the public good. When the CRTC ruled against their application for an FM radio licence in Saint John in December and awarded the station to a group that will be affiliated with Maclean Hunter Ltd., the Irvings squawked. Even though they own one of the city's few AM radio stations, hold its major television licence and own its two daily newspapers, they have appealed the FM decision. In a statement akin to the pot calling the kettle black, they argued, among other things, that granting the licence to a Maclean Hunter subsidiary would give that company an increased concentration of radio ownership in the region (it has interests in nine other stations in the Maritimes) and, therefore, their own degree of concentration was irrelevant.

"He is a genius, an absolute genius," Saint John Mayor Elsie Wayne enthused about Mr. Irving. "You only have to look at what he's done for the city and province to know that. Without him, we'd be dead. We'd simply be dead."

Still, some New Brunswickers think they could get along without him very nicely. They say his monopolies inhibit economic growth; that a single businessman should not possess so much power over the lives of so many people. They say Mr. Irving abuses his power; that he is known to go out of his way to fight even his most insignificant competitors.

"If I was in Toronto and I had a problem," one Saint John businessman complained, "at least I could tell my story in the media. And I can't go to the (authorities) here because they are all '. . . well . . . sort of hamstrung.' " An example. Last April 19 [1986], large quantities of fuel leaked from an Irving gasoline station into the city's sewer system, causing a series of explosions that destroyed two buildings and damaged two others. The centre of the city was evacuated for two days.

An engineer's report made public by city council in September said the explosions had been caused by the Irving company's having ignored several fire code regulations in installing and maintaining its gasoline storage tank. But Environment Minister Robert Jackson had already stood up in the Legislature in June to say the province would not take action against the company because the leak had occurred not from the storage tank but from a pipe connected to the tank, an eventuality not covered by provincial laws.

The city launched a suit to recover from Irving its expenses in cleaning up the damage. One independent weekly newspaper reported that Irving's insurance company was planning as a defence to allege that the city was responsible for the inci-

dent, by failing to enforce provisions of the building code in the construction of the buildings—two of which the Irvings themselves owned—into which some of the gasoline had leaked.

K.C. Irving with sons James (left) and Arthur (centre).

Little attention was paid to these developments in the Irving-owned local press. The city's lawsuit has been tied up in an increasingly complex court battle that now involves ten parties and at least eight sets of solicitors. . . .

The Irvings and McCains, [another Maritime family empire] may, indeed, own too much and affect the lives of too many people. But they provide jobs and industry in the land that gave them their start. In a sense, they are ardently loyal to the Maritimes. And as long as they keep the business wheels turning, the Maritimes are inclined to return the favor.

—*THE GLOBE AND MAIL*, TORONTO, FEBRUARY 21, 1987

RESPONSES

1. Because the information in the 1981 chart (p. 227) may have changed, do some research in your library about ownership of the media in Canada. Find out who the owners of Canadian newspapers and TV and radio stations are and what else they own. Try to find out who owns some of your favourite magazines. Do they own any other publications? Discuss your findings in class.

2. If you have not already done so, find out who owns the media in your area. Divide the class into groups to investigate one newspaper, radio station, television station, or magazine in your community. Find out who owns it and, if possible, what other businesses or media they own.

3. Why is there such concern about the concentration of media ownership? In a 1945 judgment of the United States Supreme Court, Justice Hugo Black wrote, "Freedom of the press from governmental interference . . . does not sanction repression of that freedom by private interest." In groups or as a class, discuss Black's statement. What are the possible problems of monopolies in the news media? How might such monopolies affect the news you receive?

PUTTING THE NEWS TOGETHER

The owner's influence on a news operation may vary depending on the owner and on the business itself. The people whose job it is to gather and present the news, however, have direct control over what news you receive through the media. This is called a "gatekeeping" function, a monitoring of what information is in the news. Editors and reporters decide which issues and events will be covered. Reporters judge what information is necessary for each article, and editors decide which stories will be published or broadcast. In newspapers, for example, most stories are never printed. An editor receives an estimated five stories for every one that is put in the paper.

Because the media are profit-oriented businesses, editors have to juggle the economic necessity of advertising, the demands for up-to-date news, and the need for good stories—those that will interest the audience and those that the audience needs to know. Time (in the electronic media) and space (in the print media) also influence what news is presented.

WHAT IS NEWS?

What is interesting and important enough to be researched and reported by the media? While their influence may vary from story to story, the following factors usually determine whether an issue or event is considered newsworthy.

Timeliness Considering the speed that characterizes the transmission of news today, it is obvious that news is very perishable. The issue or event must be current, or the story should contain new information about an issue or event that has already been reported.

Proximity How close to home is this news item? This often affects our interest in a story.

Prominence   While our reaction can be subjective, we are more likely to pay attention to news about world leaders and celebrities than people we do not know. Although they are less famous, we are often also interested in local persons of prominence.

Consequence   News about items that may affect us directly is news that matters, e.g., a tax increase, a new medical cure, the implications of a heat wave, a series of crimes in our neighbourhood.

Human interest   Stories that deal with our basic needs—clothing, food, shelter, affection, recognition—will always interest us. The subject can range from the pathetic to the humourous. Some of the more predictable players in human-interest stories might include a child, an animal, someone who has just reached his or her 100th birthday, and reunited relatives.

These have always been accepted as the elements of a good news story, but with television news, a sixth factor must be considered—is the story visual? Newspapers and magazines use photographs and illustrations, but stories that are visually interesting are especially important in a TV newscast.

RESPONSES

1. Clip some newspaper and magazine articles and/or write a brief summary of television and radio news items that contain one or more of the elements of a good news story listed previously. Explain how each item captures the audience's interest.

2. There is an old saying in the news business that if a dog bites a person, it's not news; if a person bites a dog, however, that's news. Another saying states that "good news is no news." What do these statements imply about what is considered newsworthy? Do you agree? Why? Compare these statements and the elements of a good news story with the material about violence in the news (pp.340-344). What conclusions can you draw?

3. As a member of the audience, you also play a gatekeeping role. As you may have seen in your survey, not everyone reads all the articles in a newspaper or magazine, or watches or listens to an entire newscast. What stories interest you? What stories don't interest you? Read a newspaper or magazine and/or watch a television newscast and note the stories covered. Note which ones interested you and why. Compare your notes with those of your classmates. How do the stories that interest you relate to the elements that make a story newsworthy?

CONSIDER THE SOURCE

Prime Minister Brian Mulroney in a reporters' "scrum"—one way of getting the news.

Where do the news media get their news? One news operation cannot afford the staff and equipment necessary to cover all the local, national, and international issues and events. The news media often rely on syndicated material and wire services such as Reuters, UPI (United Press International), CP (Canadian Press), and AP (Associated Press). There are also wire services used by the broadcast media, and TV news operations will sometimes use film or videotape fed from American networks.

Much of the news, as much as 50 percent, is a result not of reporters uncovering stories, but of their receiving news releases. Sending news releases to the media is standard practice with government departments, special interest groups, social service agencies, and large institutions and corporations. These documents are sometimes tied in with news conferences where the release of information to the media can be stage-managed as carefully as possible. The following is a sample news release from Alberta Environment Communications Branch.

 **NEWS RELEASE**

ENVIRONMENT

Date: October 19, 1987
Subject: RESPONSE SOUGHT BY ALBERTA ENVIRONMENT REGARDING ENVIRONMENT AND ECONOMY REPORT

Environment Minister Ken Kowalski is seeking provincial-wide input and discussion regarding the report of the National Task Force on Environment and Economy recently released by the Canadian Council of Resource and Environment Ministers (CCREM).

The report, viewed by many Canadian environment specialists as one of the most significant and far-reaching environment initiatives of the century, is part of the Canadian response to the World Commission on Environment and Development (Brundtland Report).

"It's difficult for me to dampen my enthusiasm or support regarding this report because implementation of many of its recommendations will influence and touch generations of Canadians to come," said Kowalski, adding that Alberta's pivotal role in encouraging the establishment of the Task Force at the 1986 annual meeting of CCREM held in Banff further demonstrated Alberta's leadership in encouraging federal-provincial dialogue on environmental issues of national and international concern.

The Minister noted that response to the report to date by provincial environmental organizations has been "extremely positive."

"However, every avenue must be taken to assure debate and discussions continue amongst all sectors of Alberta's population and that the Government of Alberta encourages public opinion to be expressed about the report," Mr. Kowalski said.

In order to stress the significance of the report and encourage discussion, Alberta Environment is currently distributing a copy of the report to more than 700 organizations within Alberta. Distribution includes major industrial and manufacturing interests, municipalities, universities, colleges and technical institutions, and environmental special interest organizations and associations. Those receiving the report are being asked to submit comments and observations to the Minister.

The Canadian delegation headed by federal Environment Minister, the Hon. Tom McMillan, will place Canada's response to the Brundtland Report before the United Nations General Assembly today in New York.

RESPONSES

1. Examine a daily newspaper to identify the sources of its articles.
   a) Compare the number of articles written by staff members with those from other sources.
   b) Find several examples of stories that you think came from news releases. Look for items that begin something like this: "The Minister of Natural Resources announced today . . ." Present your findings to the class.

2. In television and radio newscasts, the sources of items are not usually indicated. Have a representative from your class speak or write to the news director at a TV or radio station near you and ask him or her how many of the news items in a typical broadcast are generated by the station's staff. How many are based on news releases? How many came from other sources? If possible, tape the interview (with the person's permission) to play for the class.

3. A TV news show may use film footage from an American network. A wire service story may be written by a reporter who is not Canadian. Discuss how this might affect what information is given and how it is presented. Refer to the articles you have examined to support your opinion.

4. In groups, discuss the advantages and potential dangers of news releases and news conferences. If you were an editor, what suggestions might you make to offset the tendency of having too much "managed" news? Share your conclusions and possible solutions with other groups.

WRITING THE STORIES

Virtually every good news story contains answers to what journalists call the 5 W's: Who, What, Where, When, and Why. There is also an H— How. The arrangement of those facts differs depending on the type of story (e.g., straight news, feature) and the medium.

For example, the information in a news story for a paper is generally arranged in inverted pyramid style. In this method, the information is given in order of importance, with the most important information first. The facts that explain or support the lead follow. The story is written this way so that, if necessary, an editor can reduce the length of the article simply by cutting the material at the end without harming the substance of the story. The following sample uses the inverted pyramid technique.

Dr. David Suzuki, a noted authority on genetics and Canada's best-known scientific reporter, will be the guest speaker at the science curriculum conference, "New Directions," to be held at the University of Toronto next Thursday and Friday. In his talk, Dr. Suzuki, host of the popular CBC program, *The Nature of Things*, will present his views on the teaching of science in Canadian high schools. Recently returned from several continents where he has just completed the series, *A Planet for the Taking*, Dr. Suzuki is hoping that these television programs will reach a large audience. There will be a brief question-and-answer period following Dr. Suzuki's talk.

For some stories, especially when there is time and space, reporters will organize their information differently. For example, they may use an anecdote or develop the story chronologically. In hourglass style, the most important information comes at the beginning, and other important and interesting information is given at the end of the story.

RESPONSES

1. Clip eight to ten articles from a variety of newspapers. Study them to see if they use the inverted pyramid structure, and see what information you could cut from them without destroying the story. Compare your decisions with those of your classmates.

2. To see more clearly how the inverted pyramid works, select a short story you have read this year and, using the principles of the inverted pyramid form, briefly summarize its plot. By doing this, what did you learn about traditional story plots versus the nature of newspaper stories?

3. Take one of the following events and, using the inverted pyramid structure, write a lively piece which could be submitted to a class editor for revision and/or publication. Make sure you provide all the necessary information—the 5 W's and the H. Describe any photograph(s) you would include with the story. When you have compared stories with your classmates, discuss how using a different structure might have changed the story.

   a) A well known soap opera star visits a local shopping mall and creates a near-riot by his or her presence.

   b) A popular teacher is retiring this year. A surprise party is held which features former students from the past 25 years.

   c) A major fire occurs in a local restaurant. Arson is suspected.

4. It is not possible to print all the news. Inevitably, there is a selection process at work. What is left out of a story may, by some criteria, be more important than what gets printed. Working in groups, examine several recent news stories and speculate about what things have been left out. In each case, explain your opinions to the rest of the class.

PRESENTING THE NEWS

In the print media, news items fill up the space left over from advertising. In the electronic media, the news must fit into a specific amount of time, and is also influenced by advertising and time factors in terms of when the program appears. Operating within these limitations, editors must make even more decisions about how prominent each item should be.

Editors of television newscasts must decide the order of the stories and how much time each item will be given. Whether or not there will be visual material (film, video, graphics) also influences the decision. Newspaper editors consider the amount of space an article will be given, what page it should go on, whether there are photographs or illustrations, what the headline should be like (e.g., size and style of type), and where the article might go in relation to other stories.

The decisions that are made can affect the way we see the news. For example, the layout of a newspaper page affects how we perceive the content. If articles are arranged side by side, or juxtaposed, additional meanings or inferences are sometimes created. A newspaper editor might, for example, put a story about banning smoking in the workplace close to a report on funding for cancer research. A television or radio news editor might run one of those stories after the other.

RESPONSES

1. a) Bring several issues of two or more daily newspapers and a weekly newspaper to class. Work in groups and for each paper, note:

• page size

• number of pages

• front page layout

• index size and location

• number and names of sections

• which items are always located on the same page

b) Take a more detailed look at the papers by studying a few pages in each of them (including the front page) and answer the following. Your group may want to record some of your findings in chart form.

• How many stories per page?

- How many photos per page? What size are they? What are the sources of the photos?

- Examine some of the photographs. Consider the choice of subject, the details of the photo, the camera angle, the distance from the subject, and the caption. Using two or three examples, explain how the photos support the stories.

- Describe the size and styles of headlines, and the use of borders, artwork, and colour.

- Describe any interesting juxtapositions you find. Note the variety of interpretations they might imply.

- How many advertisements per page? Are there any full-page ads? Half-page ads? Who are the advertisers?

- How many stories are by staff writers? From wire services? Possibly from press releases?

- What are some of the regular columns? How many are written by staff writers? Syndicated columnists?

- Are there any "filler stories"—brief items with little news value, used to fill up column space?

2. In groups, collect a supply of newspaper articles, photographs, and ads. Create a series of interesting juxtapositions. Show the results to the class and ask them to give their perceptions of the effects you created.

3. Find some newspaper articles that do not have photos accompanying them. For each one, describe a photo you would choose to run with the story, and write the caption. Discuss why you chose the information to include in the caption and how it affects the meaning of the story.

4. Working in groups, examine a television newscast. If possible, have members of your class study the news from different stations. Record an outline of the newscast, showing each item in order. For each item, note the amount of time given and whether it was accompanied by film or videotape or graphics. Record whether each story was local, provincial, national, or international. Note how much time was spent on commercials. Share your findings with the class. Was the "top story" (the first and most important story) the same for each newscast? Do you think that story was the most important? Why? What was the relationship between the importance of a story and how much time it was given?

5. Compare a television newscast with a daily newspaper from the same day. How does their coverage of the news vary? Consider the prominence of items they have both carried. Suggest reasons for the similarities and differences.

6. a) Examine the following news items. Imagine you are a newspaper editor who can use only eight of the ten stories. Working in groups, decide which stories you would use and why. (You may find it helpful to refer to the elements of a good news story, p. 233). Create a chart that lists the stories in order of prominence and indicate how you would suggest their relative importance (e.g., through the layout, headlines, use of photos).
b) Would your decisions be different if you were producing a television newscast? If so, create another chart for your TV news.
c) With the class, discuss the decisions your group made and your reasons. What additional information about each item might have helped you make your decisions?

• Canada's national curling team has just won the world championship.

• A major accident tied up traffic on a nearby highway for three hours this morning.

• A business in a city near you has gone bankrupt. Two hundred employees will be out of work.

• The will of a popular American movie star, who died a week ago, has just been made public: all the celebrity's money and possessions have been left in trust to be used to care for his pets.

• The provincial government has just announced a commitment to improve health care.

• A drop-in centre for single parents is being shut down due to lack of funds.

• The mayor of a nearby city has announced her resignation.

• Two teenagers from a local high-school have started a program to reduce drunk driving in the community.

• Several delegates from a foreign country have arrived to discuss increasing trade between their country and Canada.

• A Canadian film production company has announced that it will begin filming some scenes for its latest movie in your area next month.

MAGAZINES: SOME ISSUES

Most newspapers and television and radio newscasts are aimed at a general audience. Magazines, however, are usually aimed at specific audiences. This is reflected in the articles and the advertising. Consider your favourite magazine. How specialized is it? Why does it appeal to you? How much attention do you pay to the ads?

To get an idea of the many kinds of magazines that are published, choose an area of interest, such as sailing, books, or woodworking, and see how many magazines on that subject you can find. You could check the periodical indexes in your library, or go to a bookstore that might also have a large selection of magazines.

Now, focus on one magazine. In groups, decide on a Canadian sports, fashion, or recreation magazine that you would like to study. Try to choose one you do not usually read. Obtain several issues of the magazine and examine them carefully. Look at the table of contents and the masthead (the section that names the publisher and editors), as well as the articles and advertising, and record as much of the following information as possible.

- name(s) of owner and publisher

- average number of pages

- regular features

- circulation

- the percentage of space given to ads, articles, and photos or illustrations

- price per issue/per year

- major advertisers

- general format/style/aims of the magazine

- who you think the target audience is

Plan the stories for the spring issue of this magazine. Choose the stories you would include and write heads (the main title of the articles) and decks (the explanatory line under the head) for them. Indicate what photographs and/or illustrations might accompany each article. Design the cover and contents page. (You may want to use a computer for this part of the assignment if you have access to one.) Share your work with other groups. Discuss the decisions you made.

HOW OBJECTIVE CAN WE BE?

Objectivity in story reporting was one of the crucial aims of professional journalists for many years. They believed that a good reporter never let his or her beliefs, feelings, or opinions influence a story. Today, most journalists would probably agree that complete objectivity is an impossible goal. In deciding on the angle of a story and on what information will be reported, a person's biases do have some influence. It is still a general rule, however, that a reporter should try to be impartial as well as accurate and honest.

There are some journalists who have taken the argument that a reporter cannot be objective even further. In the 1960s, several writers (primarily from New York) stated that since complete objectivity was impossible to attain, it was misleading to present news stories as though they had been recorded and presented by a machine-like reporter, uninfluenced by feelings and opinions. It was not enough simply to acknowledge the reporter's presence; his or her perceptions were part of the story.

Their style of writing, called new journalism, includes some of the elements of traditional news reporting. In fact, the research for these stories is often more extensive than for others. However, new journalism also borrows devices from fiction, such as first person narration. The writing is notable for the way it tries to "get inside" the thought processes of the people portrayed. Reporters are frequently participants in the events of the article. They often reconstruct their experiences scene by scene and include highly emotional description and dialogue. New journalism gives the sense that the writers are "telling it like it is."

As Time Goes By

by David MacFarlane

Consider the elements of new journalism as you read the following excerpt from an article by David MacFarlane. While you are reading, you could make notes in your media log of your opinion of MacFarlane's style and of the emotions his writing evokes.

Mrs. Drew-Brook

But in the middle of the night there is this voice.

5:00 A.M. In the very early morning, you sometimes hear a voice. It is as thin as a kazoo. It comes from one of the twenty-six rooms on the floor, but you can't be quite sure who it is.

The corridor is empty. The panels of lights are never off. Each of the numbered doors is closed. Most of the time, the only noise is the hum of the refrigerator. The refrigerator is where residents keep the gifts that visitors bring. The night shift has stacked the breakfast trays in front of the elevator. The trays bear the typewritten names of residents and what they like for breakfast: orange juice, Special K, milk. When the morning shift comes in, they will get the toast and coffee from the kitchen in the basement. They will deliver the trays to each room. "Good morning," they will say, "Good morning." Their singsong voices will sound like holidays in Jamaica, long ago.

But in the middle of the night, there is this voice. You can't be sure. It might be only a dream. "Help," you think it says. "Help me."

9:00 A.M. Miss Emory and Mr. Macphee are two residents who like to go down to the dining-room for their breakfast. In the dining-room, which is in the basement, they can have bacon and eggs. When they come up, they sit for a while in the lobby and read the newspapers. The lobby is decorated in autumnal browns and oranges. Miss Emory reads the *Report on Business*. Mr. Macphee reads *The Financial Post*. Beyond the windows at the front, students are hurrying down Spadina Road to the university. The traffic in the street is heavy with the morning rush. Buddy is the budgie. The only sound in the lobby is his chirping.

Miss Emory graduated from nursing school one year after the outbreak of the First World War.

She is a Professor Emeritus of the University of Toronto's faculty of nursing, and holds an honorary LL.D. She is a vice-president of the Canadian Red Cross. Miss Emory has the commanding look of a strict educator and a laugh of sudden and surprising gaiety. There are a good many things that amuse Miss Emory, not the least of which is her being alive. Her voice has a flat tremulous emphasis. "When we were young, you know, we used to think we'd be lucky to get to sixty. Now, here I am at ninety-four. *I'm ninety-four.*" Mr. Macphee, who is ninety-two, joins in with Miss Emory's laughter.

Mr. Macphee was born in Scotland, and he describes himself as "a Highlander with an English sensibility." He was once a great cricket player and a keen figure skater. As a young man in London during the First World War, he helped reorganize the pay system of the Canadian army. "Before we straightened it all out," he says, "it was pande-bloody-monium." Now, he moves gingerly in his slippers, as if the lodge's carpets were pebbled beaches. Occasionally, a name will slip his mind. His left hand is mostly paralyzed. But he still writes poetry. "Literature. That is my one great interest."

A truck has pulled up in front of the lodge. Two movers arrive at the desk and ask the receptionist which room is being emptied out. She checks her list.

Mrs. Rowe, in her pink cardigan, has taken her customary seat beside the reception desk. She often

Mr. Van de Walle makes a point of saying hello and asking people how they are.

Mrs. Edmunds

sits there, and always asks if it's still too early to go down for lunch, or dinner, or afternoon tea. Her voice is loud and out of key. Some people are surprised that Buddy has never learned to say "Is it still too early to go down?" She was once a champion golfer and an ice-hockey player. She watches the movers, as she watches everyone, with an odd combination of indignation and amusement. . . .

9:30 A.M. When Mr. Van de Walle comes to work, most people in the lobby are not sure who he is. He has only recently been appointed manager of the Spadina Central Park Lodge. In a very short while he will move on again, but the news of his arrival was announced happily in the monthly bulletin: "We are all delighted with the arrival of our new manager, Mr. Roger Van de Walle, who has come to us from Central Park Lodge in Windsor." Passing through the lobby, Mr. Van de Walle makes a point of saying hello and asking people how they are. . . .

Central Park Lodges is the longest-established chain of private nursing and retirement homes in Canada. The company is twenty years old. It thinks of itself, says its vice-president, Bill Jappy, as "the Cadillac of the business." Central Park Lodges built its reputation with comfortable homes for elderly people who required only minimal nursing care. These are called retirement homes. Recently, Central Park Lodges has increased the number of its nursing-home facilities to fifty per cent of its holdings.

This is a shift of some significance.

The distinction between a retirement home and a nursing home is clear enough on paper. A nursing home provides its residents with 1½ to three hours of nursing care a day; a retirement lodge can provide only up to one hour. The size of a retirement home is measured in rooms. In a nursing home you count beds. The distinction is not so clear in practice. . . .

When residents first come to Spadina, they know exactly where they are and why they are there. But the average age at Spadina is 86.4 years. There is the problem of deterioration. . . .

"If we have someone who deteriorates," said one staff member, "we give the family a choice. If they can supply the nursing we need—I mean, they need—then the guest can stay. But we can't look after those who become helpless or incontinent or uncontrollable. The sad thing is, when they're at the nursing-home stage they're better off in a nursing home. It's not fair to them or to the other guests to let them stay."

Guarding the border of deterioration is a difficult task for the management. There are, on the one hand, complaints of table-mates who drool or don't know where they are. The elevator sometimes smells of urine. On the other hand, the cost of living at Central Park Lodge is, along with death, responsible for the thirty-three per cent annual turnover. "And therein," says Mr. Van de Walle, "lies the problem."

The distiction between a retirement home and a nursing home is clear on paper.

Miss Tew

The first responsibility of the manager is to increase the rate of returns by achieving a balance between revenue and expenses. The second is to maintain occupancy through marketing and public relations. With an uncertain economy, increased rates are already coming to mean increased vacancies. No one is going to be asked to leave because he or she drools at the table. Central Park Lodge will accommodate itself as much as possible to a resident's infirmity. At Spadina there are staff members who are greatly admired by residents for their patience and concern. But when the cost of care exceeds the monthly payments— payments that can be as high as $2 300—a resident has to go. This is called effecting a transfer. "It's a sad thing," says Mr. Van de Walle. "It's an emotional thing. But you're in business. You gotta make a buck." . . .

11:00 A.M. All the residents call Mary Allen, Mary Allen. It is rarely Mary or Mrs. Allen. She is a pert, good-looking woman with a friendly, open face. She is the social and activities director, and everyone says, "Mary Allen does a wonderful job." . . .

Every weekday morning Mary Allen puts on her green jogging-suit and running shoes and leads the exercise class. Miss Tew, who once taught school in the tiny Alberta town of Anselmo, often plays the piano. She plays, "The Bonny Bonny Banks of Loch Lomond" and "Coming Through the Rye." The fifteen people who go down to the recreation room do their exercises sitting down. The room has a brown and orange carpet and a low, white panelled ceiling. In the corner there are three trays of potted plants under fluorescent lights. Ladies' purses sit on the floor. Canes are propped against the chairs. . . .

Every morning they do "The

"Ah," he says, "Ye'll have to be on your toes to keep up with the likes of us."

Miss Emory and
Mrs. MacQuarrie

Grand Old Duke of York." They sing the words: "The Grand Old Duke of York, he had ten thousand men . . . ." When he was up, their hands go up. When he was down, their hands go down. In the recreation room on a weekday morning, if you shut your eyes, the quavering straggle of voices sounds exactly like a kindergarten class. . . .

2:00 P.M. The Reminiscence Group meets once a week. Fourteen people sit in a circle in the recreation room. Two sets of double doors open out to the hall and the dining-room. The doors on the other side open onto the Happy Hour room. The windows look out on a small grey patio. The white curtains are usually closed.

The Reminiscence Group is run by two students from George Brown College and one volunteer. Of the ten residents in the group, seven have either walkers or canes. The students are called activation coordinators. Jennifer MacEachern and Denyse Burgess are both twenty-one. They study geriatric impairment, psychology, sociology, communications, adult learning, and group processing. Part of the two year course includes work in the field. They have to get in 500 hours before the end of term.

"All right," says Denyse. "Let's begin. Can anyone tell me what day it is?"

Mr. Macphee looks across the circle to a young man with a note pad. He has seen him before but isn't quite sure where. "Ah," he says, leaning forward. "Ye'll have to be on your toes to keep up with the likes of us."

When Denyse asks what year it is, Miss Davis answers. Miss Davis is short and hunched, and can often be seen working her way along the wooden handrails that line the corridors of Central Park Lodge. She always wears a crumpled sun visor and a dusty blue raincoat. "It's 1893," she says. Eventually there is some gentle laughter. "Oh. No." She laughs herself. "Now, that's the year I was born."

Today the subject is what they did before they came to Central Park Lodge. Last week it was the sinking of the *Titanic*. The stories go counter-clockwise. The first woman who speaks wears a purple cocktail dress. She clutches the purse in her lap. Her wedding band is now too large. Her smiles increase the tension in the fine lines of her face. She is asked about her family. "I think I had a boy and a girl." She smiles a quick, frightened smile. Her face has a tremble, as if holding back tears. The dignity of her bearing will admit neither the embarrassment nor the terror of having forgotten so much.

The stories go round the circle. Mrs. Allen, neatly dressed and articulate, recalls that her mother rented a house in Grimsby for nine dollars a month. She speaks of the years she lived in Haileybury. Mr. Macphee asks her about the great fire. Mrs. Maltby, who grew up in Tokyo and who has a voice like a fairy godmother, speaks some Japanese. Miss Standing, who was a teacher and who wears pant suits, sings the North Toronto Collegiate Institute school song. Mr. Macphee recounts a history that roams from Skye to Ohio, tracing as he goes the battles of the Picts, the development of the English economy, and the great depression of 1904. His reminiscence ends with "And then we came to Canada." That was 1911. . . .

3:00 P.M. The visitor is in the elevator. She is coming from a relative who is crossing the border between

There are bouquets of irises on the tables. The ceiling is low and white.

Mrs. Maltby

retirement home and nursing home. She has been up in the room all day. "Dear God in heaven," she says.

The decision to come to Central Park Lodge is difficult enough for a family. "You tell a white lie. You say, 'We're going to try it for two or three months. It's just an experiment. And if you don't like it, we'll try something else.' But you know in your heart there is nothing else." The decision to make the next move will be harder still.

There are waiting lists for nursing homes and chronic-care hospitals. There will be little chance of a private room. More possessions will have to be abandoned. The people at a nursing home will not all be the kind of people one is used to. There will be no white lies. . . .

5:30 P.M. Tuesday is a Birthday Dinner, and Miss McLaren is the last person to arrive at her table. She has been across the hall at Happy Hour. The slow procession of walkers and canes has already made its way from elevator to dining-room when she takes her usual place.

Miss McLaren sits with Mrs. Willson, Miss Foot, and Mrs. Hyde. There are two sittings, and 5:30 is the second dinner. There are four people at each of the twenty tables. Residents always sit in the same place. They are usually on time, or even a little early, for their meals. "It's what they live for." said one staff member. There are some guests who would beg to differ.

There are bouquets of irises on the tables. The ceiling is low and white and studded with sprinklers.

The waitresses wear pale-blue uniforms and dark hairnets. There is a large photograph of autumn trees on the brick wall that Miss McLaren faces. Sometimes the joke is that the picture is the central park. There are no windows in the dining-room. . . .

Miss McLaren has looked poorly ever since she came back from the hospital. She had never been much of a dinner companion, but recently there has been a noticeable change. Mrs. Willson, who used to be a nurse and who always sits to Miss McLaren's right, thinks she has been looking particularly gaunt. She hasn't been eating. Her eyes have seemed wild. Mrs. Hyde, who faces Miss McLaren, thinks she has been talking to herself more than she had before. She is always mumbling something you can't hear. Everyone feels the hospital has let her out too soon.

Carol Jones is the health-care coordinator at Spadina. She is a registered nurse. Carol Jones estimates that fifteen to twenty per cent of Spadina's population dies each year, and she agrees that sometimes residents are returned from hospitals too soon. "I've had some real doozies of fights with hospitals," she says. Frequently it is assumed that Central Park Lodge provides more care for its residents than it does. There is always one registered nurse in the building and a guest attendant for each floor. The guest attendants make beds, clean rooms, give baths, do laundry. They must have a grade-ten education. The doctor comes

"You've come a long way if you're 101, and you just have to make the best of it."

twice a week. . . .

Miss McLaren hasn't touched a thing, but Mrs. Willson has encouraged her to have some custard for dessert. "Miss McLaren," she says, "you really should eat something." Miss McLaren has eaten several mouthfuls when, abruptly, she stops. Her eyes roll and her head lolls back. The custard comes in small hiccups from her mouth. Mrs. Hyde calls for help but no one hears.

Mrs. Willson knows that someone should hold up Miss McLaren's head. She also knows that no one at the table has the strength. She pulls her walker to the side of her chair and rises more quickly than she has in years. When she crosses the dining-room, a few people look up. They have never seen her in such a rush. By the time Mrs. Willson reaches the staff tables, Miss McLaren is unconscious. By the time people come running and Miss McLaren is carried in her chair to the hall, she is dead.

9:00 P.M. After dinner there is never very much to do. On Saturdays there are singsongs. On Sundays there are hymn sings. Sometimes there will be a game of bridge, but it's hard to find a foursome. Someone always forgets what's trump.

The corridors are brightly lit. Behind each of the numbered doors there are the voices of TV sets. If visitors drop by, someone will go to the refrigerator and get some ice. Drinks are served in glasses faintly marked with lipstick. At eight o'clock the nurse brings round the medication.

A young man is visiting Mrs. Whiteside. He is writing an article for a magazine. The magazine was founded in 1887. That was the year Mrs. Whiteside was five. She was born in Dundas, Ontario, where her grandfather owned a large store. It was called Grafton's. On the wall behind her chair, there is a pretty water colour of a stream and a bridge. The bridge was near the old Dundas canal. Mrs. Whiteside painted the picture herself. "Oh, long ago," she says.

Mrs. Whiteside and the young man are talking. He is taking notes. Mrs. Whiteside's companion sits near the window by a folded wheelchair. She doesn't say very much. Mrs. Whiteside sits up in a chair, surrounded by papers and pictures of grandchildren. Her face has a calm strength. Sometimes, when you think she doesn't know what's going on, she'll give a girlish laugh to let you know she does. "I think we've had Trudeau long enough," she is saying.

Mrs. Whiteside is as optimistic as her maxim: "Laugh and the world laughs with you, weep and you weep alone." She spends her days in her room with a companion, perusing newspapers with a magnifying glass. She often says, "You've come a long way if you're 101, and you just have to make the best of it." But when the young man asks if she finds it frustrating to be lame, she looks at him as if he's asked an orphan whether parents are sometimes missed. The problem with young people is not so much that they think they will always be young as that they think old people have always been old. "How would you like to sit in a chair all day?" she says.

In the evenings Mrs. Whiteside

Mrs. Whiteside and companion

usually keeps her door slightly ajar. She likes to see what's going on. Mrs. Willson and Miss Tew have passed by, pushing their walkers. Somebody has had some visitors. Miss Davis, in raincoat and sun visor, has struggled past. Now the corridor is empty, except for Mrs. Maltby. She is standing in front of the elevator. Outside Mrs. Whiteside's door, the only sounds are the hum of the refrigerator and the low jibberish of television shows. Sometimes you hear a voice. Mrs. Whiteside doesn't hear a sound. Nor does she hear the young man's question.

"You will have to speak more loudly," says Mrs. Whiteside's companion.

"So, how does it feel to be 101?" he asks again.

"It feels fine," Mrs. Whiteside says.

"Do you like it here?"

"Oh, wonderfully."

"Do you have any complaints?" he asks.

"Nothing of importance." Mrs. Whiteside studies the young man. He was born the year that she turned seventy-one. She doesn't think there is much of a story, and besides it's getting late.

"It's a funny way to end your life," she concludes. "But what can you do?"

—*SATURDAY NIGHT*,
OCTOBER 1983

RESPONSES

1. The deck (the article introduction that follows the head, or title) for this article was: "Inside a retirement home for the old, where the residents have everything but a future, a community of remarkable strength and diversity creates itself." Using examples from the article, explain why you think this is or is not an accurate summary of the piece. (You might want to find and read the entire article.) Write your own deck for the article and compare it with those of your classmates.

2. How do you think the staff and residents may have reacted to the article? How would you feel if one of the residents David MacFarlane described were related to you? Discuss your answers in groups.

3. Referring to several characteristics of new journalism, indicate how David MacFarlane has made effective use of these stylistic features. What parts of the story do you consider to be well written? Select several examples and indicate what effects the writer achieved. What are the advantages of the reporter's use of chronological order as his basic structural device?

4. Have a group or class discussion about the idea of objectivity in news reporting. Is it possible? Is it necessary? Can you be subjective and fair? Support your answers with references to MacFarlane's article.

5. Find examples of new journalism; in newspapers or magazines, or research the development of new journalism. Using this style, write a short feature on a topic which lends itself to vivid description, e.g., a rock concert, a final basketball game, a parade, or a public rally.

If impartiality is a concern in reporting the news, just the opposite is true of opinion pieces. These articles are usually written as editorials or columns and are indicated as being separate from the regular news stories. In opinion pieces editors encourage staff writers, and sometimes guest writers, to express their own viewpoints. If those viewpoints are controversial, so much the better. Controversy often attracts readers.

Some magazines, like *Maclean's*, feature well-known columnists who express their opinions in a way that usually provokes strong reactions in readers. The following *Maclean's* article is an account of Barbara Amiel's experience in a Mozambique jail in 1981. Amiel is an editor and regular columnist for *Maclean's*. This account is followed by excerpts from an article by Rick Salutin, a writer and editor at *ThisMagazine*. Salutin criticizes Amiel in the article, and this excerpt is his response to Amiel's account of her time in Mozambique.

Make notes about your reactions to Amiel's and Salutin's articles as you read them. Be prepared to discuss the conflict between the two writers' points of view.

A Flagrant Violation of Rights

by Barbara Amiel as told to Jane O'Hara

It seemed like a perfect holiday at the time. When Maclean's senior writer Barbara Amiel, with travelling companions Toronto tour operator Sam Blyth and American Jim Basker, drove from Johannesburg to Mozambique, they were three keen tourists

sampling a little African culture. Formalities were swept aside. On entry, they were waved through three checkpoints without having their passports stamped. After luxuriating for a few days under the African sun on the bleached beaches of the Indian Ocean, whatever reservations they had about the political situation seemed a trifle. It was not until they tried crossing the border into Swaziland that the trouble began. First with Mozambique's immigration officials, then with the secret police. Amiel, who is now in Johannesburg, told her story to Maclean's Jane O'Hara.

"When we were delivered to secret police headquarters, my greatest fear was that authorities would find out I was a journalist. I had been warned that Frelimo (the governing party of President Samora Machel) was wary of even Soviet-bloc journalists and was worried that it might be impossible to extricate a western journalist who had run afoul of the government. At headquarters, we were put in separate cells, and while Sam and Jim were being grilled for long periods over the next 36 hours, I began eating my notes and anything that might identify me as a journalist, including the guest list I had taken from Maputo's Palona hotel and my plastic-coated *Maclean's* I.D. card. Oddly enough, our interrogators seemed uninterested in me as a woman and directed most of their questions at the two men. It was one of the few times I had been grateful for being under the control

Previous page: author and journalist Barbara Amiel

of a male-chauvinist regime.

"When the secret police had finished their questioning, we were told to take only our necessities and ordered to follow two machine-gun-toting soldiers. We were not told where we were being taken. No phone calls were allowed. Mozambique is a country in which the Western concept of due process of law is unknown, and although we had been warned earlier to be careful not to break any laws—that there were no trials, no judges—the concerns had seemed foolish under the blue skies and hot yellow sun that inspired an awe of the beauty, not the terror, of Mozambique. From headquarters we were put in a vehicle with one other black man, a Mozambique-born South African, who exclaimed: 'O God. We are going to Machava.'

"Machava is the largest political prison in Mozambique, a vast compound surrounded by a 12-foot wall and fortified with barbed wire. There are nine cement cell blocks, each housing 20 to 30 prisoners. I was prisoner number 975 in cell block one. Sam and Jim, at times together, at times in solitary confinement, were placed in number eight. My cell mate was Tombe, a 45-year-old Mozambican woman whose crime was her suggestion of an alternate political party to Frelimo. She had been there six months, and, like most prisoners, had no idea when she would be released.

"Our cell was seven feet by ten feet, and specifically padlocked to keep the men from getting at us. In the daytime, it was like an oven and we would take off our clothes, although we had to suffer the indignity of having the guards peep at us through holes in the wall. The bed matting was full of lice. And most prisoners had contracted dysentery from the dirty water, a part of our dietary fixture which was supplemented twice a day with indigestible rice, bread, and two ounces of meat. Despite the appalling conditions, there was a great spirit of camaraderie among the prisoners. A prisoner in the cell next to Sam made him a pair of laces for his running shoes after the guards had taken his away so that he would not hang himself.

"Sam also managed to conduct a little business behind bars. During our holiday in Maputo, he had tried contacting the minister of information and tourism to discuss tour possibilities but to no avail. According to aides, the minister was either out or busy. Sam discovered how busy he really was when the minister, who happened to be imprisoned two cells down at Machava, introduced himself one day.

"On the third day of our imprisonment, Tombe became alarmed. Blood was coming out of my mouth while I lay sleeping. She called the guards, who looked worried that they might have an ill gringo on their hands. And so they bundled me up and prepared to take me to the military hospital in Maputo. My first instinct was to stay at the prison, thinking that our one chance was to stick together, but at the guards' insistence, I was led away.

"Within hours of my arrival at the hospital, I went into an intense malarial fever. Since most of the country's doctors fled the country in 1975, at the time of the Frelimo take-over, I was treated for six hours by three Bulgarian doctors who doused me with buckets of rain water to suppress my fever. Throughout, the most haunting spectacle was the

On the third day of our imprisonment, Tombe became alarmed.

faces of the armed soldiers who stood by laughing.

"Meanwhile, thanks to the help of the U.S. vice-consul, Howard Jeter, and the diligence of U.K. High Commission officials in Maputo, our release was arranged. The proper phone calls were made and Sam and Jim were told to pack their things. The car we had rented was waiting outside the prison for them. The luggage minus two pairs of men's shoes and a watch which had been stolen, was still there. When Sam and Jim came to the hospital to collect me, I was still not convinced that the ordeal was over. I had been a week without food, hooked up to an intravenous unit with unsterilized needles, and had been forced to use the most primitive of sanitary facilities. I know we have no recourse for what has happened. I can only feel sympathy for the people we have left behind in Machava."

—*MACLEAN'S*, JANUARY 19, 1981

Amiel: Beyond the Fringe

by Rick Salutin

I t is implausible . . . that any-one, much less a travel agent, would approach such a sensitive border crossing (weeks later the South Africans sent an armed raid through) without a visa. It is, how-ever, plausible that people without visas would cross the border sur-reptitiously if they wanted to get in but *lacked* visas. . . .

The trio were arrested for lacking visas when they tried to leave the country. Amiel says her "greatest fear was the authorities would find out I was a journalist." She'd "been warned" (naturally, we're not told by whom) that Frelimo "was wary of even Soviet-bloc journalists," and she worried "it might be impossible to extricate a Western journalist." Here we start to feel we are with Barbara in Wonderland. For a scant two years ago a *Maclean's* jour-nalist, Dan Turner, made an accredited (i.e., by those same "authorities") visit to Mozambique

Rick Salutin—journal-ist, playwright, author, and editor at *This-Magazine. ThisMag* features investigative stories and is an alternative to main-stream news magazines.

and wrote rather positively about his trip in an issue which lists Barbara Amiel as "senior writer." Surely Amiel has read this article, given her areas of interest and her literacy. . . .

In prison, by her account, Amiel was placed in a cell "padlocked to keep the men from getting at us," and fed a diet of water plus, twice a day, "indigestible rice, bread and two ounces of meat." When she began coughing blood (that ID card?) she was taken to a military hospital where three East European doctors attended her. Now it seems to me there might have been a story were the men and women thrown *together* in jail, had she been starved (the diet is more than substantial by African standards), and had she been left to rot when she got sick. By her own account, it seems to me, the three day prison stint fails to shock. In the hospital she tells us armed soldiers stood by laughing at her. But she doesn't explain how she knew what they were laughing at, and she also says she was in an "intense malarial fever" at the time. She spent a week in a hospital "hooked up to an intravenous unit with unsterilized needles and . . . forced to use the most primitive of sanitary facilities." It isn't clear just what this last prissy phrase means, or where Amiel in her delirium thought she was—the Cote d'Azur? . . .

She passes off unsubstantiated and even nonsensical claims as fact. (That she was in jail along with the Mozambican minister of Information and Tourism, for example. This is ludicrous. At the most someone *said* he was that. There is not even such a ministry as "Information and Tourism" in the Mozambican government.) She loads her language for bear. . . (guards at the Mozambican border are "machine-gun toting"—though machine guns are toted all over South Africa, including the Johannesburg airport). And she blandly presents all this as objective and reasonable. . . .

—MARGINAL NOTES,
1984

RESPONSES

1. Barbara Amiel is known not only as a columnist and media personality but also as a defender of right-wing views. Similarly, Rick Salutin, who is known for representing politically leftist, anti-establishment views, describes himself as being "marginal." How might this knowledge influence the reader's response to these writers' material?

2. What do you think Amiel's and Salutin's objectives were in writing these articles? Refer to specific examples to explain how they tried to achieve them. How successful were they?

3. Did Salutin's criticism change your views of Amiel's column? If so, to what extent? Discuss the credibility of each article.

4. Read other columns in newspapers or in magazines such as *Maclean's*. Find one with which you disagree. Write a column that provides a detailed, critical response. In your response, try to describe the point of view and ideology that is presented in the article with which you disagree.

The news media provide so much information that it is virtually impossible to read and watch and listen to all of it, to get a "total picture." In addition, the factors that you have been examining influence that information, further altering the picture of reality that the news presents. How can we make sense of and assess the information we receive? In the following article, David Suzuki suggests that an understanding of the media and their limitations is necessary to help us take advantage of what the news media provide.

Television's Electronic Curse: Views of World are Distorted

by David Suzuki

The major way we get our information today is from television. We watch TV in large blocks of time—it is the main way we learn about ourselves and the world. And it's easy to see why. Television is an almost effortless way of being informed, it's pleasant, and pictures make a powerful impression.

But if we are to be well informed, we must understand the medium, its limitations and modus operandi. Of most importance, we must realize that television does not reflect reality. Television reports are artificial, just as movies are. We don't have zoom lenses in our eyeballs; we don't live in a world where we can "cut" from one place to another or from one time to another. Yet that is what television does, and our brains fill in all the spaces.

Try watching a report of a single event, such as a pole vaulter clearing the bar or a theatrical performance. It can be an illusion created by the juxtaposition of several cameras or repetitions edited together into an apparently single continuous piece. News reports themselves are fabrications.

From the decision as to what is newsworthy to the availability of a crew, the cost of doing the report and deadlines for editing and broadcast, stories sometimes are made or broken for reasons that have nothing to do with the significance of the events themselves.

Once something is judged worthwhile (and that is often arbitrary and subjective), the item's length may be determined as much by whether an interview subject is articulate, or by the kinds of supporting visual material available, as by the inherent merits of the story.

And most important, if the researchers, writers and reporters are upper middle-class white males, chances are their unconscious social and cultural biases and values will color the way the report is finally presented. I say all this not to denigrate the medium, but to point out the many constraints impinging on the profession. It is simply not possible to cling to the notion that there is such a thing as objective report-

ing on television, and people should understand that as they watch.

When I began my career in television in 1962, it was my conceit to think that through quality programming, it would be possible to educate the public and raise its general awareness of the kinds of issues I was interested in. A quarter of a century later, *I* have been educated about the severe constraints in this endeavor. The problem is one of sheer *volume* of information. We live in a world that has become fragmented into little bits of information that no longer hang together within a coherent framework of values and perspectives.

Change is what characterizes our lives—all about us, change is the one dependable feature of our social landscape. And because of rapid change and turnover, we acquire bits of information and quickly sift through them, retaining only those that happen to strike a chord.

So often we repeat a "fact" that we justify with "I read somewhere that . . ." or "I saw on TV that . . ." without regard to the quality of the source. If the *National Enquirer* is viewed as being of equal credibility with *The Globe and Mail*, information becomes totally devalued.

I am constantly surprised when in letters, phone calls or encounters I am credited with all kinds of reports from programs I had nothing to do with. Often I am told, "I saw on your show . . .", but it is a story we have never covered. People do not watch TV with concentration; there are interruptions—phone calls, getting a snack, putting the children to bed. We tune in and out, watching when something interesting comes up and slacking off at other times. By the time we go to bed, the contents of a four-hour viewing block may be completely mixed up, and it is easy to assume that something remembered from one show was actually seen on another.

We do it with other media as well, retaining little nuggets of information. This came home to me once when my wife, who teaches expository writing to science students, brought home a copy of the *National Enquirer* that she had used as a class exercise. I perused it with interest and found it was full of fantastic stories on medicine (woman inseminated by robot) and science (Soviets capture UFO crew). Three days later at work, I found myself mentioning that I'd read there are toxic chemicals in the nipples of baby bottles. Midway through I realized with a shock that I was repeating a story from the tabloid.

So while we have access to more information than ever in human history, rather than educating and informing us, "infoglut" makes life much more complex and difficult because it is all fragmented. If we are going to take advantage of this information, we have to understand the media and their limitations.

I realized with a shock that I was repeating a story from the tabloid.

We have to assess the source of information. We have to believe in our own ability to judge the pros and cons of controversial issues and to demand access to primary information. That is precisely what scientists do in their profession. They are skeptical of any new claims, demand to see the evidence for themselves and are confident enough to trust their own judgment. It's an attitude that the general public should find of great value in a time of information overload.

—*THE GLOBE AND MAIL*, TORONTO, AUGUST 22, 1987

RESPONSES

1. a) According to David Suzuki, what factors affect the way the media process information? What problems does this cause?
b) How does Suzuki think the media contribute to "information overload"?
c) What does he recommend to deal with the problems he identifies? How practical do you think these suggestions are? What other solutions would you recommend?

2. By referring to the key concepts of media, comment on Suzuki's observations about the nature of the news media.

ISSUES FOR FURTHER STUDY

Does news exist simply because the media are there to report it? Does media coverage define how important an issue or event is?

The activities in this chapter have helped you to investigate what news is, and why and how it becomes "the news." The factors that affect all media may have no less influence on the news media simply because the news is "real" and not fictional, e.g., like a novel or sitcom.

As you continue observing the news media, and as you work on the following questions, try to determine how your perceptions and reactions to the news are affected by your awareness and understanding of these factors.

1. Newspapers must be profit-making enterprises or they will not stay in business. Investigate the financial base of your local newspaper(s). You may be able to obtain an annual financial report from them or from your library. How much of their revenue comes from advertising? from subscriptions? Find out their rates for advertising.

2. No matter how much journalists try to be objective, no one can be completely unbiased. The articles and editorials in a newspaper often reveal different points of view, but some papers are known to show certain biases on specific subjects. To help you uncover the range of bias present in a typical newspaper, examine one and try to answer the following questions: Is the paper sympathetic to government positions? to big business? What is its attitude to minority groups and the rights of the oppressed? to the arts? to national aspirations? to Third World countries? Do the major advertisers in the publication tell you anything about the values of the publisher or the editors? What is the tone of the headlines? How have they used emotionally loaded language? Are there any juxtapositions of photographs or columns that might influence your response to the issues? How does the meaning of the photographs depend on the captions? What other observations might help you determine a newspaper's biases?

3. Television news has often been accused of being more entertainment than news. This is partly because the limited time given to news means that only a certain amount of information can be revealed and that complex subjects are usually covered superficially, if at all. Critics also say the need to keep ratings high means that TV journalists are more concerned with style than with substance. Is this criticism justified? Why can similar criticisms be aimed at the other news media? Explain.

4. Try to obtain copies of magazines which contain an alternative point of view to the mass circulation publications. (In Canada, these would include magazines such as *ThisMagazine* and *Canadian Forum*; in the United States, *The Nation, Mother Jones*, and *The Village Voice*.) Compare the way one or more of these magazines treats a controversial issue with the way a mass circulation magazine such as *Time, Maclean's*, or *Newsweek* treats the issue. Write your findings in a report and present it to the class. What do you think is the value of "alternative magazines"?

5. Obtain copies of at least two different newspapers and try to determine each one's point of view on some current topic. Try to follow their coverage of the topic for at least a week. Compare the quality of the reporting, the use of editorials, and photographs. Or, do a comparative study of the ways different media—television, radio and newspapers—treat the same topic. Suggest reasons for any differences you find. Individually or in groups, summarize your information for the class.

6. According to media writer Joshua Meyrowitz, the media often imitate the kind of information television provides and the way in which the information is presented. The traditionally more formal and abstract print media have turned towards issues of personality. Magazines such as *People* explore the personal lives of public figures. Print journalists and scholars have adopted a more personal and subjective style. Newspapers now often describe events in a manner that imitates what one might have seen and heard on television. . . . The sweat on a politician's brow, a tear running down a face, or a nervous twitch may become part of the print description—because the event is now defined in terms of how it appeared on television.

Find your own examples of this imitation. Debate the effectiveness of this approach. To what extent does it make a report more interesting? Discuss other ways in which the news media influence each other.

7. In a symposium on journalism entitled "Can the Press Tell the Truth?" published by *Harper's* magazine in 1985, the editor, Lewis Lapham, made the following observations: "Today's journalism is increasingly an amalgam of fact and fiction. This isn't done with intention; but because journalists work in the usual alloys of flawed information and unconscious bias. . . . Journalism is sculpture in snow. To have the expectation that it's somehow cast in stone—that it will reveal the truth to us—is to load it down with a burden it can't carry." Use this quotation as a starting point for a study of the role of journalists today and readers' expectations of them. In what ways does the quote illustrate the notion that the news media "construct" reality?

CHAPTER 6

Advertising

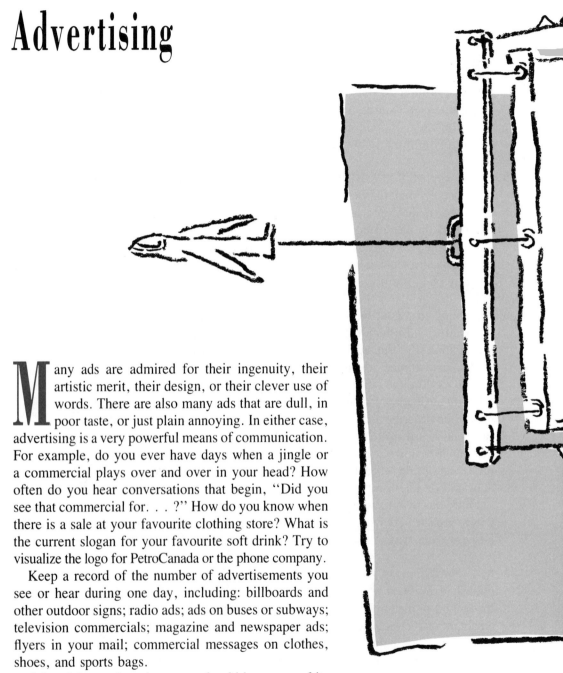

Many ads are admired for their ingenuity, their artistic merit, their design, or their clever use of words. There are also many ads that are dull, in poor taste, or just plain annoying. In either case, advertising is a very powerful means of communication. For example, do you ever have days when a jingle or a commercial plays over and over in your head? How often do you hear conversations that begin, "Did you see that commercial for. . . ?" How do you know when there is a sale at your favourite clothing store? What is the current slogan for your favourite soft drink? Try to visualize the logo for PetroCanada or the phone company.

Keep a record of the number of advertisements you see or hear during one day, including: billboards and other outdoor signs; radio ads; ads on buses or subways; television commercials; magazine and newspaper ads; flyers in your mail; commercial messages on clothes, shoes, and sports bags.

Advertising surrounds us; we should be aware of its impact. To understand the influence of advertising, we should become familiar with advertising techniques and be able to "decode" the many ads we see and hear daily.

ON SALE

STOKELY

THE CRAFT OF ADVERTISING

In groups, study current ads—some of you could make notes while watching and listening to television and radio ads, some could clip ads from newspapers and magazines, while some could record information about ads on billboards and on the public transit system, if there is one in or near your community. Examine and compare the ads by discussing points raised in the list that follows. You might want to record your findings in chart form. Keep the ads and your notes in your media log for future use.

- where and when the ad appears

- what characters are used (number of people, male or female, age, and so on)

- size of print ad or length of time of TV or radio commercial

- number of times the name of the product appears or is spoken

- in print ads, the location and prominence of the product itself

- in print ads, how much copy (written material) is used

- in TV commercials, how the product is displayed (how often, how prominently, and so on)

- what special effects are used, if any

- logos or symbols used, if any

- how it "hooks" us (gets our attention)

How to Produce Advertising That Sells

by David Ogilvy

David Ogilvy is one of the best-known figures in the advertising world. In his books, he defends advertising in a provocative way, and reveals how to succeed in the business. In the following selection from *Ogilvy on Advertising*, Ogilvy gives his formula for successful advertising. It is advice worthy of your attention—Ogilvy's advertising agency, Ogilvy and Mather, is the fourth largest in the world.

You don't stand a tinker's chance of producing successful advertising unless you start by doing your homework. I have always found this extremely tedious, but there is no substitute for it.

First, study the product you are going to advertise. The more you know about it, the more likely you are to come up with a big idea for selling it. When I got the Rolls-Royce account, I spent three weeks reading about the car and came across a statement that "at sixty miles an hour, the loudest noise comes from the electric clock." This became the headline, and it was followed by 607 words of factual copy.

Later, when I got the Mercedes account, I sent a team to the Daimler-Benz headquarters in Stuttgart. They spent three weeks taping interviews with the engineers. From this came a campaign of long, factual advertisements which increased Mercedes sales in the United States from 10 000 cars to 40 000.

When I was asked to do the advertising for Good Luck margarine, I was under the impression that margarine was made from *coal*. But

The Rolls-Royce Silver Cloud—$13,995

"At 60 miles an hour the loudest noise in this new Rolls-Royce comes from the electric clock"

What makes Rolls-Royce the best car in the world? "There is really no magic about it— it is merely patient attention to detail," says an eminent Rolls-Royce engineer.

1. "At 60 miles an hour the loudest noise comes from the electric clock," reports the Technical Editor of THE MOTOR. Three mufflers tune out sound frequencies—acoustically.

2. Every Rolls-Royce engine is run for seven hours at full throttle before installation, and each car is test-driven for hundreds of miles over varying road surfaces.

3. The Rolls-Royce is designed as an *owner-driven* car. It is eighteen inches shorter than the largest domestic cars.

4. The car has power steering, power brakes and automatic gear-shift. It is very easy to drive and to park. No chauffeur required.

5. The finished car spends a week in the final test-shop, being fine-tuned. Here it is subjected to 98 separate ordeals. For example, the engineers use a *stethoscope* to listen for axle-whine.

6. The Rolls-Royce is guaranteed for three years. With a new network of dealers and parts-depots from Coast to Coast, service is no problem.

7. The Rolls-Royce radiator has never changed, except that when Sir Henry Royce died in 1933 the monogram RR was changed from red to black.

8. The coachwork is given five coats of primer paint, and hand rubbed between each coat, before *nine* coats of finishing paint go on.

9. By moving a switch on the steering column, you can adjust the shock-absorbers to suit road conditions.

10. A picnic table, veneered in French walnut, slides out from under the dash. Two more swing out behind the front seats.

11. You can get such optional extras as an Espresso coffee-making machine, a dictating machine, a bed, hot and cold water for washing, an electric razor or a telephone.

12. There are three separate systems of power brakes, two hydraulic and one mechanical. Damage to one will not affect the others. The Rolls-Royce is a very *safe* car—and also a very *lively* car. It cruises serenely at eighty-five. Top speed is in excess of 100 m.p.h.

13. The Bentley is made by Rolls-Royce. Except for the radiators, they are identical motor cars, manufactured by the same engineers in the same works. People who feel diffident about driving a Rolls-Royce can buy a Bentley.

PRICE. The Rolls-Royce illustrated in this advertisement – f.o.b. principal ports of entry—costs **$13,995.**

If you would like the rewarding experience of driving a Rolls-Royce or Bentley, write or telephone to one of the dealers listed on opposite page. Rolls-Royce Inc., 10 Rockefeller Plaza, New York 20, N. Y. CIrcle 5-1144.

Ogilvy's first piece of advice: Do Your Homework. He read about the Rolls-Royce car for three weeks before he came up with this factual ad.

ten days' reading enabled me to write a factual advertisement which worked.

Same thing with Shell gasoline. A briefing from the client revealed something which came as a surprise to me; that gasoline has several ingredients, including Platformate, which increases mileage. The resulting campaign helped to reverse a seven-year decline in Shell's share-of-market.

If you are too lazy to do this kind of homework, you may occasionally *luck* into a successful campaign, but you will run the risk of skidding about on what my brother

Francis called "the slippery surface of irrelevant brilliance."

Your next chore is to find out what kind of advertising your competitors have been doing for similar products, and with what success. This will give you your bearings.

Now comes research among consumers. Find out how they think about your kind of product, what language they use when they discuss the subject, what attributes are important to them, *and what promise would be most likely to make them buy your brand.*

If you cannot afford the services of professionals to do this research, do it yourself. Informal conversations with half-a-dozen [consumers] can sometimes help a copywriter more than formal surveys in which he or she does not participate.

Positioning

Now consider how you want to "position" your product. This curious verb is in great favor among marketing experts, but no two of them agree on what it means. My own definition is "what the product does, and who it is for." I could have positioned Dove as a detergent bar for men with dirty hands, but chose instead to position it as a toilet bar for women with dry skin. This is still working 25 years later.

In Norway, the SAAB car had no measurable profile. We positioned it as a car for *winter*. Three years later it was voted the *best* car for Norwegian winters.

To advertise a car that looked like

an orthopedic boot would have defeated me. But Bill Bernbach and his merry men positioned Volkswagen as a protest against the vulgarity of Detroit cars in those days, thereby making the Beetle a cult among those Americans who eschew conspicuous consumption.

Brand Image

You now have to decide what "image" you want for your brand. Image means *personality*. Products, like people, have personalities, and they can make or break them in the market place. The personality of a product is an amalgam of many things—its name, its packaging, its price, the style of its advertising, and, above all, the nature of the product itself.

Every advertisement should be thought of as a contribution to the brand image. It follows that your advertising should consistently project the *same* image, year after year. This is difficult to achieve, because there are always forces at work to change the advertising—like a new agency, or a new Marketing Director who wants to make his or her mark.

It pays to give most products an image of quality—*a First Class ticket*. This is particularly true of products whose brand-name is visible to your friends, like beer, cigarettes and automobiles: products you "wear." If your advertising looks cheap or shoddy, it will rub off on your product. Who wants to be seen using shoddy products?

Take whiskey. Why do some

Think small.

Our little car isn't so much of a novelty any more.
A couple of dozen college kids don't try to squeeze inside it.
The guy at the gas station doesn't ask where the gas goes.
Nobody even stares at our shape.
In fact, some people who drive our little flivver don't even think 32 miles to the gallon is going any great guns.
Or using five pints of oil instead of five quarts.
Or never needing anti-freeze.
Or racking up 40,000 miles on a set of tires.
That's because once you get used to some of our economies, you don't even think about them any more.
Except when you squeeze into a small parking spot. Or renew your small insurance. Or pay a small repair bill.
Or trade in your old VW for a new one.
Think it over.

This ad "positioned" the Volkswagen as an economical alternative to large, conspicuous cars.

people choose Jack Daniel's, while others choose Grand Dad or Taylor? Have they tried all three and compared the taste? Don't make me laugh. The reality is that these three brands have different *images* which appeal to different kinds of people. It isn't the whiskey they choose, it's the image. The brand image is 90 percent of what the distiller has to sell.

Researchers at the Department of Psychology at the University of California gave distilled water to students. They told some of them that it was distilled water, and asked them to describe its taste. Most said

Grethe Meyers nye stel "Rødtop" fås i 38 dele til både bord og køkken.

Sådan fornyer man en klassiker
designet af Grethe Meyer.

Det er tyve år siden Grethe Meyer lavede "Blåkant" for Den Kongelige Porcelainsfabrik. Og lige fra starten var vi klar over, at her stod vi overfor en klassiker på linie med Børge Mogensens møbler og PH's lamper.

Tiden har givet os ret. Grethe Meyers rene, gennemtænkte formgivning og diskrete dekorationskunst er blevet højt præmieret og højt elsket i mange lande.

Men kunst er fornyelse, og Grethe Meyer har netop fornyet "Blåkant"'s tidløse former med en glad, rød kant og en lysere bundfarve. Ændringen er lille, men virkningen stor, og "Rødtop" er næsten lige så forskellig fra

"Blåkant" som sommer fra vinter. Hvad De foretrækker, ved vi ikke. Vi er bare glade og stolte over at kunne give Dem muligheden for at vælge.

DEN KONGELIGE

"Sometimes the best idea of all is to show the product—with utter simplicity."— David Ogilvy.

---

it had no taste of any kind. They told the other students that the distilled water came out of the tap. Most of them said it tasted *horrible*. The mere mention of *tap* conjured up an image of chlorine.

Give people a taste of Old Crow, and *tell* them it's Old Crow. Then give them another taste of Old Crow, *but tell them it's Jack Daniel's*. Ask them which they prefer. They'll think the two drinks are quite different. *They are tasting images*.

I have always been hypnotized by Jack Daniel's. The label and the advertising convey an image of homespun honesty, and the high price makes me assume that Jack

---

Daniel's must be superior.

Writing advertising for any kind of liquor is an extremely subtle art. I once tried using rational facts to *argue* the consumer into choosing a brand of whiskey. It didn't work. You don't catch Coca-Cola advertising that Coke contains 30 percent more cola berries.

Next time an apostle of hard-sell questions the importance of brand images, ask him how Marlboro climbed from obscurity to become the biggest-selling cigarette in the world. Leo Burnett's cowboy campaign, started 25 years ago and continued to this day, has given the brand an image which appeals to smokers all over the world.

What's the big idea?

You can do homework from now until doomsday, but you will never win fame and fortune unless you also invent *big ideas*. It takes a big idea to attract the attention of consumers and get them to buy your product. Unless your advertising contains a big idea, it will pass like a ship in the night.

I doubt if more than one campaign in a hundred contains a big idea. I am supposed to be one of the more fertile inventors of big ideas, but in my long career as a copywriter, I have not had more than 20, if that. Big ideas come from the unconscious. This is true in art, in science, and in advertising. But your unconscious has to be *well informed*, or your idea will be irrelevant. Stuff your conscious mind with information, then unhook your rational thought process. You can help this process by going for a long walk, or taking a hot bath, or drinking half a pint of claret. Suddenly, if the telephone line from your unconscious is open, a big idea wells up within you.

My partner Esty Stowell complained that the first commercial I wrote for Pepperidge Farm bread was sound enough, but lacking in imagery. That night I dreamed of two white horses pulling a baker's delivery van along a country lane at a smart trot. Today, 27 years later, that horse-drawn van is still driving up that lane in Pepperidge commercials.

When asked what was the best asset a person could have, Albert Lasker—the most astute of all advertising people—replied, "Humility in the presence of a good idea." It is horribly difficult to *recognize* a good idea. I shudder to think how many I have rejected. Research can't help you much, because it cannot predict the *cumu-*lative value of an idea, and no idea is big unless it will work for 30 years.

One of my partners came up with the idea of parading a herd of bulls through Merrill Lynch commercials under the slogan—"Merrill Lynch is *bullish* on America." I thought it was dopey, but fortunately it had been approved before I saw it. Those bulls are still parading, long after the account moved to another agency.

It will help you recognize a big idea if you ask yourself five questions:
1. Did it make me gasp when I first saw it?
2. Do I wish I had thought of it myself?
3. Is it unique?
4. Does it fit the strategy to perfection?
5. Could it be used for 30 years?

You can count on your fingers the number of advertising campaigns that run even for five years. These are the superstars, the campaigns

Good ideas, says Ogilvy, come from the unconscious. The image of the horse-drawn bakery van came to him in a dream. Over 25 years later, the image is still used.

that go right on producing results through boom and recession, against shifting competitive pressures, and changes of personnel. The Hathaway eyepatch first appeared in 1951 and is still going strong. Every Dove commercial since 1955 has promised that, "Dove doesn't dry your skin the way soap can." The American Express commercials, "Do you know me?," have been running since 1975. And Leo Burnett's Marlboro campaign has been running for 25 years.

Make the product the hero

Whenever you can, make the product itself the hero of your advertising. If you think the product too dull, I have news for you: there are no dull products, only dull writers. I never assign a product to a writer

> *Every time I have written a bad campaign, it has been because the product did not interest me.*

unless I know that he or she is personally interested in it. Every time I have written a bad campaign, it has been because the product did not interest me.

A problem which confronts agencies is that so many products are no different from their competitors. Manufacturers have access to the same technology: marketing people use the same research procedures to determine consumer preferences for color, size, design, taste and so on. When faced with selling "parity" products, all you can

hope to do is explain their virtues more persuasively than your competitors, and to differentiate them by the style of your advertising. This is the "added value" which advertising contributes, and I am not sufficiently puritanical to hate myself for it.

"The positively good"

My partner Joel Raphaelson has articulated a feeling which has been growing in my mind for some time:

"In the past, just about every advertiser has assumed that in order to sell his goods he has to convince consumers that his product is *superior* to his competitor's.

"This may not be necessary. It may be sufficient to convince consumers that your product is *positively good*. If the consumer feels certain that your product is good and feels uncertain about your competitor's, he will buy yours.

"If you and your competitors all make excellent products, don't try to imply that your product is *better*. Just say what's good about your product—*and do a clearer, more honest, more informative job of saying it*.

"If this theory is right, sales will swing to the marketer who does the best job of creating confidence that his product is *positively good*."

This approach to advertising parity products does not insult the intelligence of consumers. Who can blame you for putting your best foot forward? . . .

—OGILVY ON ADVERTISING, 1983

RESPONSES

1. In groups, select a few ads from the ones you examined earlier and explain to the rest of the class how they use some or all of David Ogilvy's advice for good advertising. Discuss the target markets of the ads and the image the product sells. Suggest areas in which you think the advertisers could have improved their campaign.

2. In what areas do you agree with Ogilvy? Disagree? Why? You could write your answer in a brief essay, and share it with others.

3. Being knowledgeable about brand image is crucial to successful advertising. Using the results of the taste-test of some whiskeys, Ogilvy suggests that people are just "tasting images."
   a) How does this make you feel about the ad business? About our impulses to buy because of brand image?
   b) Discuss the image of the Marlboro man, an ad campaign that has been running for over 25 years. Why do you think that image has been so successful? To whom does it appeal? Does it appeal to you? Explain your answer.

4. Using the list of five questions that help to "recognize a big idea" in advertising, discuss several of the big ad campaigns in recent years. (Campaigns for fast food restaurants, soft drinks, beer, cars, and jeans are some suggestions.) In groups, establish a consensus on ad campaigns that you would rate as "big ideas." Present your choices to the class, and give your reasons. See how many of your classmates agree with you.

5. Ogilvy asserts that "there are no dull products, only dull writers" and that an ad writer must have enough interest in the product to "make the product itself the hero of [the] advertising." Keeping that in mind, choose a product or a service (such as a travel agency or laundry service). You may use one that is currently available or create a new one. Write the copy for an ad that would appear in a magazine.

6. Assess the Coke-Pepsi ad competition—the Cola wars—in light of the insights that Ogilvy provides. Consider both companies' current ads and some ads they have used in the past (you could look through old magazines and newspapers or ask some older people about them) to determine their brand images, and to compare their styles. How much does advertising affect which soft drink you buy?

MUNCH MU

60g
Doritos
FROMAGE NACHO CHEESE
FREE GRATIS
Rick A&A
$25 MILLION

The world according to VALS is simple. There are essentially five basic groups of citizens in this nation—Belongers, Emulators, Emulator-Achievers, Societally Conscious Achievers, and the Need-Directed. Each segment of VALSociety is driven by its own special demons, demons that the advertising industry seeks to exorcise with its 30-second television commercials and print ads. . . .

VALS tells us that almost one out of three citizens in the United States is a *Belonger*—the typical traditionalist, the cautious and conforming conservative. Archie Bunker is a Belonger; he believes in God, country, and family. The lifeblood of the Belonger's world is a strong community consciousness. Change is his or her archenemy. Without a secure, stable, and structured society, this staunch defender of the status quo is unable to cope.

The Belonger's consumer profile reflects his old-fashioned view of things. He usually drives a Dodge or a Plymouth; he drinks Coke, Pepsi, or Budweiser; he eats at McDonald's with the family; he loves Jell-O; . . .

In the 1970s, Belongers were caught by surprise as their sheltered environment, so carefully con-

Psychographics
by William Meyers

structed through the years, was dismantled bit by bit. . . .

Madison Avenue rescues Belongers and helps bind their psychic wounds with commercials that offer a world of idealized images. McDonald's, for example, uses the Big Mac in its campaigns to lure the shattered family back together. Pepsi and Coke have traditionally featured picnics and Frisbee flings. Ma Bell eases the loneliness of long-distance relationships with its "Reach Out and Touch Someone" campaign. And Miller Beer's advertising reinforces the warm glow of fraternity to help lessen the pressures of the workplace.

William Meyers's _The Image-Makers_ is a book about advertising and the major campaigns from New York's Madison Avenue (Ad Alley)—home of the major advertising agencies in the U.S. Meyers says that in the mid-'70s, many of the ad agencies were experiencing a "crisis of confidence." Economically, North America was reeling from inflation and recession. Many people had become cynical about and disillusioned with the advertising business and perceived that it was overly manipulative. Many young people dropped out of the consumer culture, believing that advertising and the accumulation of material goods were shallow. In order to win them back and restore the industry, advertisers needed a new strategy. They started to use "psychographics" instead of "demographics" for their marketing research; that is, instead of relying on statistics, they analyzed the population's attitudes, beliefs, desires, and needs. One of these psychographic approaches is called VALS (Values and Life-Styles), designed by SRI International (formerly known as Stanford Research Institute) in California. As you read about VALS in the following excerpt from _The Image-Makers_, see if you agree with the approach and the presumptions it makes. Try to determine to which group(s) you and people you know belong.

Which of the five VALS groups do you think this Ford Motor Company ad and the ad for Frito Lay (on the previous page) are aimed at?

THE
DESIRE TO SUCCEED
DOESN'T STOP
HERE.

OR HERE.

Emulators are not so set in their ways. They are a small but impressionable group of young people in desperate search of an identity and a place in the adult working world. These kids, who represent about 15 percent of the American population, will do almost anything to fit in. Most of them lack self-confidence and are discouraged about their prospects. They envision little future for themselves in our society. They compensate for this pessimism with unabashed personal hedonism. Confused and vulnerable, Emulators will purchase products from advertisers who offer solutions to their postadolescent dilemmas. In dealing with Emulators, advertisers prey on their insecurity.

Chevrolet, for example, has sold

hundreds of thousands of Camaros to these uncertain youngsters by positioning the vehicle as the coolest car on the market. Dr. Pepper became a major soft drink in this country with its "Be a Pepper" campaign, which offered teenagers the reassurance of group acceptance and friendship. The tobacco business also capitalized on this segment's precarious sense of self-worth. . . .

Emulator-Achievers, America's materialists, have already made it. These acquisitive consumers often own a Mercedes; they feel most comfortable with such "uptown" brand names as Dom Perignon, Tiffany, or Gucci; and they have to have the latest in high-tech toys. . . .

Although they have reached a prosperous plateau of middle-class success and status, Emulator-Achievers still want to derive even greater financial rewards from the system. But the new era of limits has cramped their hard-driving style, making additional monetary gains next to impossible. Emulator-Achievers, approximately 20 percent of the population, are in a funk. Once they believed the sky was the limit; today they feel frustrated, perhaps a bit cheated, stuck just below the top rung of the economic ladder. Despite their relative affluence, three quarters of them feared they wouldn't be able to attain their fiscal goals during the coming decade.

Madison Avenue cheers up Emulator-Achievers with commercials that transform everyday items into accoutrements of accomplishment, success, and taste. Advertisers convince these compulsive consumers that by purchasing certain products they will be seen as the modern aristocrats they seek to be.

Societally Conscious Achievers are the flower children of America's consumer culture.

Clothing manufacturers such as Ralph Lauren and Izod, who put little polo players and alligators on the breast pockets of cotton shirts, offer simple togs with fancy prices that give consumers a sense of upper-crust respectability. And one recent ad for Johnnie Walker Black showed a picture of a mansion with a lawn stretching as far as the eye could see. The caption informs covetous Emulator-Achievers, "On the way up, the work may not get easier, but the rewards get better." The message was clear: Serve this scotch to your friends, and you'll be just like the landed gentry—even if you do live on half an acre in the suburbs. Ad executives know that to get Emulator-Achievers into the stores, you've got to offer them the opportunity to be king or queen for a day.

Societally Conscious Achievers are the flower children of America's consumer culture. They are members of the post-World War II baby-boom generation who care more about inner peace and environmental safety than about financial success and elegant surroundings. Personal, not professional, fulfillment matters most to these individualists. Societally Conscious Achievers, constituting approximately 20 percent of the U.S. population, are experimental—they will try anything from acupuncture to Zen, as long as it fits into their uncomplicated life-style. Unlike the Emulator-Achievers, whose materialistic drives are constrained by the economy, these gradually graying hippies are self-constrained in their purchasing behavior. Many of them are dropouts from the world of commerce—reformed strivers who no longer see the need for conspicuous consumption. . . .

The Need-Directed aren't driving new cars or acquiring state-of-the-art personal computers . . .

Societally Conscious Achievers often shop for their clothing by mail, choosing L.L. Bean moccasins over Gucci loafers, and they usually drive small foreign cars—Mazda, Honda, Volvo, or Subaru. Lighter wines or such wholesome beverages as herbal tea, fruit juice, or bottled water are preferred by these inner-directed citizens. . . . If they smoke at all, . . . [they] generally puff on "healthy" low-tar Merits. These fitness-oriented citizens also take their exercise seriously; Nike and New Balance running shoes are essential parts of their athletic wardrobe.

Societally Conscious Achievers are the ad industry's toughest challenge. They turn a deaf ear to advertising unless it whispers softly. They need to be told in their own iconoclastic language that their low-key values and attitudes make sense. Several imported car manufacturers have won the confidence of Societally Conscious Achievers by emphasizing counterculture buzzwords as "simplicity" and "integrity." Volvo calls itself "a car you can believe in." Subaru says it's "inexpensive, and built to stay that way." . . .

Need-Directed Americans are the survivors, the people struggling to sustain themselves on subsistence incomes. Mostly welfare recipients, Social Security beneficiaries, and minimum-wage earners, these citizens, who represent close to 15 percent of the country, aren't consumers in the true sense of the word. They're so busy trying to make ends meet that they don't really have time to worry about the type of beer they drink or the image projected by the cigarettes they smoke. The Need-Directed aren't driving new cars or acquiring state-of-the-art personal computers, and they rarely have enough money to take the family out for even a fast-food meal.

As far as Ad Alley is concerned, the Need-Directed don't exist. They are the people who are least affected by television commercials in this country. When you're . . . poor, a dollar will only stretch so far, and you buy what you can afford. Even the wizards of Madison Avenue can't find a cure for poverty.

—*THE IMAGE-MAKERS*, 1984

RESPONSES

1. a) Think of some characters in popular TV shows who would fit into each of the four groups.
b) Assess the use of VALS to determine audiences for consumer products. How do you feel about slotting people into groups such as these?

2. With each group surveying one medium, collect a number of ads that you think appeal to each of the groups. Discuss your findings as a class.

3. Discuss the following comment from advertising executive Jerry Della Femina. "Everyone has a button. If enough people have the same button, you have a successful ad and a successful product." Does this observation make you feel cynical about the ad world? Or do you think one could argue that advertisers are simply working effectively to appeal directly to your interests and aspirations?

4. In groups, choose one of the following products: a) a breakfast cereal, b) a soft drink, c) a car, d) a watch—or think of your own product, and create an ad campaign that appeals to each of the four VALS groups. Write the copy for a print ad or the script for a radio or TV ad and, if you have the equipment, film or tape it. Show your ads to the other groups, and have them guess to which VALS group each appeals.

AND NOW . . . THESE MESSAGES

Being aware of advertisers' strategies can help you to "deconstruct" some of the ads you see. To increase your awareness of the "logic" of advertising, study the following examples of advertisers' claims. You might find that the language of persuasion used by advertisers is not always rational, and is often more emotional than logical. Analyzing ads for their logic can be an amusing and, perhaps, a money-saving pastime.

"*It's the answer*"

"To what?"

"*This car has power*"

"Don't all cars have power?"

"*It fights tooth decay*"

"But does it prevent tooth decay?"

"*It's clinically proven*"

"What does that mean?
What clinic proved it?"

"It's thicker and richer"

"Than what?"

"It's part of a nutritious breakfast"

"Maybe the orange juice, toast, and milk are the nutritious parts?"

"It's the one"

"The one what?"

"Eight out of ten people prefer the better taste"

"The other two people prefer the worse taste?"

RESPONSES

1. Think of your own examples of advertising language and add them to the list. Read the print on the containers of some products at home and ask yourself if the claims are reasonable. Share your sample claims and disclaimers with your class.

2. Obviously, advertising copywriters choose their words very carefully. Words like "virtually," "helps," "acts," "tastes," "can be," are sometimes called "weasel words." They sound convincing, but really mean very little. Write some ad copy for products of your choice, using these weasel words. Then rewrite the copy without them. Share your ads with others in your class. How effective are the ads without the weasel words?

"Has real fruit goodness"

"But does it have real fruit?"

Meet Me Tonight in TV Dreamland by John Fisher

Advertising creates a world of its own by establishing its own images of men and women, the family, teen-agers, and the elderly. It defines for us the so-called "good life" and tells us what kind of behaviour is socially unacceptable. Are we aware of the impact of these images? What messages are we really receiving? Do we accept this mythic world, this "TV Dreamland," created by consumer goods? John Fisher described this "world according to advertising" in the 1960s in an article that appeared in the then-popular Canadian publication, *Weekend Magazine*. The following is an excerpt from that article.

It is a comfortable world with no poverty—a sort of affluent womb. Almost everyone is young. Mother, especially, is young and very blond, with a lithe 110-pound figure. She dresses in Paris originals and smiles a lot with her excellent bridgework.

She is an expert cook—lovely 12-inch-cakes—and is sometimes accompanied by a smaller blond version of herself who is rarely dirty, wears a freshly starched dress, and smiles a lot too, sometimes with the beginnings of excellent bridgework.

Dad is usually a bumbling idiot shaking the last two corn flakes out of the package, or bewailing the loss of his deodorant. Or he's a shadowy figure of no real importance except as a prop, like the furniture and bathroom fixtures.

Fortyish, terribly handsome in a distinguished way, he wears casually expensive clothes (even when using that fast drying paint) and smokes a pipe. He drives a large, expensive car (he didn't really think he could afford it), owns a palace of a house sitting in the middle of an empty field and has a taste for antique cars and oil paintings.

Generally, everyone is white. Minority groups pop up every so often, but usually as caricatures. . . .

For Mom, Dad, kiddies, and caricatures, it's first class all the way; everyone has his own bathroom, with cans of deodorant cluttering the shelves. (Having one of anything, or a small anything, is a negative thought.)

Kitchen floors that pretty blond Mummy struggles with, and occasionally breaks pitchers on, are of colossal size. Sometimes the blond girl-child will have a faintly grubby brother who owns a purebred sheepdog, and they all troop across this freshly shined surface leaving footprints, dollops of ice cream and a variety of spills, all of which vanish after one spray from an aerosol can.

The living room has the same huge proportions, with a massive cut-stone fireplace and crackling log fire (winter or summer). Furniture is obviously chosen by an interior decorator with unlimited charge accounts—windows stretch from floor to roof. Flanked by $1000 drapes.

Nothing is dirty, except perhaps after parties where people over-indulge and the occupants momentarily slip from their pedestals to allow a fascinating peek at dirty dishes, cigarette butts, empty bottles, caps, paper hats, crumpled tissues, and cold leftovers congealed in gravy.

> *Dad is usually a bumbling idiot, shaking the last two corn-flakes out of the package . . .*

The garage contains two cars, several thousand dollars' worth of tools, power mowers, bicycles, garden implements, furniture, and fishing gear. The cars are never dirty, nor does Dad seem to do much actual work about the place with all that equipment. The garden is usually a kind of Shangri-La of massive proportions, with the 20 people needed to tend it hidden from view.

The world outside is reserved for individuals strolling across empty fields or driving fast convertibles on empty highways. People sometimes dine outdoors by candlelight in full evening dress, with their new car parked in the foreground, amid forest glade surroundings as the sun sinks magnificently. Mosquitoes are not allowed, nor does the slightest breeze dare to flicker the lights of their table candelabra.

Their religion is the hysterical rite of the annual new car. The fever begins in the latter part of the summer, fed by shots of chromium grilles, trunk insignia, tail light assemblies, and slogans: "Coming soon—the TAKE CHARGE car." Hysteria reaches a peak as new models are launched into history with leaping tigers, blond . . . dream girls sagging over the hoods misty-eyed, and handsome middle-aged men in full evening dress leering at them.

An automobile is fun. Convertibles barrel along sun-lit roads with dutch-bobbed blondes whose hair blows merrily; never a traffic jam, a line-up at gas stations or a flat tire. . . . And, ah, those beautiful empty coastal roads. Not a soul in sight; no stop signs, traffic lights, pedestrians or policemen.

All take-charge men are Outdoors Men, smoking cigarettes by the dozen, all crinkly-faced and square-jawed, terribly virile, adult, and glamorous—with limpid-eyed teen-age girl-women lingering self-confidently near. All approach middle age with slightly greying hair and wearing yachting caps. They suck their cigarettes out of the package with one hand, light them with a sneer.

They snap fingers at ball games, grateful for the true taste in a filter cigarette, examine antiques, ride old fire engines, or casually dash off oil paintings and sculptures. They are with it.

When not smoking at the ski lodge, these virile males sit about unshaven and dirty, clad in scruffy plaid sports shirts, alternately drinking beer, playing cards and fishing. Never actually drinking, but [there are] bottle openers tossed across the room, coasters, wet rings, bright-eyed looks of expectation as a waiter walks by carrying the stuff on a tray, and dirty glasses galore.

But it's the young who are really alive. They live it up. Anyone over 25 is out. Being young means a mad whirl. Everybody runs everywhere, laughing madly to vibrant guitars. People dance night and day, sometimes on empty beaches, sometimes in recreation rooms the size of an auditorium, and occasionally they frug wildly at expensive ski lodges.

Being young has something to do with drinking ice-cold beverages from the bottle in a snow storm, driving an amphibian car across a beach and into a lake (both utterly deserted, of course) or being glad he came back.

Everyone is healthy. Not a symptom in sight, unless it's poor Suzie with all sinuses plugged again. Girls are all white-skinned blondes with . . . dark mysterious eyes, perfect teeth and moist, perfumed breath. The take-charge-male-to-be is baby-faced . . .with perfect teeth, immaculate clothes, a convertible, a good credit rating, and a carefree existence.

He rarely shows interest in these perfect girls, except perhaps in an athletic sense—he's always racing them somewhere: into the lake, out of the lake, into a car, out of a car, up a hill, down a hill.No wonder he rarely has time for actual romance, just a polite peck on the cheek under the porch light or an old-fashioned squeeze of the hand.

Being old isn't exactly a crime, but older people rarely appear unless grandmother wants to blow out all those candles for the insurance company or grandfather gets grouchy about instant coffee. Being old has something to do with false teeth whiteners and crunching apples to prove that your teeth stay in. . . .

—*WEEKEND MAGAZINE*

RESPONSES

1. What images from this "dreamland" of the 1960s remain true today? What images have changed? How has the awareness of multiculturalism and women's issues changed the portrayal of people in today's ads?

2. a) By referring to your collection of print ads and your notes on billboard, TV, and radio ads, make a list of generalizations about the following:

• What constitutes happiness and the "good life"?

• What makes us feel guilty?

• What are things we fear?

b) Refer to the foreign-language ads you studied earlier (you may need to collect more) and make a list of similar generalizations. Compare the two lists.

3. How do you think the "yuppie"—young urban professional—market has affected advertising? List some ads that you think are aimed at this group. You could try to interview some people who are part of that group and ask them for their views of advertising and how they feel about being a major target market. See page 212 for tips on conducting interviews.

4. Write an updated version of "Meet Me Tonight in TV Dreamland" using techniques similar to the author's. You could choose similar or different products and services. Don't hesitate to use humour and exaggeration. Share your writing with the class and choose the best selections to make up a composite portrait.

5. In groups, write and perform a short play in which all the characters and situations are drawn from the world of advertising. If you have the equipment, videotape the play and show it to the class.

Television viewers and magazine readers reacted sharply in 1980 when teenage actress and model Brooke Shields appeared in a North America-wide advertising campaign for Calvin Klein jeans. At the time, she declared, "Nothing comes between me and my Calvins." But that once provocative line now seems understated as ad agencies increasingly resort to raciness—mainly nudity and, in one controversial instance, thinly disguised obscenity—to sell products.

The competition—and the advertising excesses—are particularly intense in the crowded $5.2-billion North American fragrance industry, which generates large ad revenues for newspapers and magazines. But *The New York Times* and *Womens's Wear Daily* in the United States have refused to accept an ad which features a model swearing as he talks about designer Perry Ellis's fragrance for men. And although the cologne's distributor will not use the ad in Canada until the fall, some Canadian publishers may reject it. Declared Bruce Drane, publisher of Maclean Hunter's *Chatelaine* magazine: "We have turned down softer stuff. These guys are going too far." . . .

The text in most other ads is less pungent, but half-dressed men and women also sell such items as Guerlain perfume, Pierre Cardin musk for men, Anne Klein bath

Sex and a New Hard Sell

by Anne Steacy

Sexuality in ads is not new, but ever since Brooke Shields appeared in her Calvins, ads have become increasingly sexually suggestive, even explicit. Some people in the advertising industry suggest that sexuality in advertising is just another "gimmick" to get people to pay attention to ads and their products. Some advertisers say that consumers become bored with advertising very easily and ads need to be provocative. But how real are advertising's portrayals of sexuality, and what effects do they have on viewers? Find some magazine, billboard, TV, and radio ads that you think depict sexuality in advertising. In groups, discuss your reaction to the ads. What kind of products are being advertised? Describe any recurring patterns you see in the ads, e.g., the poses and expressions of the models, or the language used. How are the messages conveyed? Is the sexuality in the ads relevant to the products? How? Take notes during your discussion and refer to them when you study the chapter, "Gender Roles." After you have talked about the ads, read the following article excerpt from *Maclean's* and see if the author raises any issues similar to the ones raised in your discussion.

products, Piz Buin suntan lotion and Guess? jeans. And New York-based fashion designer Calvin Klein has once again caught consumers' attention and drawn criticism from women's organizations for his recent offerings: ads with nude and semi-nude models promoting Obsession fragrances for men and women. One ad for the men's fragrance appears in such U.S. publications as *Glamour and Cosmopolitan*. It features four nude women posed together on one page. But Edmund Pearce, a spokesman for Toronto-based Comac Communications Ltd. said that his company's nine magazines likely would not accept such explicit ads. Said Pearce: "There are lines that I think you shouldn't cross in a publication." Still, another Obsession ad—with a nude woman entwined with two nude men—encountered no difficulty gaining acceptance in 10 Canadian magazines, including Comac's *City Woman* and Maclean Hunter's *Flare*.

For her part, Teresa Chan, product manager for Limoges Cosmetics Ltd. in Toronto, said that the Obsession ads especially draw consumers' attention to the perfume, which costs $240 for a 30-mL bottle. Said Chan: "You want them to look and look again, so that they ask themselves, 'What the hell is he doing?' " But Tova Wagman, a spokesperson for MediaWatch, a Vancouver-based organization which monitors sexual stereotyping in the media, said that she had received complaints about the Obsession ads. Said Wagman: "All imagery is prone to teaching behavior. The Calvin Klein ads are straight objectification—women as decorative objects." . . .

For Rochelle Udell, the New York art director who helped create the Perry Ellis ad, the controversy demonstrates that words can be as effective as scantily clad models. Said Udell: "Most fragrance advertising is based on visuals. My feeling is that words are quite powerful." Indeed the ad has met one of Madison Avenue's primary objectives: getting customers to notice the product. Added Udell: "I would much rather have people be delighted or enthralled or detest the stuff than to turn the page."

—*MACLEAN'S*, JUNE 9, 1986

Taking Action

What do you do if you find an ad sexist or offensive in its portrayal of sexuality? If you want to take action, you can write a letter to, or telephone, the company or organization responsible for the ad. Or, you can contact MediaWatch, the National Watch on Images of Women in the Media Inc. Read the following excerpt from an article entitled "Strategies for Social Change: MediaWatch (and other) Complaint Actions" by Tova Wagman, a proponent of positive and non-sexist images of women in the media. The excerpt shows how effective MediaWatch, and taking action, can be.

A Success Story

We received an ad for Western Boot Liquidators and complaints from 16 people in Edmonton. The ad shows a young girl standing sideways wearing only a hat, boots and underwear. MediaWatch sent off the ad and complaints with a note expressing the need for action against the ad. We received the following letter from the Advertising Advisory Board:

We agree with the complaint completely...in fact, it's being turned over directly to the Advertising Standards Council for handling under Clause 15. The ad probably will not appear again anyway as it seems to have been for a special sale. However, this kind of complaint is still valuable because it provides an opportunity to contact the advertiser and work towards ensuring this kind of message isn't used again. The Edmonton Sun and the Canadian Daily Newspaper Publishers Association are being advised too.

You *can* achieve success in getting media changed or removed through complaint action.

When you are launching a complaint, remember; the more people who complain about the same thing, the better; always make sure you include a copy of the ad, article, picture, etc. with the complaint (unless it's a billboard!); if you see something in the media that deserves praise, praise it.

—*Canadian Woman Studies*, Spring 1987

RESPONSES

1. Discuss the idea that sexually explicit ads are "gimmicks" that will eventually come to an end. In groups, design a jeans or perfume ad that is not sexually suggestive. If you have a computer, you could use it when designing the ad for a magazine, newspaper, or billboard. Or you could create the storyboard for a TV commercial. See page 218 for tips on storyboards.

2. Look closely at the way models are posed in a few ads and list any recurring patterns. Try doing a light-hearted pantomime of these poses.

3. In groups, look up and discuss the word "voyeurism." Find some examples of ads that contain elements of voyeurism and discuss your responses to them. Who do you think is the voyeur in the examples you find? Why do you think ad agencies use this style of advertising?

CONTROVERSIES IN ADVERTISING

While the images and messages of advertising are controversial in themselves, there are other aspects of advertising that can cause public concern. For example, you have seen that ads often promote a particular lifestyle. How do you feel about ads that promote a lifestyle that is potentially harmful? As you study these issues, consider if, and how advertising should be regulated.

Cigarette and alcohol advertising have been with us a long time. The Marlboro man and all those "happy" people cavorting in beer commercials are now pop icons—images that are an integral part of our culture. There are several reasons for the current controversy about the advertising of these products, among them, the convincing medical evidence of possible harmful effects of the products and the morality of pitching ads for these products to youth. At the same time, many have argued that we have the right to make our own choices. In any case, if some ads were banned, as many critics have proposed, would that help consumers stop smoking and drinking? Think about these issues as you read the following excerpt.

Battle of the Booze ads

by Elaine Carey

Gordie Howe stickhandled his way through hundreds of battles in his hockey career but Ontario's liquor laws have left him in the penalty box.

Ontario's first beer commercial featuring ex-athletes showed former superstars Howe and Bobby Hull savoring a Miller Lite beer in a bar. It ended with the infamous line from Hull: "We all know you and I packed away a little more than our equipment after the game, didn't we, Gordie?"

Attorney-General Ian Scott, whose ministry includes the drinking and driving countermeasures unit, reacted immediately.

Bypassing the Liquor License Board of Ontario, Scott urged the beer company to can the commercial because of its appeal to young people, and the link between sports and drinking.

But Carling O'Keefe continued to air the commercial throughout the National Hockey League playoffs and may persist next fall, says Drew Knox, brand manager for Carling O'Keefe Breweries.

Howe maintained in an interview that the commercial was "done in

FIRST,
HE KILLED THE BOTTLE...

IF YOU DRINK, DON'T DRIVE.

Ministry of the
Attorney General

fun and the line itself was to get a laugh out of people.''

This latest bout in the beer sale wars comes as both the provincial and federal governments are reviewing their stand on so-called lifestyle-promoting alcohol advertising.

The three major breweries, Car-ling O'Keefe, Molson's, and Labatt's, insist that their commercial efforts go toward persuading beer drinkers to switch brands, not to attract new drinkers.

But fuelled by a growing anti-drinking-and-driving lobby, critics such as Scott and federal Health and Welfare Minister Jake Epp charge the commercials are aimed at young, underage drinkers, the group most vulnerable to the happy, handsome, fun-loving messages they portray. Already, they say, half of all young people are drinking at 16.

"Linking alcohol consumption to social acceptance, success, romance and friendship has a great impact on impressionable teens," Epp says.

Every beer and wine commercial must be approved by both the federal Canadian Radio-television and Telecommunications Commission (CRTC) and every provincial liquor board, each of which has different regulations. It means an advertiser must produce four versions of a beer commercial to get it on the air nation-wide.

The new Liberal-appointed board of directors of the LLBO quietly lifted the long-standing ban on the use of celebrities in beer and wine commercials last month [May 1986], provided only athletes no longer involved in the sport are used, the ads don't appeal to young people, and the athletes don't attribute their success to drinking.

But from day one there were problems.

John Bates, president of PRIDE (People to Reduce Impaired Driving Everywhere) charged the Hull-Howe commercial was "in very poor taste when you think it's only been a year since (Philadelphia Flyers' star goalie) Pelle Lindberg was killed in a drunk-driving crash. Lifestyle advertising has hit a new low." . . .

Meanwhile, the CRTC held a week-long hearing last month into its proposal to get out of the business of regulating beer and wine commercials, leaving it to advertisers and broadcasters, with a voluntary code of ethics administered by the Advertising Standards Council. A decision is expected this summer.

The proposal brought outraged reaction from Epp, who said alcohol abuse has become such a severe problem that the number of radio and television commercials should be cut in half and the CRTC should continue regulating it.

"It's not that I'm cynical or negative, but television self-regulation only works if the market is expanding," Epp says.

The proposed code would allow actual beer drinking now prohibited, on the screen, as well as the use of celebrities and ex-athletes, provided they are not role models for young people.

"It's not that I'm cynical or negative, but television self-regulation only works if the market is expanding," Epp says. Broadcasters netted $88 million from beer commercials alone last year, he says, and they have too much of a vested interest to effectively regulate them.

Do lifestyle ads actually persuade young people to start drinking?

The brewers argue there are no studies that positively link drinking and advertising, and point to a Canada Health survey that found the highest level of drinking by minors and young people was in B.C., where no advertising is allowed.

> *The breweries argue that governments raise $5 billion a year in taxes on beer and wine and some of that could be directed toward moderation messages.*

Per capita beer consumption has fallen 5 percent since 1983, according to the Brewers' Association of Canada, but there have been dramatic swings of up to 20 percent in a beer company's share of the market because of television and radio commercials. A change of only 1 percent represents 60.4 million bottles of beer or $48 million.

Fewer Calories

Light beers, which contain less alcohol and fewer calories, start to appeal to regular beer drinkers at the age of 28 to 30, says Knox of Carling O'Keefe.

But, in his brief to the CRTC, Epp said the department is "convinced that the brewing industry, which is spending millions of dollars on advertising and promotion aimed at young people, is involved in a deliberate attempt to expand their market by promoting their products to this target group."

Epp says this makes sense only in a declining market.

"How do you maintain your market if you don't attract people under 18?" he asks. A study by his department last year found the ma-jority of rock shows on television are sponsored by breweries and for many of them, 70 percent of the audience is under 18.

In addition, hockey and baseball games are sponsored by beer companies, he says, adding, "How can they say baseball isn't viewed by minors? We've tried to get moderation ads run during Blue Jays baseball games and we can't do it. If they want the freedom to advertise, fair ball. We should have the same right."

PRIDE also argues that beer companies should not be allowed to sponsor car races, stunt drivers, and other sporting events that link beer and driving.

"An automobile race sponsored by a beer company is nothing short of obscene," Bates says.

Epp insists that if the number of commercials isn't reduced, the beer companies should direct some of their money to moderation advertising.

The breweries argue that governments raise $5 billion a year in taxes on beer and wine and some of that could be directed toward moderation messages, "but that doesn't fly with me," says Epp. "If $5 billion was all we had to spend on lost productivity and health-care costs, I would accept it. But you can't place a value on a human life. I think they've got a very direct responsibility and I'm simply saying to them, 'You can't have it both ways.' The consumer is paying those taxes, not the beer companies." . . .

—*THE TORONTO STAR*, JUNE 24, 1986

RESPONSES

1. Cigarette and alcohol ads usually use the "lifestyle" approach. Examine a number of these ads and describe the people who appear in them. Note their appearance and age, the activities in which they are participating, and the setting. Is there a similarity in the slogans or the ad copy? When you have studied all these details, list some generalizations about the brand image and lifestyle associated with these products and discuss your observations.

2. Write an essay or a letter in which you present a thesis about the ethical implications of one or more of the following: the target market of potential teenage smokers; the exchange between hockey stars Gordie Howe and Bobby Hull in the beer commercial; the right of beer companies to sponsor sporting events.

3. In groups, do a satire of cigarette or alcohol lifestyle ads. You could create a storyboard for a TV commercial and enact it or write and perform a radio script. See page 217 for information on script writing. You might want to perform a play based on the ads. (You could use approaches similar to satirical groups such as *The Second City* troupes or the cast of *Saturday Night Live*.) If you have access to the equipment, you might want to produce a video or make an audiotape of your work.

4. The article is from 1986, and it applies to Ontario only. Research the present regulations for alcohol and tobacco advertising in your province.

5. Have a class debate about one or more of the following statements. "Resolved that: a) all cigarette ads should be banned; b) there should be stringent health warnings about the possible dangers of alcohol; c) since cigarette ads are banned on TV, alcohol ads should also be banned; d) government regulators should stay out of the way of the advertising industry."

6. Discuss the effectiveness of the "Don't Drink and Drive" campaign or similar government campaigns against drinking and driving. What do you think about the use of pictures of real auto accidents as a warning to people against drinking and driving? Write a script for a television or radio commercial that could be used to launch a similar anti-smoking or anti-drinking campaign. See page 217 for tips on script writing. Include a slogan for your campaign. You might want to produce the commercial and present it to your school.

We often take advertising and the promotion of a consumer culture for granted, but in developing countries the phenomenon is relatively recent. The trend towards products being available worldwide and the expansion of international marketing can profoundly affect local cultures. Many of the consequences are negative, but are not apparent until too late.

The arrival of television and extensive advertising automatically introduces images of a lavish lifestyle. This pattern of transnational culture or global culture is potentially destructive—things do not always go better with Coke. Perhaps because of our closer similarities to the U.S., the situation is less dramatic for Canada than, for example, Third World countries. It is still important, however, to ask ourselves if transnational culture, which is largely American, represents our best interests. Consider some of these issues as you read the following article excerpt.

Cloning the Consumer Culture—

How International Marketing Sells the Western Lifestyle

by Noreene Janus

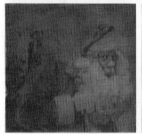

The common theme of transnational culture is consumption. Advertising expresses this ideology of consumption in its most synthetic and visual form.

Advertisers rely on a few repetitive themes: happiness, youth, success, status, luxury, fashion, and beauty. Social contradictions and class differences are masked and workplace conflicts are not shown. Cam-

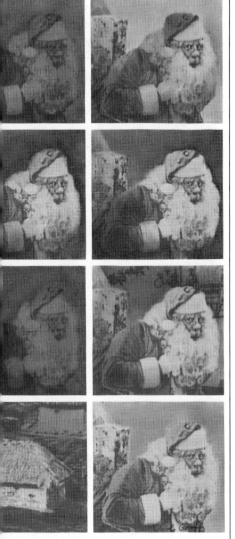

formed the U.S. Pepsi ad campaign "Join the Pepsi Generation" for use in Brazil as "Join the Pepsi Revolution" explains, most people have no other means to express their need for social change other than by changing brands and increasing their consumption.

Transnational advertising is one of the major reasons both for the spread of transnational culture and the breakdown of traditional cultures. Depicting the racy foreign lifestyles of a blond jetsetter in French or English, it associates Western products with modernity. That which is modern is good; that which is traditional is implicitly bad, impeding the march of progress. Transnational culture strives to eliminate local culture variations.

Global marketing strategy is so effective that conscious subversion is hardly needed. The message "we will sell you a culture," has resulted in the global advertising campaign, a single advertising message used in all countries where a product is made or distributed. Worldwide advertising is more economical and more efficient, although it may clash wildly with local conditions.

Thus, farmers facing an intensification of violence in rural Guatemala may gather around the only TV set in their village to view an ad for Revlon perfume showing a blond woman strolling down Fifth Avenue in New York.

Transnational corporations and international advertising agencies work hard at creating a consumer culture. Increasingly, advertising

paigns suggest that solutions to human problems are to be found in individual consumption, presented as an ideal outlet for mass energies . . . a socially acceptable form of action and participation which can be used to defuse potential political unrest. "Consumer democracy" is held out to the poor around the world as a substitute for political democracy. After all, as the advertising executive who trans-

campaigns are aimed at the vast numbers of poor in Third World countries. Even poor families, when living together and pooling their incomes, can add up to a household income of more than $10 000 per year, making them an important

Leo Burnett's Marlboro-man campaign is known internationally and has been running for over 25 years. Why do you think this cowboy image has been promoted so successfully in countries outside the U.S.?

advertising target.

As one advertising professional commented, "Once the TV set goes to work, the family is like a kid in a candy store. They're pounded by 450 commercials a week. They see all the beautiful things. And what they see, they want."

Since an important characteristic of transnational culture is the speed and breadth with which it is transmitted, communications and information systems play an important role, permitting a message to be distributed globally through television series, news, magazines, comics and films. The use of television to spread transnational culture is especially effective with illiterates. Grey Advertising Inter-

national undertook a worldwide study of television to determine its usefulness as an advertising channel and reported that:

"Television is undisputedly the key communications development of our era, shaping the values, attitudes, and lifestyles of generations growing up with it. In countries where it operates as an unfettered commercial medium it has proven for many products the most potent of all consumer marketing weapons as well as a major influence in establishing corporate images."

Anyone who has heard children singing along with television commercials and introducing these themes into their daily games begins to see its impact. Pierre Thizier Seya studied the impact of transnational advertising on cultures in the Ivory Coast. He notes that transnational firms such as Colgate and Nestlé have helped to replace traditional products—often cheaper and more effective—with industrialized toothpastes and infant formulas. As the report put it:

"By consuming Coca-Cola, Nestlé products, Marlboro, Maggi, Colgate or Revlon, Ivorians are not only fulfilling unnecessary needs but also progressively relinquishing their authentic world outlook in favor of the transnational way of life."

Advertising of skin-lightening products persuades the African women to be ashamed of their own color and try to be white. Thus, Seya said, Ivorians relinquish their racial identity, one of the most powerful weapons available for safeguarding their human identity.

He also mentions that advertising is helping to changing the Ivorian attitude toward aging, making women fear looking older and undermining the traditional respect for elders.

The consumption of soft drinks and hard liquor points to another social change. Traditionally drinks are consumed only in social settings, as evidenced by the large pot where they are stored. Yet, the advertising of Coca-Cola and Heineken portrays drinking as an individual act rather than a collective one. . . .

—*CULTURAL SURVIVAL
QUARTERLY*, 1983

RESPONSES

1. The author, Noreene Janus, suggests that transnational advertising implies: "That which is modern is good; that which is traditional is implicitly bad." a) Discuss the examples she uses to illustrate this observation and b) Think of your own examples of ads that "sell a culture."

2. If any of you have lived or travelled in a non-North American country, you might like to describe what you think are the effects of North American consumer culture on other countries. Imagine scenarios—outlines of a series of events—in which people from a developing nation are exposed to current ads. Refer to what you studied in the Television chapter about stereotyping, and write about your responses. Your writing could be in the form of a dialogue, play, poem, essay, or short story.

3. If you have access to the ads from a non-North American country, or if there are students in your class who have lived or travelled abroad, make some cross-cultural comparisons. Can you understand the message of the ads even though you can't understand the language? How is this achieved? (Keep the ads for future use.)

MUSIC & SFX

ANNCR: The next time...

you choose a leading
soft drink...

SFX: ICE CUBES DROPPING

SFX: OPENING

you can't...
SFX: FIZZ

top Canada Dry Ginger Ale.
Ahhhhhhh

SUPER: YOU DON'T
HAVE TO BE SWEET
TO BE GOOD.

JULY IS EGG MONTH

Veggies GET CRACKING

Based on what you have learned in this chapter, discuss and evaluate these ads. For which medium do you think the ads are intended, e.g. transit ad, poster, magazine ad, billboard? At what target markets are they aimed?

Food for thought.

À TOUTE HEURE
DU JOUR OU DU SOIR

JE REPARS EN
OEUF

ONCE AGAIN OUR INNOVATIVE DESIGNS ARE RAISING EYEBROWS AND THE BEST OF AUTOMOTIVE STANDARDS.

1988 unveils an extraordinary variety of technological and design advancements in the Ford and Lincoln Mercury line-up.

You'll see Canada's best selling car, Ford Tempo, take on a beautiful new windswept exterior. And the sophisticated Mercury Topaz sports a dynamic new shape.

This year also brings the world's most advanced luxury automobile, the incomparable new front wheel drive Lincoln Continental.

Later in the year, the futuristic Ford Probe will arrive bringing with it one of the lowest drag co-efficients anywhere.

In fact, you'll find innovative design in everything we build.

So come to the Show at the PNE Grounds, January ... we have the high designed and built 7 years running ...

Ford
Quality is Job 1.

Whose European decaff process leaves the flavour of the beans untouched?

GEVALIA

G E V A L I A

Possibly the world's finest coffee.

NOT OUT OF REACH, JUST OUT OF SIGHT. THE 1989 FORD PROBE.

The new Ford Probe is more than just a high performance road machine, it's tangible proof of a new philosophy.

A philosophy that departs from the common wisdom that high performance comes a bit ... wisdom that high performance comes a bit. Winter Probe LX, GT and GT-2 new examples of bold, move to design, leadership and performance. Probe is collection of drag is a remarkable. 261

In driver ergonomics are among the most advanced. But to really appreciate this departure from the ordinary, leave the Probe GT's personal cockpit ... functional feeling, comfort with available integrated anti- port electronic fuel injection controlled a ... four wheel independent suspension, with dispower stabilizer bars and coffee bushings.

Antilock adjusting suspension with 3 drive modes for variable driving conditions.
Four powered ... with performance and anti-sway steering ... lock brake system ...
Speed rated high performance tires on 16 inch aluminum wheels.

Finally, high tech high performance is not only within your reach, it's at your fingertips too.
And that's true of sight.
For more information, call ...

Ford
Quality is Job 1.

ISSUES FOR FURTHER STUDY

Certainly advertising is a helpful channel of information and a very powerful means of communication. We are all consumers, and thus, all targets of advertising—you have seen how we all receive many messages from sponsors daily. From your studies in this chapter, you should now be able to interpret, decode, and be aware of the effects of those messages. The following questions allow you to explore more fully some of the issues raised in the chapter. You could brainstorm to raise some of your own questions.

1. Advertising is an expensive business. Study the following charts. Choose one of the top Canadian advertisers and do some research to give an in-depth "profile" of the organization. Try to obtain an annual report (sometimes found in the Business section of your library) or find some articles about the organization or company in newspapers or magazines. List some of their most well-known campaigns. Present your profile to the class.

Top Canadian advertisers

The 15 largest buyers of space and time in 1986:

Company		$ millions
1	Government of Canada	63.7
2	Procter & Gamble	51.1
3	John Labatt	37.5
4	Molson	32.0
5	General Motors	27.3
6	Unilever	27.1
7	Ontario Government	26.0
8	The Thomson Group	24.0
9	McDonald's Restaurants	21.0
10	Bell Canada Enterprises	20.1
11	Ford Motor	19.4
12	Coca-Cola	18.7
13	Dart & Kraft	18.4
14	Rothmans	18.4
15	General Foods	18.4

—MEDIA MEASUREMENT SERVICES, INC.

Where money goes

Percentage of net advertising revenue by media:

Electronic media	%
Radio	9.1
Television	16.6

Print media	%
Newspapers:	
Dailies	22.7
Weekend supplements	0.7
Weeklies	5.6
Business papers	2.9
Farm papers	0.4
General magazines	4.3
Directories	6.3
Catalogue, direct mail	23.7
Outdoor	7.3
Other	0.4

—MACLEAN HUNTER RESEARCH BUREAU

2. The government is the number one spender on advertising. Research some of their campaigns and ads. Why do you think the government spends so much on advertising?

3. Do some research to find out just how expensive advertising is. For example, you could find out advertising rates for radio and television stations (try the business section of your local library or contact the stations). Find out the advertising rates of your local newspaper or of some magazines. (Some of you may have done similar research for the Journalism chapter.) Try to find out who owns billboards, and how much it costs to rent space on one. You could find out how much it costs to have an ad placed in your public transit system. Research the cost of the production of an ad. How much money do models make? photographers? copywriters? How much does it cost to rent a recording studio to produce a jingle for an ad? Write your findings in a report, and present it to the class.

4. Investigate further the issue of transnational advertising. What is the impact of the images of North American consumerism on people who cannot afford such lifestyles? What are the problems arising from the clash between a country's local culture and the culture of consumerism? Interview people who have emigrated from developing nations, or find books and newspaper and magazines articles that deal with this problem.

5. Have a class debate on the following statement by advertising critic Judith Williamson, "Advertising sells ourselves to ourselves."

6. In groups, create an ad campaign for an event at your school. Before you begin the creative process, discuss the market, and the purpose of the campaign, and refer to what you have learned about value creation in ads and the myth-making tendencies of advertising. If you have access to the equipment, you could make a multi-media presentation: you could produce a videotape; broadcast a "radio" ad on your public address system; create billboard-like signs; and/or use computers to design ads for bulletin boards or your student newspaper.

7. There are many positive and negative aspects in advertising. While it is essential to our consumer society, its enemies suggest that it creates needs and tries to sell "the impossible dream." Write an essay on how you perceive the role of advertising.

8. There are awards given in the advertising business, both for print and television ads. Some international award-winning television ads appear on video and may be available from video outlets. Try to obtain one of these videos, or find publications that show the award-winning print ads. Compare the ads and assess them in terms of their appeal, art, ingenuity, and design. You might want to investigate some of the techniques used in print ad design, such as air-brushing, typography, lay-out, photographing techniques, and so on. Prepare a report for the class.

CHAPTER 7

Violence

Violence in the media and popular culture is not new, but the concern about its effects seems to be much stronger today. If there is concern, there is also some heated controversy. Some people view the depiction of violence as, for the most part, simply entertainment. Others, though, are concerned that violence in the media and popular culture makes the idea of using violence to solve problems acceptable or even that it causes aggressive behaviour. Even the people who research violence in the media are not in agreement over its effects.

The issue is not a simple one. Just establishing a definition of violence is difficult because violence covers such a wide spectrum and varies in context and degree. Critics are often as concerned about how violence is depicted as much as how frequently it occurs.

A question that has been raised frequently in this text is also central to the study of violence in the media: Does the violence depicted in the media merely reflect our society or does it shape our society? Is the world a dangerous place, or does the media make it seem more dangerous than it really is?

Another concern is the fact that most media products we see are from the U.S. and the violence they may portray might not be part of Canadian culture. To what extent is American culture—and its media—affected by a heritage that gave a "wild west" mythic dimensions? To what extent is Canadian culture affected by a heritage that gave the R.C.M.P., and law and order, mythic dimensions?

There are no simple answers to these questions, but an examination of how violence is constructed and used in the media and popular culture is important if only to help us refine the questions we should be asking.

DEFINING VIOLENCE

Defining violence is not easy; there are problems just in deciding what this territory might include. For example, are natural disasters such as tornadoes or earthquakes forms of violence? Is substance abuse violence against oneself? Are verbal attacks a type of violence? In some cultures, violence is closely linked to the defence of one's honour, or family, or religious beliefs. Is violence acceptable in some situations? Violence may be determined by degree or context. What may be a playful tussle for some people could be a serious fight for others. Blowing up a building might be seen as more violent than throwing a brick through a window, but what if the building were empty and the brick hit someone?

Read the following scenarios and for each one, decide whether its presence in the media is acceptable or unacceptable to you. In groups, try to place the scenarios on a scale from "most violent" to "least violent."

1. A newspaper publishes a picture of an armed and distraught man holding his young son by the feet from a third-floor window.

2. A nature program on TV shows footage of lions killing and eating their prey.

3. An "outdoors" TV show depicts a hunter shooting a moose.

4. During a concert, a rock performer verbally abuses and spits on his audience.

5. In a TV comedy show, one character throws a pie in someone's face.

6. An album cover shows a woman cowering in front of a man who is threatening her with a whip.

7. A film depicts a stabbing, complete with sound effects.

8. The TV news shows footage of a hijacker shooting a hostage.

9. A made-for-TV movie drama about wife-battering shows graphic scenes of a man hitting his wife.

10. In an episode of a children's cartoon show, the villains destroy an entire city.

11. A newspaper uses a picture of a crosscheck that resulted in injury as its only photo coverage of a hockey game.

What was the basis for your decisions? Have a class discussion and see if there is a consensus for any of these cases. Brainstorm to develop a list of criteria you could use to establish what violence is acceptable or unacceptable.

Before you read the following definitions of violence, see if your group or class can establish its own definition. What did these exercises tell you about personal perceptions of and subjectivity toward violence?

In Canada, one of the most important investigations into the nature of violence in the communications industry was led by a Royal Commission in Ontario. The commission took a rather broad definition of violence in order to make the scope as comprehensive as possible. The following is an excerpt from the commission's report:

- Violence is action which intrudes painfully or harmfully into the physical, psychological or social well-being of persons or groups.

- Violence or its effects may range from trivial to catastrophic.

- Violence may be obvious or subtle.

- Violence may take place against persons or against property.

- It may be justified, or unjustified, or justified by some standards and not by others.

- It may be real or symbolic.

- Violence may be sudden or gradual.

—*REPORT OF THE ROYAL COMMISSION ON VIOLENCE*
IN THE COMMUNICATIONS INDUSTRY, 1977

American researcher George Gerbner defines violence as follows:

"We define violence as the overt expression of physical force,with or without a weapon, against self or other; compelling actions against one's will on pain of being hurt or killed; or actually hurting or killing."

Gerbner applied this definition not only to serious and realistic depictions of violence, but also to comedy and slapstick, accidents, and acts of nature such as floods, earthquakes, and hurricanes.

In groups or as a class, study your original definition of violence and make any changes you wish. If you were unable to reach a consensus before, write the definition now.

THE LANGUAGE OF VIOLENCE

Consider the language of some sportscasters. What words do they use to describe a body check in hockey, or a tackle in football? What words come to mind when you think of the portrayal of cartoon or comic book battles? What words are often used in newspaper headlines to describe acts of violence? Our perceptions of violence are often influenced by and reflected in the language we use to describe it.

In the following excerpt from an article, an American psychology professor suggests that people use defence mechanisms to justify acts of violence and make them more acceptable. As you read this excerpt, consider whether the defence mechanisms he describes are equally applicable to Canadians.

The Enemy Within

by Robert S. Moyer

DEHUMANIZATION This defense mechanism, a popular propaganda tool, leads people to regard or portray others as subhuman. If we view our enemies as beasts we don't feel so guilty about killing them. . . .

We and the Soviets . . . denigrate each other's attitudes and ethics. The Soviet press in July 1982 implied that President Reagan is a "pygmy," saying, "Pygmies have often tried to cast aspersions on the immortal name of V.I. Lenin." Reagan, for his part, dehumanizes the Soviets when he says things like " . . . we have a different regard for human life than those monsters do."

PROJECTION We tend to attribute our undesirable characteristics to others. If we have aggressive impulses, or if our group has done terrible things, we can allay our anxiety by believing that our enemies are guilty of the same offenses. Our enemies, naturally, purify themselves by attributing their misdeeds to us.

Pravda, for example, announced in July 1982 that "it is against the Afghan people that an undeclared war is being waged, the main inspirer and organizer of which is, once again, Washington." And it asked, "How many million dollars have been spent in an attempt to use counterrevolutionary forces to crush the socialist system in Poland?" But it was the Soviets who sent troops to Afghanistan and the Soviets who have been the prime manipulators of events in Poland. The United States may make mischief in Afghanistan and Poland, but it hardly measures up to the level of Soviet meddling.

> **Once we have reduced our adversaries to subhumans and projected many of our evils onto them, it is easy to see ourselves as good, peace-loving . . .**

We, too, practise projection, as Reagan did in a May 1982 speech: "The Soviet Union continues to support Vietnam in its occupation of Kampuchea and its massive military presence in Laos. . . . The Soviet Union has provided toxins to the Laotians and Vietnamese for use against defenseless villagers in Southeast Asia." We attack them for the kind of intervention we took in Vietnam years before.

Dehumanization and projection work together: evil actions can be more readily projected onto subhumans, and people already cloaked with undesirable qualities are easier to dehumanize. Further, since projection often produces a response in kind, a spiral of insults and defamation results, simultaneously widening the gulf between adversaries and aggravating existing tensions.

Once we have reduced our adversaries to subhumans and projected many of our evils onto them, it is easy to see ourselves as good, peace-loving and self-defense-oriented, and portray our enemies as evil, aggressive and warlike. Our adversaries' view, naturally, is a mirror image of our own. Almost any Soviet or American foreign-policy statement will illustrate this point. Reagan, for example, remarked in March 1983, "We will never stop searching for a genuine peace . . . [the Soviets] are the focus of evil in the modern world." He also warned the United States not to "ignore the facts of history and the aggressive impulses of an evil empire, to simply call the arms race a giant misunderstanding and thereby remove yourself from the struggle between right and wrong, good and evil."

The Soviets, of course, have a different view. As Yuri Andropov explained in September 1983, "The course that the present U.S. administration is pursuing . . . is a militarist course, one that poses a serious threat to peace. . . . The U.S.S.R. wishes to live in peace with all countries, including the U.S. It does not nurture aggressive plans, does not impose the arms race on anyone and does not impose its social system on anyone." . . .

—*PSYCHOLOGY TODAY*, JANUARY 1985

RESPONSES

1. Investigate the use of language to describe acts of violence or aggression against "the other side" or the "out group." Examine media coverage of an event or issue such as a war, a strike, a riot, the peace movement, feminism, a summit conference, or an incident of international terrorism. Record any evidence of dehumanization and projection. Present your findings to your group or class.

2. In the twentieth century, there are many examples of this dehumanizing of "the other side," whether it is in the treatment of the Jews in the Second World War or the so-called "Red Menace."
a) Investigate and write a brief essay about how one or more of these groups was treated and how language has been used to dehumanize them. Or
b) Describe some of today's target groups. Find examples in newspapers and magazines to support your ideas. Write your findings in a short essay.

3. a) In your group, discuss the formula for writing propaganda that follows this question. If you examine a print story in the first question, compare its headline with the formula.
b) Write some propaganda headlines of your own. Apply the formula to a current situation of conflict, such as a riot. Compare your headlines with those used for newspaper stories about that conflict. (This formula for making headlines comes from a description of actual techniques used widely in Latin America by various sources of propaganda.)

THE HEADLINE = SUBJECT + VERB + OBJECT

Scapegoat term	Groundless accusation in future	Generality
SUBJECT	VERB	OBJECT
Terrorists or Extremists	Plan to attack	Political System Public Education System
Guerrillas or Socialists	Threaten	Armed Forces Freedom
Secret Communists	Plan to infiltrate	Supermarket Middle Class National Security

FANTASY VIOLENCE

Much of the violence we see in media and popular culture is not real; it is violence as entertainment. Its purpose and effect on the audience is a subject of considerable controversy. Some people view this fantasy violence as harmless fun, not meant to be taken seriously; others consider it exploitative. Some people see violence in the media and popular culture as a healthy outlet for normal human aggression; others are concerned that it makes people more aggressive and makes acts of violence more socially acceptable.

The issue is further complicated by the fact that the audiences and consumers include children as well as adults. Does this make any difference in our perception of violence as entertainment?

THE GAMES WE PLAY: A SURVEY

Before you begin to examine how violence in the media and popular culture might affect children, complete the following survey in your media log.

1. List some of the toys you played with as a child.

2. List the cartoons and television shows you watched as a child.

3. Describe the games you played with your toys. Indicate if any of them were imitations of TV shows that you watched or films that you saw.

4. Were any of your games violent? If so, describe how they were.

5. Do you think your toys or the shows you watched encouraged you to be more violent in your play? Explain your answer.

6. Describe the effect, if any, that you think your toys and the games you played with them had on the development of your character.

Share your response with the class. How do the views of the females in the class compare with those of the males? Compare your ideas with those presented in the following quotations.

CHILDREN AND VIOLENCE

Since children learn by watching and by doing, the issue of children being exposed to violence is an important one. Some children's shows and toys provide role models or examples of behaviour and beliefs for children to follow as they grow up. It is not surprising, therefore, that there has been a great deal of controversy about the war toys (and children's TV programs with similar themes) that have flooded the market. Do children learn unrealistic ideas about war and aggression through G.I. Joe and *Star Wars* toys? Does violence in our society begin with war toys and children's television programs? How do these American products affect children outside the United States?

"Playing with violent toys increases the risks that children are going to use aggression in real life at a later time."

—CHARLES W. TURNER, UNIVERSITY OF UTAH

"Play is children's work, a prime medium through which they learn about their world and through which they rehearse and consolidate their adult role. Toys directly influence children's make-believe games and thus the lessons they learn as they play. When children play war, they learn war's language, its meanings and the beliefs which give rise to it. . . . No wonder it is claimed the Pentagon supports war toys. The Pentagon's viewpoint should not dominate over others in a young boy's or girl's play world. Indoctrination occurs, however unintentional. . . . Children deserve a broader range of toys which accord a greater variety of viewpoints, toys which help to develop respect and appreciation for other human qualities than violence."

—DIANNE O'CONNOR, *CCAVE*
(CANADIANS CONCERNED ABOUT VIOLENCE IN ENTERTAINMENT)

"Our in-depth research with youngsters told us (in 1981) that boys spend as much as a fourth of their leisure time fantasizing; most of this fantasizing represented some form of good against evil, and their imaginations were not limited to the world around us."

—RESEARCH FROM THE MATTEL TOY COMPANY

"There is no doubt that children become more aggressive when they are playing with war toys. The question that everybody asks is, does that make the children more aggressive in the long term?"

—JEFFREY DERENSKY, PSYCHOLOGIST, MCGILL UNIVERSITY

In a study of children's television, Tom Englehardt suggested that children's TV can be divided into four zones: action-figure superhero shows; specials aimed at little girls; Saturday morning network shows; and the advertisements. The following excerpt is from his description of "The Universe of the Action-Figure Superhero."

The Shortcake Strategy

by Tom Englehardt

Once upon a time, there was a series of soldier figures made by Hasbro and sold to little boys under the name of G.I. Joe. Then came the post-Vietnam War period, not a propitious selling atmosphere for a "real American hero," whereupon in 1978 Joe and his ilk were quietly retired. Now G.I. Joe is back, this time with his own daily afternoon show. He is a bit smaller—perhaps due, as Peggy Charren of ACT [Association for Children's Television] says, to inflation—but he comes equipped with a sort of animated A-Team pitted against a group of international terrorists (acronym: COBRA), that great Reagan-era bogeyman, and armed to the teeth. As the *Wall Street Journal* describes it, Joe's arsenal includes "a 7 1/2-foot G.I. Joe aircraft carrier—a toy behemoth, Pentagon-priced at about

$100. The toy can carry up to 100 Joes, at $3 each, and several Sky-striker jets at $19 a piece. A fleet of 100 000 aircraft carriers is planned."

In fact, the fall 1986 toy-and-TV season is highlighting terrorism, with Rambo and his Force of Freedom bursting onto the afternoon screen locked in daily combat with General Terror and his S.A.V.A.G.E. terrorist group. . . . *Advertising Age* reports that this year more than $40 million may be spent on ads supporting terrorism-related toy lines, "more than President Reagan wanted to send to Nicaraguan rebels for weapons."

Most action-adventure shows, however, have snubbed this somewhat more conventional sector of the defense budget, preferring the world of Star Wars first envisioned as a fantasy by George Lucas and only later promoted by Reagan's High Frontiersmen. Reagan himself clearly feels safest in space, and the producers of these shows still tend to agree that outer space, high tech, and faraway enemies in a distant future are a safer, tidier, less complicated way to turn after-school TV into a war zone.

A composite show would look something like this:

On the idyllic planet of Eternia (*He-Man*), Arcadia (*Voltron*), or even Earth (*M.A.S.K.*). . .

Lives an intrepid blond prince named Adam (*He-Man*), a blond hulk of a freelance scientist (*M.A.S.K.*), a blond warrior-prince named Dargon (*Sectaurs*), a blond

princess (*She-Ra*), "a real American hero" (*G.I. Joe*), a superforce of space explorers representing a galaxy alliance (*Voltron*), an intrepid group of space explorers representing the United Planets (*Mighty Orbots*), a "true hero of pure heart and purpose" named Jayce, representing the Lightning League (*Jayce and the Wheeled Warriors*), a group of friends able to transform themselves from inane teenagers. . .

Into power superheroes (*Superfriends*), into the strongest man in the universe (*He-Man*), into a "heroic team of armed machines" (*M.A.S.K.*), into "a mighty robot loved by good, feared by evil"

(*Voltron*), into a mighty robot that "protects the world from the shadow of evil" (*Mighty Orbots*), into mighty armed warriors, the Autobots (*Transformers*). . . .

Locked in mortal combat with them are the evil, black-eyed Skeletor (*He-Man*), the evil, yellow-eyed Lotar and his evil, blue-faced father from Planet Doom (*Voltron*), General Spidrax, lord of evil, master of the Dark Domain's mighty armies

> **"Ready to form Voltron! Activate interlocks! Dynotherms connected! Infracells up! Megathrusters at go!"**

(*Sectaurs*), the evil, red-eyed Darkseid of the Planet Apokolips (*Superfriends*), the treacherous Miles Mayhem, head of V.E.N.O.M.—the Vicious Evil Network of Mayhem—from the Contraworld (*M.A.S.K.*), the evil Monster Minds (*Jayce*), the evil Decepticons (*Transfomers*), the evil, many-eyed Umbra and his Shadow Star (*Mighty Orbots*). . . .

In this struggle between Good and Evil, light and darkness, blondness versus purpleness (or sickly yellowness), blue-eyedness versus glowing red-, purple-, or yellow-eyedness, what is at stake is nothing less than "the secrets of the universe" (*He-Man*), "the universe" (*Voltron*), "the destruction of the universe" (*Jayce*), "the ultimate battle for survival" (*Sectaurs*), "the fate of the entire world" (*Robotech*), "the ultimate doom" (*Transformers*). . . .

The actual episodes revolve around a series of evil plans to loose havoc on innocent planets (metal-eating bugs, froglike "Robeasts," and so on), or to trap the hero and deny him his transforming powers, or to stop the mighty robots from being assembled, or to kidnap a friend of the superheroes, or to steal something so powerful, dangerous, radioactive, death-dealing that it will destroy the earth/planet/galaxy/universe or alternately turn it into a world of slaves/zombies at the service of the Evil Force. . . .

All of which results in a series of chases and battles with techno-wonder weapons—space stations, laser beams, harnessed black holes, assorted yet-to-be invented and never-to-be-invented megaweapons—and a final withdrawal by the forces of evil, muttering curses and threatening to return, followed by a prosocial message, often not obviously related to the show, or perhaps a "safety tip" by the show's hero. . . . The program writers must find not so much plots as strings of team-action sequences.

It is in these sequences with their explosively animated displays of technoweaponry that kids' TV comes alive, however momentarily. Approximately twice per show, for instance, the blond leader of the Voltron force issues some version of this order to the other four space explorers (including one blond princess), each already seated in his or her own powerful robot lion: "Ready to form Voltron! Activate interlocks! Dynotherms connected!

Infracells up! Megathrusters are at go!"

The others respond, "Let's go, Voltron!" and the screen bursts into a riot of violent colors to a rock beat, flashes of lightning, odd camera angles, vivid cuts, and suddenly, to a cry of "Form blazing sword!" there emerges from the five lions a single awesome robot being with a glinting double-pronged . . . object of monstrous proportions that cuts through the enemy in a blinding, screen-filling flash of white-yellow light which can be nothing but an atomic explosion. . . .

The increased fears of nuclear war . . . permeate action-adventure shows: the daily use of nuclear threats as plot elements (stolen plutonium, radioactive death-rocks, radioactive sun creatures); the superweapon destruction of whole planets by the forces of evil (a direct theft from *Star Wars*); scenes like one in *Dungeons and Dragons* in which the good teenagers are saved from a harpylike evil spirit by a blinding explosion which leaves them "safe" in a desert landscape; the upping of the stakes in all these shows to the Fate of the Universe; constant, vague references to an ultimate battle for survival or an ultimate destruction, past or future. ("But then, technological experiments went wildly out of control, the Ancients' paradise began to collapse and a great Cataclysm began.") Indeed, the whiz-bang technoexplosions which dot these action-adventure cartoons, while

often not explicitly nuclear, are clearly routinized dress rehearsals for the ultimate Big Bang. Such nuclear devastation is so overused, so banal, that it is as taken for granted in these shows as the existence of the magical box itself. . . .

Nuclear menace has, in short, become a fixture of kids' television life—yet it has scarcely been remarked upon either by the producers of the shows or, more interestingly, by the critics. On the face of it, this omission is curious, given academic, critical, parental, even official alarm about "violence" on television. Millions of dollars have been spent on social-scientific studies that demonstrate the seemingly obvious: there is some correlation (often contradictory from study to study) between viewing TV violence and aggressive behavior in children. However carefully tabulated and studied such TV acts of violence may be, the category of "violence" itself is almost meaningless, covering as it does anything from the total destruction of a planet to Miss Piggy hitting Gonzo with a pillow. Such "violence" floats in an abstract space conveniently uncoupled from the real world. The category, by omitting distinctions, leaves no opening to explore, for instance, the obvious parallels between the Reagan-era military budget and the increase in violent acts and baroque weaponry in these shows; or to compare this sort of TV violence with violence elsewhere in media history—in silent film comedies, to take an example,

Children could interact with the TV program *Captain Power and the Soldiers of the Future* by shooting light beams at the characters on the screen. During a five-minute segment of the show, the characters appeared to shoot back.

where it was certainly just as prevalent though of a far more subversive nature, or in the violent world of the comic strip from the moment Krazy Kat first picked up a brick (to say nothing of a previous generation's experiences at shooting galleries and in penny arcades). The scholarly literature is not interested in the links between violence and authority, violence and power,

violence and the Good on kids' TV. Perhaps most important, no one mentions that this on-screen "violence" is of a strangely ritualistic and utterly unconvincing nature. Nor does anyone seem to wonder whether such convictionless mayhem induces in children an indifference to suffering in the real world, some strange form of visual pleasure or some utterly unexpected set of reactions.

"Violence" is simply a catch-all category that allows moral crusaders to vent their displeasure without either analyzing what's really going on in front of our kids' eyes or discussing why and how it gets there.

In fact, the only place where violence on kids' TV doesn't seem utterly antiseptic is in the ads for the action-figure toys on which the shows are based. Only there do we sense real aggression, some actual human venom at work. A few years ago, these commercials were little films about kids playing with their toys. Now they are tiny ritual outdoor battles among three or four usually white, mostly blond boys (never a girl) in vaguely suburban settings. Each holds a Transformer or a GoBot or a He-Man figure on a "stage" of uneven rocks. Grimacing and growling, the boys insult each others' figures, exchange oaths and curses ("Next bash is on you, boneface!") while parading their toys, often to the crushing drumbeat of Japanese-style background chants for the product. Only here, in the ads, can you actually *feel* the urge to smash, insult, destroy—all connected to the urge to rush out and buy.

How children sort these shows out, and what their impact might be, can be little more than speculation. How the industry reacts to the periodic studies of "violence" that lead to outraged articles in the media and then cries for reform in Congress, is clearer. Under fire, the producers begin to tag "prosocial messages" onto their shows. Typ-

ically, *M.A.S.K.* has its safety tips (moreover, it's the first first-run cartoon series to be closed-captioned for the hearing impaired), while *He-Man* has its final homilies urging respect, politeness, or some similar value. These messages and

> *Only here, in the ads, can you actually feel the urge to smash, insult, destroy . . .*

tips are so dissociated from what's of interest about the shows (special effects, robots, toys to buy) that they can clearly only have been designed as ammunition for future congressional hearings on the responsibilities of broadcasters.

Their minimal links to the shows are living proof, however, that the attack on "violence" misses the point. Were someone to come up with another formula guaranteed to attract boys two to eleven to licensed-character products, the mesh of toy companies, card companies, advertising agencies, and film production companies that make TV's violent shows would abandon them in a minute—and what would be the result? We already know part of the answer: Rainbow Brite, Strawberry Shortcake, the Care Bears, and all their "non-violent" ilk, the sort of shows so sickly sweet, so poorly made, and so obviously false that a viewing adult almost yearns for the Incredible Hulk or Skeletor or the Monster Minds to land in their midst and tear the place to bits.

—*WATCHING TELEVISION*, 1986

RESPONSES

1. Note the key elements in the definitions of violence presented at the beginning of the chapter and in the definition that your group or class created. Determine to what extent they apply to a) the ways that children use their war toys and b) the plots and characterization in action-figure superhero cartoons.

2. Why do you think Tom Englehardt brought a cross section of the characters together to make a composite cartoon? In groups, use the same technique, but update the material and create your own patterns. You might shape it into a short play in which you use dialogue that would be appropriate to the characters. You might present the events as a newscast.

3. Englehardt is concerned about the tendency of the plot lines of these shows to involve a nuclear threat. What is the basis of his concern? Explain why you agree or disagree with him.

4. Examine the language used in children's shows and in commercials and advertising for war toys. Find any evidence of the defence mechanisms of dehumanization and projection described in the excerpt from ''The Enemy Within.'' Discuss your findings with members of your group.

5. In groups, compare the characters and plots of children's cartoons and war toys with those of movies like *Go-Bots* and *Star Wars*, or those of children's adventure comic books like *Spiderman*. Present your findings to the class.

6. Violence is described simply as ''fantasy'' by one well-known developer of instructional microcomputer software. Explain why you agree or disagree with this description. In what ways do computer or video games resemble children's cartoons?

7. In groups, devise a non-violent, fantasy-type board, video, or computer game that is challenging and interesting. You could use a storyboard to present your ideas for the video game. Think of a name for the game, and write the advertising copy for it.

ADULTS AND VIOLENCE

The controversy about the effects of fantasy violence in popular culture and media on children extends to the possible impact on teenagers and adults. Music videos, song lyrics, slasher films, action/adventure television shows, computer games—is the violence in these and other media simply harmless entertainment or a cause for concern?

The presence of violence itself is not new. There have been war films and westerns and detective shows almost since the beginning of movies and television. War films, for example, have almost always been popular with many people, whether they showed John Wayne leading the U.S. Marines in an attack on the beaches in the Second World War or Sylvester Stallone as Rambo, a one-man army gunning down hundreds of sinister-looking North Vietnamese soldiers. In fact, film audiences often cheer heroes like Rambo, a Vietnam war veteran who, in the sequel to *First Blood*, returns to Vietnam to liberate American prisoners of war. Read the following comments about *Rambo: First Blood Part II* and notice how some people see the film as the embodiment of current cultural trends.

"*Rambo* is an effort to deal with a complex, painful and deep wound with simple and sentimental responses. Part of the psychological potency of fairy tales such as these is that they dramatize our own inner struggles."

—*HEALING FROM THE WAR TRAUMA AND TRANSFORMATION*
AFTER VIETNAM BY ARTHUR EGENDORF

. . . "Rambo has echoes of half a dozen movie heroes of old, from Tarzan to Shane, and his Vietnamese and Soviet foes are updated versions of the malevolent Japanese and Germans from World War II films. The cheers that erupt in the theatre as the body count soars are coming largely from young moviegoers whose only previous encounter with Vietnam may have been a question on *The Hollywood Squares*.". . .

—*TIME*, JUNE 24, 1985

"These films (*Rambo, Red Dawn, Rocky IV*) are rabblerousers in a dangerous game of oneupmanship. And they benefit from bandwagon timing, making the martial approach seem inevitable and calling it bravery instead of its true name: bully."

—MARCIA PALLY, *FILM COMMENT*

"It may be that Rambo is particularly appealing at a moment when we are mightily frustrated about the threat of terrorism and the stubbornness of certain Third World Countries. The White House strives day and night to create an image of Fortress America, besieged on many sides."

—FRED BRUNING, *MACLEAN'S*, JULY 29, 1985

RESPONSES

1. In groups, discuss why you do or do not enjoy movies and television shows that contain violent scenes. Indicate whether any of the previous comments apply to the films or shows you watch. What do you think is the appeal of these shows and films? To what extent are they part of Canadian culture? Why?

2. a) In groups, examine different types of violent TV shows and films, e.g., a war film, a detective show, a western, and a children's cartoon show. Analyze the show, answering the following questions:

• How is the hero or heroine portrayed?

• How is the villain portrayed?

• Describe the conflict briefly.

• Indicate the nature of the conflict. (For example, is the conflict presented in simple or complex terms? What are the possible consequences if the conflict is not resolved?)

• How is the conflict resolved?

• Describe any examples of dehumanization and/or projection.

• How are music and sound effects used?

b) Present your findings to the class. You may wish to create a class chart to compare the shows. Use categories suggested by the questions above and any other categories you think are important or interesting.

3. Critics have suggested that the *Rambo* films have the qualities of fairy tales and links with mythical superheroes like Tarzan. In what ways do these films and/or similar shows relate to fairy tales and myths?

4. Study several examples of one genre that uses violence, e.g., a war film, an avenger film, a western, or a detective show. Create a composite show that illustrates the formula typical of that genre. You might adapt and update the show so that it addresses the concerns of Canadian culture today. You could create a storyboard for your show, or dramatize it for the class.

5. What are the similarities and differences in the attitudes toward cultural groups in the *Star Wars* films and *Rambo*?

Perhaps because of their popularity, music videos have received a lot of attention in the controversy about the effects of violence in media and popular culture. They have been called "one of the most vital and important forms of popular culture." They have also been blamed for inciting murders and suicides. In the following excerpt, John Hofsess suggests that while it is difficult to evaluate the influence of rock videos, we should at least be examining the messages they are sending.

Do You Know What Your Children Are Watching?

by John Hofsess

In the early dark hours of an April morning last year, in a Scarborough, Ontario house, a 14-year-old boy—intoxicated with the demonic music and emblems of the heavy-metal rock group Iron Maiden—stalked through the house armed with a rifle. Voices, he would later tell police, urged him on, told him what to do: voices from Iron Maiden's mascot, Eddie. The voices told him he would feel better after he killed his sleeping prey. Eddie is depicted on Iron Maiden's albums as a ghoulish creature leashed by chains, struggling to break free. Many of Iron Maiden's songs celebrate death, satanism, and violence.

The youth began his bloody rampage by shooting and killing his 39-year-old mother and . . . his 55-year-old father. Then he went downstairs and murdered his seven-year-old sister. Psychiatrists later testified at the boy's trial that he was suffering from a "severe mental disorder." Heavy metal rock-music is not the primary cause of this familial bloodbath, but that doesn't mean there's no connection between these murders and a form of pop music, as practised by Iron Maiden, that promises impressionable fans that death is the greatest trip of all. The question that needs to be asked, but could not be dealt with by the courts, is this: Are rock musicians responsible for their cultural influence? Do the music and stage persona of Iron Maiden, among other heavy metal groups dabbling in satanism, create a climate conducive to violent crime? The suicide of a 19-year-old California youth in 1984, supposedly after listening to an ode to suicide by British rock singer Ozzy Osbourne, suggests that there may be many young people teetering on a life-and-death brink between hope and despair who are capable of being pushed over the edge by forms of pop culture that present an alluring picture of apocalyptic nihilism.

Questions about the effects of certain forms of popular culture become all the more urgent with the emergence of rock videos. Joseph Gladstone, principal author of the report *Television and Your Children* (Ontario Educational Communications Authority, 1985), states, "Combining the power of rock music with 30 years of television know-how and the pizzazz of the short high-budget commercial, rock videos are at the cutting edge of all that is new and controversial in television. Short and slick, punchy and powerful, they combine the most sophisticated video editing techniques with the most potent lyrics and the most popular melodies. They are television in the fast lane. Lasting no longer than a hit song or several commercials they are seductive and addictive to many teens and preteens."

If most rock videos were blatant incitements to psychopathic behavior, and if teenage crimes with a link to rock music were a frequent occurrence, it would be fairly easy to evaluate this new phenomenon and to propose ways in which its influence could be more carefully controlled. But, in fact, the "messages" transmitted by rock videos are generally covert, practically subliminal. It may take years of exposure to hundreds of rock videos, repeated over and over, in which, say women are depicted as sex objects, for there to be a *measurable* effect on sexual stereotyping. Similarly the glamorization of violence may have an insidious *cumulative* effect when it is presented as a stylish attitude, often enough and in different ways—and yet, no one rock video will be culpable.

Robert Jay Lifton, a professor at John Jay College of Criminal Justice in New York and an analyst of world renown for his studies on violence (and the effects on children living with the omnipresent threat of nuclear war), says, "Nobody knows exactly what [rock videos] are doing to us. If anybody says he or she knows, I don't believe it. It's too new."

What is not in dispute is the fact that many rock videos are sexist, racist panderings to the basest of human tastes. Consider the following:

In a rock video called *Looks That Kill*, by Mötley Crüe, a group of barely clad women are rounded up like cattle and put inside a pen. The women cower before their heavy metal masters, eager to please so that they won't be abused. Suddenly, an Amazonian superwoman appears and frees the other women with a laser blaster. But she herself is then stalked by the men and forced to lie down on a bed of shiny metal spikes. There is a flash of fire, a puff of smoke, and an overhead shot of Mötley Crüe turns into a demonic pentagram, apparently inviting viewers to associate the group with black masses and devil worship. All this in the space of three minutes in a video that drums home its dubious message like a television commercial. . . .

Barry Sherman, assistant professor of telecommunications at the University of Georgia, evaluated 366 videos aired in 1984. Sherman reports that the view they present is that of a "predominantly white, male world." Sixty percent of the music videos showed violence, and men were usually the aggressors. Fifty percent of the women depicted were provocatively clothed.

The intertwining and repetition of the themes of sex and violence is regarded with concern, even alarm by many parents. David Scott, chairman of the Media Action Group in Toronto and a media violence researcher there and at the Child and Family Protection Institute in Washington, D.C., contends that rock videos are yet another means (in conjunction with movies and prime-time television shows) by which people become "increasingly desensitized [to violence]."

Rock videos have "an enormous potential for teaching," he says. "By the very virtue of having that potential for teaching they also have an enormous potential to allow society to regress into levels of violence that could be quite frightening."

Other observers of the rock video phenomenon take a less censorious view of their contents, yet they too feel that the line should be drawn somewhere. Daniel Richler, a freelance rock critic and a host for *The New Music*, argues that rock'n'roll "has always been a fusion of sex and danger. Without those elements it doesn't work very well. It is deliberately subversive; it tries to make trouble." Kids need an outlet for aggression "and rock'n'roll provides that. And perhaps the most difficult thing to come to terms with is the fact that videos are the word made flesh." Whereas rock'n'roll lyrics were often ambiguous, they are no longer ambiguous when made into visual images.

Richler is making the valid point that popular music has long contained pathological elements in its lyrics, especially in what used to be called "torch songs," which, if made visually explicit, could strike many people as offensive. Even a line like "I don't want to set the world on fire, I just want to start a flame in your heart" allows itself to be visually interpreted in ways that may seem shocking. The Mötley Crüe video referred to earlier is one that Richler feels is particularly offensive. Last year he started a rock video eduation project in which he regularly visits Toronto-area high schools and special interest groups, shows examples of questionable videos and invites the students to "talk back" to what they see and hear rather than passively accept it.

—HOMEMAKER'S, APRIL 1986

RESPONSES

1. Discuss why you agree or disagree that violence in music videos has negative effects on the audience. Consider how the influence of these videos might change depending on the age of the audience and the degree to which the audience likes the artist.

2. Have a debate on this topic. "Resolved that: The violent content in some music videos is justified as a release of rebellious feelings in adolescents."

3. Do you think that music videos impose a visual interpretation on lyrics that the audience might otherwise not share? Explain your answer. In groups, listen to some song lyrics and then watch or think about the videos for those songs. Note whether there is violence depicted in the song and whether the violence in the visuals reflects or increases the violence in the lyrics. Present your findings to the class.

4. a) In groups, choose a song and create a storyboard that shows the major scenes of the video you would make. If the equipment is available, you might like to tape or film your video.
b) Present your storyboard to the class. See whether you agree with the visual interpretations of other groups. Compare the visual techniques used by the groups in your class with the techniques used in the videos you see on television.

5. If you were part of a rock video education project, such as the one started by Daniel Richler, how would you teach students to "talk back" to rock videos?

6. Choose a video and write a review of it, pointing out any questionable or negative images it may contain and showing how you might explain the video to children to lessen its negative impact.

7. Choose a favourite pop song and write the script for a video that avoids clichés and sexism. If feasible, film the video by lip-synching the song.

REAL VIOLENCE

The violence you have been examining until now has been the fantasy violence of toys, cartoons, movies, TV shows, and music videos. The blood has been fake, if there has been any blood at all. You have discussed this fantasy violence, or violence as entertainment and the extent to which it influences our behavior. With some of the violence you see in the media, however, the actions—and the injuries—are real. Consider violence in sports and the daily news coverage of violent events in the world. How do you think we are affected by seeing, or hearing about, real violence? Do the media show real violence to grab our attention? How do you react to seeing real violence in the media?

VIOLENCE IN SPORTS

Watching televised sports is a favourite pastime of millions of people. The behaviour of some players and the resulting media coverage have created a great deal of controversy. Some viewers consider the violence a negative influence; others see it as just part of the game.

Discuss the following questions in your group or class.

1. What do you consider violence in sports? For example, if someone is injured accidentally, is that violence?
2. Is there an acceptable level of violence in sports? How would you define it?
3. Do you think watching violence in sports leads to imitative behaviour? Why?
4. Do you think playing a rough sport releases a person's aggression in a relatively harmless way or increases a person's aggression? Why?

What role do the media play in the effect of violence in sports on audiences? In the following article, Robert Gould suggests that television both increases violence in the players and magnifies the impact of the violence on the viewer. Gould is a professor of psychiatry at New York Medical College, and director of the New York Office of The National Coalition on TV Violence.

Killing Them Loudly: TV Sports Teaches Violent Lessons

by Robert E. Gould

A Connecticut school teacher was startled by her students' aggressiveness one morning. They were trading insults, throwing objects, hitting, pushing and shoving—all to an unusual degree.

In exploring what gave rise to this behavior, she discovered one common denominator—many of the students had watched championship wrestling on television the night before.

The children's reaction shouldn't surprise anyone familiar with studies that trace a connection between viewing violence like boxing or wrestling and increased violent behavior.

During the last 20 years, for example, research has shown a 12 to 15 percent rise in homicide statistics nationwide during the four days following championship boxing matches. And wrestling fans showed a marked *decrease* in displays of social affection after watching matches.

But what is new in the 1980s is the amount of violence we are seeing in other "ordinary" sports (watch what goes on under the basket in pro basketball) and the increasing viciousness that comes through the media sports window.

Much sports/violence research concentrates on the violence that may follow as fans leave the stadium. But research by Indiana University psychologists Dolf Zillman and Jennings Bryant suggests that television coverage in and of itself may magnify effects of violence on fans viewing at home.

They note that rough plays are more apt to be picked up by the camera and instant replays are scheduled more frequently for violent plays. In addition, announcers often follow violent incidents with approving comments like, "Now that's the way to make a halfback think twice before hitting the hole again."

Sportscasters reporting on games most often speak admiringly of the athlete or team that is the more aggressive and tend to emphasize the violence as "highlights" of the game.

For example, when popular quarterback Joe Theissman of the

Watching sports can evoke strong feelings of nationalism. Sometimes these feelings become too strong, as shown by these rioting soccer fans.

Lombardi once put it, "To play football you must have a fire in you, and nothing stokes a fire like hate."

Today's most admired coaches teach their players that they must hate to win—a view that is very similar to what army sergeants teach recruits. Athletic contests are thus very similar to war, and the language used by sports commentators is filled with war imagery.

Of course, winning has always been an important part of sports contests. But sportsmanship and fair play were once part of the standards. Today's emphasis on winning for the camera and the national audience has made those ideals seem out of date and sissified. Today's accepted rules are: "Nice guys finish last" and "Show me a good loser and I'll show you a loser."

With winning "the only thing" in Lombardi's descriptive phrase, sports' symbolism has changed from a way to build character to a way of winning at all costs. Even non-contact sports such as tennis now tolerate temper tantrums in their star athletes like Jimmy Connors and John McEnroe. And again, the TV camera hones in on every thrown racket or hostile display of anger.

Washington Redskins had his leg badly broken after a vicious tackle, sportscasts repeated the violent tackle over and over again, including slow motion reviews that made the most of every graphic detail.

Ultimately, the camera focuses on the violence because of the excitement and interest it evokes in the viewer. But from a psychological point of view, TV sports violence also increases in intensity as it explodes out of the little box into a relatively small viewing space.

As one of the few live events on television, sports has a rough-hewn integrity that emphasizes the lessons it teaches. All the more reason, then, to regret that it glorifies violence and encourages the reverse dogma of "hate your enemy." As legendary football coach Vince

It seems to me that as sports become more brutal, players and spectators both become dehumanized. If the point is winning without grace or dignity; if anything goes—cheating, bullying, deliberate injuries—and if violence is the name of the game, we will all be losers in the larger game of life.

—*MEDIA AND VALUES*, SUMMER 1986

RESPONSES

1. Write about an incident or incidents of violence in sports in which you were involved, either as a participant or an observer. Give as much background information as you can and illustrate how you (and perhaps the others involved) felt about the incident. You could present your story in short story, poem, or play form. Share your writing with the class.

2. In groups, analyze a variety of sports coverage by the media, including the sports highlights on the evening news. Some areas to consider are: how much of the camera time is given to rough play or behaviour; the use of instant replays; comments from the announcers and/or commentators that suggest approval of violence or aggression; the imagery used in the commentary and/or news article; and the headlines and photos used in newspapers or magazine articles. You might want to report your findings in chart form.

3. In groups, interview parents, children's club leaders (Girl Guides, Cubs), and elementary school teachers to find out if they connect aggressive behaviour in children with the children's viewing of certain TV sports events. If possible, have each of your groups interview only one or two persons, parents, teachers or leaders. Prepare your questions in advance. See page 212 in the Reference Section for interviewing techniques.

4. In a letter to a network president, write some guidelines for sports coverage that would help to overcome some of Robert Gould's criticisms.

5. There is a video available called *Great Hockey Fights*. How does the availability and popularity of this tape relate to the thesis of the Gould article?

6. Choose several sports and propose some rule changes that might reduce their violence.

HOCKEY VIOLENCE

Hockey has been considered one of the more violent sports by some viewers since at least 1907 when a player was killed—the result of a fight during a major league game. One 1976 Canadian study of males aged 12-21 indicated that the majority of amateur hockey players admitted that they learned a great deal about the practice of hockey violence through watching televised hockey. While the study does not prove that the subjects used what they learned, the following are some of their descriptions of illegal hitting learned from watching professional hockey:

"I learned spearing and butt-ending."

"Hitting at weak points with the stick, say at the back of the legs."

"Getting a guy from behind. Getting a guy in the corner and giving him an elbow."

"Butt-end, spearing, slashing, high sticking, elbow in the head."

"The way you "bug" in front of the net."

"Clipping. Taking the guy's feet out by sliding underneath."

"I've seen it and use it: when you check a guy, elbow him. If you get in a corner you can hook or spear him without getting caught."

The previous quotes and other data were collected and presented in a paper by Michael D. Smith. The following is an excerpt from the paper as it appeared in the book *Violence in Canada*.

From Professional to Youth Hockey Violence: The Role of the Mass Media

by Michael D. Smith

"Violence"—insofar as it refers to one person physically assaulting another in a manner proscribed by the official rules of hockey—was, literally, non-"violence." Most of today's players, professional and amateur, thoroughly socialized, do not consider fighting with fists "violent"; professionals claim that their games are generally not "violent." This highly charged term is reserved for only the most extreme and injurious of acts. . . .

Professional hockey's influence on youth hockey seems to operate in two main ways. The first has to do with the structure of the "system." The fifty or so professional teams in North America depended upon junior leagues for a steady outflow of "talent." Most of the ablest amateur players are strongly motivated to advance through minor hockey to junior professional and thence to professional ranks. But en route, the number of available positions progressively diminishes, and competition for spots becomes increasingly intense. Professional standards determine who moves up and who does not. These include the willingness and ability to employ, and withstand, illegal physical coercion. Some performers with marginal playing skills are upwardly mobile—even as young as fourteen—primarily because they meet this criterion.

Secondly, North Americans have been socialized into acceptance of professional hockey's values, chiefly through the communications media. Small wonder that minor hockey is the professional game in miniature when consumption of the latter has for decades been nothing short of voracious. Violence has been purveyed by an almost bewildering variety of means, blatantly, artfully, often no doubt unconsciously: attention-getting pictures of fights (sometimes without accompanying stories); radio and television "hot stove league" commentary (chuckles about Gordie Howe's legendary elbows or the hundreds of stitches in Ted Lindsay's face, a breathless report that a new penalty record has been set); the sheer amount of atten-

The 1987 World Junior Hockey championship game between Canada and the Soviet Union had a 20-minute, bench-clearing brawl that resulted in the expulsion of both teams.

tion given "enforcers" and tough guys (Dave Schultz was a virtual media "star" in his Philadelphia heyday); newspaper and magazine pieces ("Detroit's Murderers' Row," "Hit man"). In American cities full-page newspaper advertisements show Neanderthal-like cartoon characters belaboring one another with hockey sticks. "Crunching No Nos are slashing, hooking, charging and high-sticking," one legend informs, "Don't let this happen to you; buy a season ticket to the Robins' 74-75 season. Watch it happen to others." The *Atlanta Flames' Yearbook* cover of a few years ago, sold in NHL arenas everywhere, featured an eye-catch-

ing scene of a multi-player brawl. Highway billboards: San Diego's "Mad, Mean, Menacing, Major League Mariners." At least two feature movies whose major themes turn on hockey violence are currently in the making. *Blades and Brass*, the award-winning National Film Board of Canada short, highlights body-thumping and bloody faces. The Better T Shirt Company manufactures shirts emblazoned with pictures of cartoon players gleefully engaging in various dirty-work ("Hooking," "Charging," the captions read). Even the Topps Chewing Gum people are in the violence business. Consider the following, not atypical bubble gum card biography: "André is one of the roughest players in the NHL. Opponents have learned to keep their heads up when he is on the ice. André won't score many goals, but he's a handy guy to have around when the going gets tough." Whatever their form, the media messages are clear: violence and hockey go together.

Young performers, also, may learn specific behaviors from professional hockey, directly and through the mass media. The conditions for observational learning and modelling . . . via TV are almost laboratory-perfect: models who get money and attention for aggressive acts, observers' expectations of rewards for the same behavior, close similarity between the social situations portrayed on the screen and subsequently encountered directly by observers.
—*VIOLENCE IN CANADA*, 1985

RESPONSES

1. In groups, discuss your views on violence in hockey. What aspects of the game do you consider violent? If you play hockey, share with your group any incidents of violence you have encountered. Interview someone who knew the sport at an earlier time (pre-1960) and ask his or her view of the changes that have occurred in the game and its media coverage.

2. Hold a debate. "Resolved: That media portrayals of violence in professional hockey have contributed to the spread of a social climate in youth hockey that promotes violence and makes it respectable."

3. Interview some minor league hockey players and their parents, coaches, and referees about their views on imitative behaviour. You might prefer to attend a minor league game and note the behaviour of the parents, players, coaches, and referees. Present your findings to your group or class.

Media coverage of sports depends on the level of audience interest. In the following excerpt, Rocco Rossi suggests that the coverage of wrestling increased both because the participants learned to appeal to the audience and because the media capitalized on the conflict and aggression that are part of the sport.

Hype is the Key to Wrestling Mania

By Rocco Rossi

We live in an age of manias. Beatlemania, Trudeaumania, discomania—they burst on to the scene, dominate for a while, and then fade.

What explains them?

While there is no scientific theory, there are interesting insights to be found by examining yet another mania—wrestlemania.

Long a fringe activity, professional wrestling is today a marketing bonanza that features everything from Saturday morning cartoons to rock videos. And, now that wrestling star stickers are being offered as prizes in packages of potato chips, it is safe to say that wrestling has entered the mainstream of pop culture.

You don't have to take my word for it.

Ask King Kong Bundy, Big John Stud or Hulk Hogan—if you dare. These behemoths of the ring are all well over 6 feet tall, their combined weight is close to 1200 pounds, and they have become very wealthy, very quickly.

Hogan, for example, once a bank teller by the name of Terry Bollea, could now open his own bank. World Wrestling Federation (WWF) champion for the last three years, Hogan earns almost $3 million (U.S.) per year.

True, wrestling has had periods

of popularity in the past. I remember sitting in my grandfather's lap almost 20 years ago to hear stories about Canada's own Whipper Billy Watson and to watch The Beast (my favorite) take on Abdullah the Butcher.

But wrestling was never this popular. And, for over a decade before the latest renaissance, wrestling was relegated to the fringes by more "sophisticated" forms of entertainment like video games, videos, and high-tech special effects movies.

How, then, was it able to escape the fringes?

All manias begin with two components: a product and publicity.

Professional wrestling, as a product, has never varied the traditional three-part wrestling formula:

One, people love to hate villains

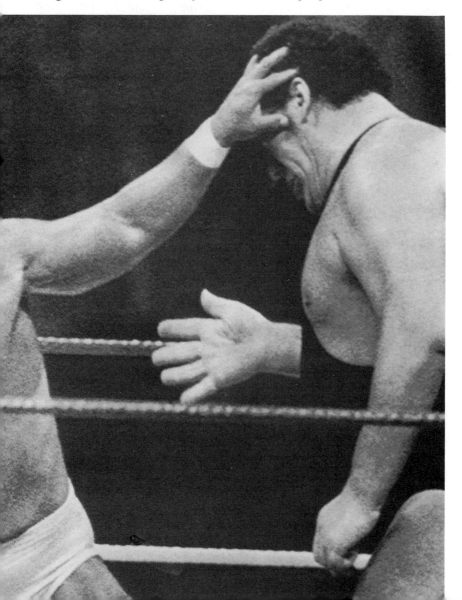

Hulk Hogan vs. Andre the Giant

almost as much as they love to cheer for heroes. Almost all wrestlers are champions either of good or evil, and carry appropriate nicknames like "The Living Legend" or "The Butcher." You can be sure that the ones who don't are there simply to serve as target practice.

Two, people love to see the unusual and the larger-than-life. Like circus freak shows, wrestling offers a cast of characters to amaze the ordinary mortal.

In Wrestlemania III, the best of the new met the best of the old.

Three, people love a spectacle. The more glitter and noise, the better.

Any formula, however, is only as good as the ingredients that go into it. The downfall of wrestling in the '70s was due to the fact that, in the face of slicker competition, wrestling failed to keep up. The wrestlers were big and had neat nicknames but, by and large, they were inarticulate lugs who failed to hold the attention of an increasingly demanding audience.

The key to the resurgence of wrestling in the '80s was the recruitment of dozens of articulate, charismatic individuals like Hulk Hogan, Rowdy Roddy Piper, Jake the Snake, and Jesse "The Body" Ventura. The pre-fight theatrics of these and others have become an even greater attraction than the matches themselves.

But the rise of these stars is no accident. For several years, wrestling schools like The Monster Factory in New Jersey have been proliferating. Just as the image makers have been retooling our politicians, these schools have been fashioning wrestling stars.

With the old formula and improved ingredients in place, all that was needed was a little publicity.

Enter Sylvester Stallone and *Rocky III*. Hulk Hogan was given a starring role and, from that point his fortune and that of the new and improved wrestling was made.

The promoters quickly consolidated this tremendous exposure by inviting Mr. T., another Stallone find, to participate in Wrestlemania, a gala tournament that was televised via closed-circuit throughout North America.

Two years later, in Wrestlemania III, the best of the new met the best of the old. Fighting for the world westling championship were Andre the Giant, a 7-foot holdover from 15 years ago, and Hulk Hogan, the central figure in the revival of professional wrestling.

Andre *is* a giant of a man who makes even Hulk Hogan look small, but the Giant is only the biggest of the big, inarticulate lugs. He had a place in the marginal wrestling of old, and his immense size gives him freak appeal even today, but without the polish of a Hogan, he could not be the central figure of a mania.

The Giant was defeated, not by superior strength and skill, but by greater marketing potential.

—ADAPTED FROM AN ARTICLE IN
THE TORONTO STAR, MARCH 17, 1987

RESPONSES

1. In groups, discuss the rise of wrestling mania. Why does wrestling appeal to its fans? If you are or were a wrestling fan, explain why you like(d) it to your group.

2. How does Rocco Rossi explain the popularity of wrestling in the 1980s? Discuss the three-part formula for wrestling according to Rossi. Consider the elements that television has added to the sport in order to "construct its reality," e.g., the use of camera techniques, the function of the interviews before and after the match, the promotion for the next event, and the behaviour of the participants during the match.

3. To what extent is wrestling mania part of, or in contrast to, the violence in sports described by Robert E. Gould? Debate the following topic. "Resolved: that wrestlemania with its mostly fake violence is a harmless diversion and should be enjoyed for what it is—a terrific spectacle."

4. In groups, write a dialogue that is a parody of the pre-match interviews. You may wish to apply this format to another sport. Have two or three people play the roles of the interviewer and the participants. If you have the equipment, film or tape the interview and present it to the class.

VIOLENCE IN THE NEWS

Real violence, whether it is in your neighbourhood or across the world, is brought to you through the news every day. How do the news media present violence? What effect does their portrayal have on our perception of it?

Survey the radio and television news over a period of two to three days. You might want to do this in groups, with each person taking responsibility for a different station or channel. Monitor the broadcasts at different times of the day, and include some American stations, if possible.

Indicate what topics were covered and how much time was spent on each. Note when film, graphics, or audiotape were used with a story and any words or phrases that suggested violence, e.g., "conflict," "threaten." You may find it helpful to create a chart similar to the one below to record the information for each station or channel you monitor. Use the categories suggested and add any other information you think is important.

You might like to conduct a similar survey of daily newspapers. Examine at least the front section and the front pages of the other sections. Note the topics of the articles and the amount of space and prominence that was given to each story. Indicate the photos used, if any.

STATION OR
CHANNEL _____

Broadcast time	Topic	Time spent on topic	Audio/Visual material used	Words/Phrases depicting violence

Discuss your survey results as a class. What kinds of events and issues were considered news? How do American news programs compare with Canadian news programs?

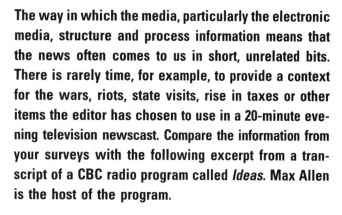

The way in which the media, particularly the electronic media, structure and process information means that the news often comes to us in short, unrelated bits. There is rarely time, for example, to provide a context for the wars, riots, state visits, rise in taxes or other items the editor has chosen to use in a 20-minute evening television newscast. Compare the information from your surveys with the following excerpt from a transcript of a CBC radio program called *Ideas*. Max Allen is the host of the program.

Sex and Violence
by Max Allen

The news is overwhelmingly about conflict—international, inter-group, interpersonal. The whole public world is transformed into a battleground. In general, world news consists of stories about catastrophes, lethal violence, and statements by politicians. Local news consists of crime reports, strikes, and statements by politicians.

Everybody's news, not just the CBC's, is fragmented and decontextualized. There is no such thing as a story that's too short. Editors think almost everything is too long. On television and radio, stories are so abbreviated that everybody relies on codes and shorthand. If I say the word "terrorist" or "guerrilla," a whole world of information comes into your mind. Guerrillas are always bad. Strikes are bad. "We" are good, "they" are bad. Radio news is full of clichés: Widespread looting. It's always "widespread." "Fierce" fighting, outbreaks of "savage" shelling, and always "tough" new economic measures.

The news really ought to be called the "olds," because anything really new is too complicated for broadcast news. Anything that's being constructed, any really new alternative, anything that doesn't already exist takes a relatively long time to describe. Anything that's being knocked down can be described much faster. Short newscasts emphasize catastrophic events

Thirteen percent were about riots and crime, and 24 percent of the stories were about war and terrorism.

because they can be disposed of in just a few seconds. Destruction lends itself to quick description. Construction is relatively complex and is seldom discussed on the news. Death is fast. Life is slow. As a result, the news likes death. Eighty-eight percent of the stories on the CBC Radio hourly newscasts are about conflict. Fifty-six percent are about death.

Here's how I know that. In June, July, and August 1985, we sampled the flow of CBC Radio news every 12 hours for 3 months, analyzing the content of 1000 consecutive stories on the 1 am and 1 pm newscasts. In 3 percent of the stories, the point was that something—any-

thing—had turned out well. Fifteen percent of the stories were about disease and disasters. Political arguments accounted for 19 percent. Thirteen percent were about riots and crime, and 24 percent of the stories were about war and terrorism. . . .

Because it presents the world as a marathon of disorder and conflict, malfeasance and distant emergencies, mass media news teaches that chaos is just around the corner. Because the news never adds up to anything, the audience can seldom figure out what to make of it, that is, what can be done. Reporters and editors rarely think of their work in these terms. The journalistic policy book at the CBC, for example, says simply that "the purpose of news broadcasts is to report events." Which events? Why do we get the particular events that are covered in the CBC Radio hourly news bulletins? A ten-year veteran of CBC News explained that to me. He said there are so many stories about death and violence because the best news is news where there is dramatic conflict. But does this "best news" make you smarter, that is, better equipped to act in your own interest? Or does it make you more frightened, more passive, more pliant? I contend that the news as a social control mechanism works like electroshock on the neural mechanisms of the body politic. It induces amnesia and paralysis. It stupefies. . . .

—CBC's IDEAS, 1985

RESPONSES

1. Discuss why you agree or disagree with Max Allen's statement that "news is overwhelmingly about conflict." How do you define conflict? What effect has the constant flood of information about conflict on the listener?

2. Allen says that on radio news, "the whole public world is transformed into a battleground." Is this true of other media? Refer to your survey results to support your answer.

3. Refer to "TV As a Shaper of Culture" in the Television chapter (p. 99). How do Max Allen's findings and your survey results compare with George Gerbner's idea that TV portrays the world as a dangerous place?

4. How might the news media answer concerns about violence in the news?
a) Write a letter to the news editor of a paper or radio or television station, suggesting guidelines for reporting on violent events.
b) Try applying your guidelines to a story—re-write a news story about violence the way you think it should be reported. Indicate how you would use headlines, photographs, illustrations, audiotape, videotape, or film. Compare the re-written stories with the originals. Decide what is most effective about each type of story and consider how the audience would respond to the violence in each.

5. a) What is "good news"? How might a reporter go about finding "good news"? Try writing a "good news" story. Describe any audio or visual material that you would choose to accompany the story.
b) In groups, compare the "good news" stories with traditional news stories. Note the similarities and differences. Are the "good news" stories as interesting as the traditional news items? If so, explain what makes them so.

ALL THE WORLD IS WATCHING

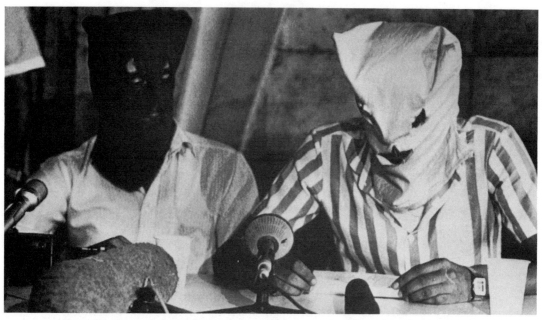

These hijackers, aware of the wide coverage they would receive, requested a news conference that coincided with the release of the hostages to publicize their cause.

The media cover conflict and violence because they are important, but also because they are usually visual and straightforward. Do the media, by their presence, encourage or intensify conflict and violence? Consider the following observations.

"I would guess that a majority of demonstrations as such wouldn't happen if the media didn't cover them. A demonstration is designed not just to get the attention of the people on the street, it's to get publicity for some cause. And if the press weren't there, I would say a majority of demonstrations wouldn't happen."

—FROM *REPORT OF THE ROYAL COMMISSION ON VIOLENCE IN THE COMMUNICATIONS INDUSTRY*, 1977

. . . "Television may contribute more to riots than liquor and beer. By showing the excitement and turmoil of riots over and over, the theory goes, TV lures imitators to the scene of future outbreaks.". . .

—COMMENTING ON THE 1985 SOCCER RIOTS IN BRUSSELS, *TIME*, JUNE 10, 1985

Investigate demonstrations in recent months that have had extensive media coverage. Note any evidence that the staging of a demonstration has become an "art." How does this affect the way you respond to any of the violence that might have occurred?

Whether the violence we see is real or fictional, it does have some effect on us. Does the impact change when we know the fight is staged and the blood is ketchup? How are our responses to real and fantasy violence related? Dr. Mike Oppenheim, the author of the following excerpt, suggests that the audience, particularly children, should be aware of just how unrealistic fantasy violence can be.

TV Isn't Violent Enough

by Mike Oppenheim

The trail of quiet corpses left by TV's good guys, bad guys and assorted ill-tempered gun owners is ridiculously unreal. A pistol is certainly a deadly weapon, but not predictably so. Unlike a knife wound, one bullet can kill instantly—provided it strikes a small area at the base of the brain. Otherwise, it's no different: a matter of ripping and tearing enough tissue to cause death by bleeding. Professional gangland killers understand the problem. They prefer a shotgun at close range.

No less unreal is what happens when T.J. Hooker, Magnum, or a Simon brother meets a bad guy in manly combat. Pow! Our hero's fist crashes into the villain's head. Villain reels backward, tipping over chairs and lamps, finally falling to the floor, unconscious. Handshakes all around. . . .

Sheer fantasy! After hitting the villain, our hero would shake no one's hand. He'd be too busy waving his own about wildly, screaming with the pain of a shattered fifth metacarpal (the bone behind the fifth knuckle), an injury so predictable it's called the "boxer's fracture." The human fist is far more delicate than the human skull. In any contest between the two, the fist will lose.

The human skull is far tougher than TV writers give it credit. Clunked with a blunt object, such as the traditional pistol butt, most victims would not fall conveniently unconscious for a few minutes. More likely, they'd suffer a nasty scalp laceration, be stunned for a second or two, then extremely upset. I've sewn up many. A real-life, no-nonsense criminal with a blackjack (a piece of iron weighing several pounds) has a much better success rate. The real-life result is a large number of deaths and permanent damage from brain hemorrhage.

Critics of TV violence claim it teaches children sadism and cruelty. The critics have it backward. Children can't learn to enjoy cruelty from the neat, sanitized mayhem on the average series. There isn't any! What they learn is far more malignant: that guns or fists are efficient, exciting ways to deal with a difficult situation.

Truth in advertising laws eliminated many absurd commercial claims. I often daydream about what would happen if we had "truth in

violence"—if every show had to pass scrutiny by doctors who could insist that any action scene have at least a vague resemblance to medical reality. ("Stop the projector! You have your hero waylaid by three thugs who beat him brutally before he struggles free. The next day he shows up with a cute little bandage over his eyebrow. We can't pass that. You'll have to add one swollen eye, three missing teeth, at least 20 stitches over the lips and eyes and a wired jaw. Got that? Roll 'em.")

Seriously, real-life violence is dirty, painful, bloody, disgusting. It causes mutilation and misery, and it doesn't solve problems. If we're genuinely interested in protecting our children, we should stop campaigning to "clean up" TV. It's already too antiseptic. Ironically, the problem with TV violence is that it's not violent enough.

—*TV GUIDE*, MARCH 31, 1984

RESPONSES

1. What does the author mean when he says that "the problem with TV violence is that it's not violent enough"? Explain why you agree or disagree with this statement.

2. According to the author, what effect does sanitized violence have on children? Discuss whether you agree with the solution he proposes and why. Suggest other possible solutions.

3. Compare the violence of a televised hockey fight with that of a staged fight in a TV drama. Do the two fights affect you in the same way? Explain.

4. How are fights in TV shows and films staged to mask the reality of their violence? Consider the special effects, sound effects, choreography, and music. To what extent does the knowledge of these kinds of special effects lessen the impact of the violence?

ISSUES FOR FURTHER STUDY

What is violence doing to us? And what should we be doing about it? This chapter has helped you examine ways violence is depicted and used in the media and popular culture. The question of its influence on audiences and consumers, however, has no easy answer. As you consider the following questions, or any other project you think is important to the study of violence, consider the ways violence influences you and whether your growing awareness of it will change its impact on you.

1. Violence in sports and the news existed before the mass media. Do you agree that media coverage encourages and/or intensifies real violence? Write an essay explaining why.

2. Critics charge that the media use violence because violence sells. Discuss why you agree or disagree with this statement. Consider why violence might sell and whether the statement applies to both real violence and fantasy violence.

3. How should the mass media balance their need for profit with their responsibility to audiences? Are the media only reflecting our culture and giving us what we want, even if that happens to be another edition of *Friday the 13th* or *The Texas Chainsaw Massacre*? Are the media exploiting their audiences and encouraging even more aggression and violence? What do you think the media's role should be? Why?

4. What are your concerns about violence in the mass media and popular culture? As a class, identify the issues you think are important. Working in groups, choose one issue to investigate. Outline the problems and propose possible solutions. You may find it helpful to consider the issue from differing points of view; for example, those expressed by a network programmer, a member of the audience, a parent of young children, an advertiser.

5. What do you think children should know about violence in the media? Make an instructional video or audiotape for children and/or their parents that presents this information.

6. Canadian communications expert, Marshall McLuhan, offers the following interesting and provocative view on the relationship between media and violence:

"The violence that all the electronic media inflict on their users is that they [the users] are instantly invaded and deprived of their physical bodies and are merged in a network of extensions of their own nervous systems. . . . The loss of individual and personal meaning via the electronic media ensures a corresponding and reciprocal violence from those so deprived of their identities; for violence, whether spiritual or physical, is a quest for identity and the meaningful. The less identity, the more the violence. Violence exerted by private individuals tends to have limited results, whereas the violence exerted by groups knows no bounds". . . .

Explain McLuhan's observation in your own words. Discuss your opinion of the observation. Relate his statement: "the less identity, the more the violence" to another of his statements: "A hijacker is a nobody who wants to become a somebody."

7. Choose a media product—a TV show (or scenes from it), cartoon, music video, scene from a film, song, newscast—that you think is too violent for children (or any audience) and make the content more suitable.

CHAPTER 8

Gender Roles

One of the most important and controversial issues in media studies is gender stereotyping, or sexism, and how it influences our perceptions of ourselves and others. Closely related to this issue is the depiction of sexuality in the media. The concern is: do the media simply mirror sexist tendencies that already flourish in our culture or do they magnify and distort these tendencies? Does the media's portrayal of sexuality give us misinformation about our own gender roles and sexuality? To what extent does objectification—the portrayal of humans as objects—occur?

Before you begin to explore these issues, make sure that you and your classmates understand and agree on the meaning of the following terms: sexism; gender; sexuality; stereotyping; masculinity; femininity. In groups, find the dictionary definitions and discuss how the words may have taken on additional meanings in today's usage.

A SURVEY OF SEXISM

While most of us are aware of sexism in our society (an awareness that is only recent), it is worthwhile to find out how extensive it is and what impact it can have. To do this, form groups and survey a variety of media, with each group focussing on one medium. For example, a group could: study a newspaper's articles and ads, including classified ads; watch an evening's television shows and commercials; study the lyrics and graphics of albums or tapes; or listen to one day's radio programs, morning and/or evening. To do your survey, ask yourself the following questions and any other questions you think are important in researching gender portrayal.

- Are males and females represented equally in terms of numbers and prominence?

- What jobs do men and women have?

- What ages are represented? Are there differences in the roles that are given to elderly men as opposed to elderly women?

- Are options for switching traditional roles ever presented, e.g., father as homemaker?

- How do men and women handle conflicts?

- Are men and women shown to use sexual persuasion to gain an advantage?

- What words are used to describe men and women?

You could also interview various people for their opinions of the way media portray gender roles. Interview parents, teachers, other adults, and peers about their opinions of sexism in the media. Interview some children about their perceptions of gender roles and try to find out if (and how) the media have helped to shape these perceptions. See page 212 for tips on interviewing.

As a class, compile the results of your surveys and interviews, and discuss your findings. Using examples from your survey, make a list of words that the media use to describe masculinity and femininity. How are they similar to and different from your definitions? As you continue this chapter, compare your survey and interview results with the ideas and information in the reading selections.

SEXISM AND STEREOTYPES

Why are stereotypes so common? One reason is that a stereotype provides us with an easy, shorthand way of looking at the world, a means of instant identification. Gender stereotypes are invariably oversimplified and convey, at best, half-truths about the nature of gender roles. Consider Chrissy, the stereotyped "dumb blonde" in *Three's Company*. She was guaranteed to commit several stupid and naive acts in each show. Or think about the concluding section of Alice Munro's *Boys and Girls*, which was made into an Academy Award-winning short film: the young daughter in the family begins to cry at the dinner table. "She's only a girl," says her father, illustrating the assumption that girls are inferior to boys ("only a girl") and their behaviour may be excused.

While some people would argue that the female stereotypes are more offensive, there are also many misleading male stereotypes. Ads often sell images of the rugged, macho loner—the Marlboro Man—or the wealthy man-about-town. Consider characters such as Magnum in *Magnum P.I.*, and James Bond—they are athletic, smart, attractive, and always tough and reliable, but have you ever met anyone who is really like them? At the other extreme, there is the "wimp" image. The question "What is a real man?" was asked often in the 1980s, and advertisers frequently tried to sell the answer.

How do you feel when someone tells you to consider only those jobs that are appropriate to the so-called female or male professions but your choice happens not to fit that mould? If you are a boy, how do you feel when you are sad or frustrated but suppress your feelings because you have heard that "big boys don't cry"? If you are a girl, how do you feel when you are called pushy or impolite if you have acted in a way that would be thought of as aggressive for boys?

The media are not the sole cause of sexism in our society, but even if they are only presenting a reflection of what already exists, they may be reinforcing gender stereotypes. It is important to be aware of what the media are saying about women and about men.

"An ad for Mr. Clean shows a woman who has gone quite bonkers over her dining room table waxing job. She sits at one end of the table and rubs it lovingly. If her husband found her this way, he most certainly would either return her to her mother or, if he were kind, suggest a shrink."

—Jane Trahey, president of Trahey-Wolf Advertising Agency

Traditionally, the male image of strength and dominance contrasted with the passive and dependent roles of mothers and homemakers assumed by many women. Women were represented as the so-called "weaker sex."

Professors of marketing Alice Courtney and Thomas Whipple, writing in *Canadian Perspectives on Sex Stereotyping in Advertising, 1978*, concluded that in print advertisements of the 1970s, four general stereotypical portrayals of women were shown:

1. A woman's place is in the home.
2. Women do not make important decisions or do important things.
3. Women are dependent and need men's protection.
4. Men regard women primarily as sexual objects.

Images of male strength and accomplishment, and of female passivity and caring, come from archetypes—models or patterns—that have been part of our culture for many years. Women as nurturing but dependent people is one such archetype. Another holds that women who are ambitious and intelligent are dangerous. Helen Porter, a Canadian story-teller, suggests that some of these archetypes were created by men who feared "the elemental power of women."

The Importance of the Archetype

an interview with Helen Porter

I think it's very important to know about the archetype today in the modern world because I think those female archetypes are still very much with us. One is that I think those archetypes were largely created by men, and the society in which those archetype stories arose was controlled by men who felt very, very frightened of the elemental power of women, so frightened of their ability to bear life and their ability to be close to nature, by the fact that they could bear children. There were many other reasons why these fearful archetypes arose. At one point women were very powerful. During the matriarchal period in history, women were very, very powerful. When the current period of history, the patriarchal period that we know now took over, men wished to control women and to control their extraordinary natural powers, and they did this by creating stories that made people frightened of women—stories such as the one of Lilith the demon woman, the one of Hecta, Queen of the Witches, and so on. In all mythology, they have these kinds of stories.

Today, we still have enormous fears of the elemental power of women. The fears, we express them in a more sophisticated way—we don't have witchcraft hunts: we don't take women and burn them in the city square. However, we do have pornography and we do have a lot of sex-role stereotyping on television and movies and in rock songs, and album covers—everywhere you look, in fact, there are archetypical messages about the dangers that lie within women, especially sexual women. Therefore, we reduce women to a very passive stereotype, a very rigid, robot-like, foolish woman that we hear in the commercials talking about Tide and Cheer or we see in fashion magazines, getting all excited over a lipstick or over nail polish. At the same time such a woman can be wearing a dog collar: it could be either a pearl-type dog collar or some kind of leather bracelet. There'll be the suggestion that even though this is a silly woman who's all excited about lipstick, this is a woman you have to control, she's going to be dangerous. Always you find those messages in advertising. Now we are starting to clear some of it up, but it's still powerful.

—MACLEAN HUNTER CABLE TV, 1986

IMAGES OF WOMEN

The images of women that Helen Porter describes in her interview may seem to be exaggerated but it was not really until the 1960s that North American men and women underwent a major reappraisal of their roles. In Canada, it was not until 1986 that the CRTC's (Canadian Radio-television and Telecommunications Commission) report called *Sex Role Stereotyping in the Broadcast Media, A Report on Industry Self-Regulation* recommended that the representation of women in the media should not be demeaning. The following is an excerpt from that report.

A. GENERAL ISSUES

i. Images

Although the word "image" tends to elicit thoughts of visual presentations, it also includes images evoked aurally. This section, therefore, applies to both radio and television. The cumulative impact of stereotyped images is of special significance, and is applicable to many of the points made in this document.

1. Broadcasting should include a wide variety of images reflecting the diversity of women in our culture. This includes:

a. women of all ages (the elderly as well as the young);

b. women of differing ethnic groups;

c. women of differing physical appearance.

2. Broadcasting should present women engaged in a wide variety of activities, including athletics.

3. Women should not be used as sexual stimuli or lures, or as attention-getting, but otherwise irrelevant, objects.

4. Broadcasting should not demean or degrade women through the images used to portray them.

ii. Language

1. Language should be inclusive and non-sexist when all persons are meant to be included. The so-called "generic" man is inappropriate, as are diminutive terms such as "girl" or "little lady."

2. Broadcasting should not demean or degrade women through language, as it does when it refers to men in the context of their accomplishments and to women merely in terms of their appearance.

iii. Roles

1. Women should not be presented only in so-called traditional roles. The role of homemaker, for example, is but one of women's contemporary roles.

2. Women should be presented in a more balanced and realistic way in

terms of their occupations or activities within contemporary society.

3. Men and children should be presented participating in household tasks.

4. Women are also authorities and experts and should be included and presented as such.

iv. Family and Interpersonal Relationships

1. When families are presented, the diversity of life styles that exist today should be reflected (for example, single parents and extended families).

2. Women should not be presented as subservient to and dependent on men.

3. Men should not be presented as always being the beneficiaries of services performed by women or products used by women.

4. No interpersonal relationship or lifestyle that is consistent with the maintenance of human dignity should be demeaned or degraded in broadcasting.

v. Personality

1. *Motive and needs*

a. Broadcasting should not play on women's fears, such as the fear of being sexually unattractive.

b. Women should not be presented as either excessively concerned with youth and beauty or neurotically afraid of aging.

c. Women should not be presented as being neurotically compulsive about cleanliness.

d. Broadcasting should not imply that the prime motivating factor for a woman is to catch a man.

2. *Traits*

a. Broadcasting should not demean or degrade women by presenting them as possessing predominantly negative traits, for example, "catty," dependent, incompetent, subservient, submissive, and so forth.

3. *Intellectual Factors*

a. Broadcasting should not involve a condescending presentation of women's intelligence and capabilities. It is demeaning and degrading to portray women as unintelligent and incapable.

b. Women should be presented as decision makers, and contributing significantly to society.

B. PROGRAMMING   In addition to all of the concerns in the above section, the following apply specifically to programming.

i. News, Public Affairs, Documentaries, Arts and/or Sciences

1. Women should be more adequately represented as news readers, reporters, and hosts.

2. Issues of special concern to women, such as sexual harassment, rape, or equal pay legislation, should receive more adequate coverage.

3. Women's events (such as conferences, demonstrations, press releases) should receive attention and coverage equal to that given to men's events.

4. Women's contributions (for example, in the artistic, scientific, economic fields) should be recognized and presented fairly.

5. Women's perspectives on issues of general interest (for example, the economy, elections, international events) should be included adequately in general reporting and comment (women as experts or authorities, and/or in giving public views).

ii. Sports

1. Participation of women in sports should receive fair and equitable coverage.

2. Women athletes should not be subject to patronizing or belittling treatment. . . .

Skier Laurie Graham. Media coverage of the 1987 Olympics was faulted for calling women athletes "girls" and "young ladies" and for referring to their physical appearance, as in "blonde bombshell."

C. COMMERCIALS

i. Women as Buyers

1. Women should not be presented in desperate need either of products or of assumed product benefits in order to meet alleged deficiencies or in order to satisfy or serve their adult companions or children.

2. Women buy a full range of products and services (including, for example, cars and bank loans), and commercials should reflect this more fairly.

3. Women are not exclusive buyers and users of products for the home, and commercials should reflect this as well.

4. Products such as cosmetics, fragrances, jewellery, and clothing should be presented as personally beneficial, not as a means to catch or please a man.

ii. Women as Sellers

1. Women should be presented as experts and authorities as well as men.
2. Voice-overs on TV and announcers on radio should be female as well as male (they are predominantly male now).
3. Women should be shown selling a wider range of products and services, not only those assumed to be for women.

D. OTHER

1. Male dominance and female submissiveness are at the very heart of the stereotypes of men and women. Pornography reflects the extreme portrayal of dominance and the exploitation of women's sexuality. Pornography, or any portrayal of violence against women, is the ultimate expression of dominance/submissiveness, the objectification of women. As such, pornography or the portrayal of violence against women has no place in the broadcast media.

RESPONSES

1. Based on your survey results, how far have the broadcast media progressed in their representations of women since Alice Courtney and Thomas Whipple's findings in the 1970s? Since the 1986 CRTC report? Use specific examples to support your answer.

2. Which media representations of women do you think are the most demeaning and/or the most harmful? Why? Why would some of the recommendations in the CRTC report be more difficult to implement than others?

3. Despite the CRTC report, the federal government has allowed media industries to regulate themselves. The CRTC usually will not intervene except in extreme cases, such as slander and obscenity. In groups, discuss why you agree or disagree with the following statement: "The media industries have not shown that they can regulate themselves; therefore, the CRTC recommendations must be made law."

4. In groups, write a short skit that deliberately uses gender stereotyping in plot and dialogue. Then re-write it without the sexist content and according to the CRTC recommendations. Share your two versions with other groups. Discuss the kinds of changes you had to make and whether everyone agreed on what was sexist.

Consider the traditional stereotypes—and archetypes—of males. You may want to refer to the survey (page 352) of gender roles you did at the beginning of the chapter. The following magazine column describes some of these roles and the progress that has been made in TV portrayals of men.

Male-Watching

by Penney Kome

Tom Selleck in *Three Men and a Baby*. This "new sexism" is big business; the film grossed $102.2 million in six weeks.

We often hear that feminists resent how women are projected in the media, but what about how men are portrayed? Most feminists would agree that stereotyping harms both sexes and presents false images of men as well as women, but I think it's time to take this a little further. The most aggressive, vicious, unprovoked violence in the mainstream entertainment media has usually been male-on-male, as in the all-male army movies and cops and robbers shows. For years, in certain shows, it was even unmanly to speak in complete sentences. Alan Alda challenged that stereotype. What is replacing it?

I speak as one who has finally moved her TV into the living room, where it gets more use. Twirling the dial, I find things have changed. Click: a talk show about men, with two men defending the feminist analysis of sports and war. Click: a program about a macho stud who behaves like a cad and loses everything including his career and his girl-

friend. Click: the A Team's Mr. T takes time out from being mean and is tender with a child. There is something refreshing—almost intoxicating—in seeing men on TV acting human. Only when they're represented that way is it apparent how many dimensions have been missing from male characterizations.

It seems to me that many people who criticize the mass media also pride themselves on never watching TV. Personally, most of the time I'd rather read a good book. But I think it's very risky to act as a TV critic without being a regular viewer. The medium, by its very nature, changes quickly. We have come a

H. sapiens (modern)

60   70   80

long way since *The Honeymooners* and *Father Knows Best*. I doubt that a current situation comedy would dare present wife battering as a joke, as in Jackie Gleason's repeated threat to his TV wife Alice: "You want to go to the moon?" And—it occurs to me now—in those programs that still present women as sexy but schizy scatterbrains, the men tend to come across as flaming idiots you'd be embarrassed to introduce to your parents. We are talking here about the lowest common denominator, with emphasis on the word low.

There is nothing new in the notion that most TV programming insults the viewer's intelligence. What *is* new is that most adventure programs have incorporated a nonviolent philosophy, and that some sitcoms now send up men's discomfort in expressing their feelings. I think that anyone who chooses carefully can finally find appropriate light entertainment suitable for any age group. Those who believe that the medium itself is pernicious, of course, will never be satisfied with the mainstream programming. But this is one person who brought her TV out of the closet, and was pleasantly surprised.

—HOMEMAKER'S,
JANUARY/FEBRUARY 1985

RESPONSES

1. Find examples of TV portrayals or ads that objectify males. Discuss your reactions to them. In what kinds of magazines or newspapers did you find the print ads? What do you think is the target market for the TV shows and ads?

2. Some of the same stereotypes that for years were used to depict women have been newly assigned to men, e.g., men as incompetent bumblers and sex objects. Discuss your opinion of "reverse sexism." Is this trend simply a new and relatively harmless advertising gimmick? Is the danger of creating and/or reinforcing stereotypes of men as great as it was for women? Give examples to support your opinion.

3. Think of media images that portray men in both traditional and "new" stereotypes. In groups, enact several of these images in short skits, or write a short play in which you imagine several of these characters at some function. What would be their typical appearance? their favourite expressions? typical conflicts? their sources of happiness and fun? If you have the equipment, videotape the skit or play and show it to the class.

4. Using the CRTC Report as a guide, write some guidelines and recommendations for the solution of the problem of male stereotyping in the broadcast media.

TV Portrayals Praised for Realism

by Associated Press

The report of the National Commission on Working Women, 1984, revealed some positive steps toward shattering sexual stereotypes, both male and female. As you read the following AP (Associated Press) newspaper article about the report, consider whether these are real steps forward or just token efforts.

Cagney and Lacey stars Tyne Daly (left) and Sharon Gless (right). The show is often praised for its progressive portrayal of women.

In its new shows, television is doing better at portraying women as they really are instead of picturing American womanhood as mostly "young, white, single, beautiful," the National Commission on Working Women said yesterday.

And TV is giving a new picture of the American male, the commission said: "Instead of being locked into aggressive roles, some male TV characters on the new fall shows actually care for their children, love their families, and do so without being objects of ridicule."

The Cosby Show was cited as an example.

The commission, a non-profit organization that does research on the status of the 60 percent of American women who work outside the home, made public an analysis of the treatment of women characters in the 1984 TV season.

It said the shows are getting away

> **Although most shows are still all white, 18% of female characters are members of racial minorities . . .**

from the pattern of the last 12 years, when "the prevailing picture of female TV characters was of young, white, single, beautiful women."

"In addition to the increasing number of female characters on television this year, they are more diverse than in years past, and more of them have strong roles," the report said. "In shows like *Jessie*; *Murder, She Wrote*; *V*; and *Kate and Allie*, females are the stars. Their characters show leadership, authority and courage."

The report welcomed "the emergence of men as nurturers" on TV as "one of the most encouraging signs this season."

The report also said:

Ten years ago, men outnumbered women in TV roles 3–1, but in the 1984 season, of 143 new TV characters, 67 are women.

Although most shows are still all white, 18 percent of female char-

acters are members of racial minorities, compared with 7 percent last year. *The Cosby Show*, a situation comedy featuring a black male doctor married to a black woman lawyer, accounts for much of the increase.

Only 36 percent of families on the new shows are traditional, two-parent families. Out of 14 families, two are headed by single men, three by divorced women, one by a widow and two by non-parent adults.

Seventy-six percent of adult female TV characters in new shows have jobs outside the home. Women are often shown at work. Many hold unusual jobs—police detective, spy, photographer-detective, helicopter pilot, musician-detective, mystery writer, model.

There has been an increase in the number of divorced female TV characters, who now account for 10 percent of all women on TV, and of female characters who are widows, 9 percent.

Issues of concern to women are the subject of some shows. "Perhaps because there is a small but increasing number of women writers behind the scenes," the report said, "some female TV characters sound less like stereotypes and more like real women and some shows' plots revolve around the actual concerns of women." Examples include divorced homemakers going back to college, working parents trying to find time together, and single mothers raising children alone.

But some stereotypes remain, the commission found. Most female characters are still young, white and single, and the "female as victim" is a major theme of action shows such as *Mickey Spillane's Mike Hammer* where "beautiful women get killed each week and the only continuing female character is the curvaceous secretary, Velda, who comes to work in extremely tight, low-cut dresses."

—AP, AS PUBLISHED IN *THE GLOBE AND MAIL*, TORONTO DECEMBER 6, 1984

RESPONSES

1. Compare the information reported by the National Commission on Working Women with your survey results. What current television shows would confirm the positive patterns the commission noted, e.g., female characters who "show leadership, authority and courage"?

2. Write a review of a current television show in which you assess the portrayal of gender roles. See page 215 in the Reference Section for tips on writing reviews.

3. The article refers to American TV shows only. Using examples, explain how the points raised in the article do or do not apply to Canadian shows.

ROLE MODELS

Our sense of identity is basic to our well-being and to our self-fulfillment. Basic to a definition of self is our gender identity. How we look and feel about being female or male is often conditioned by our role models: our parents, our peers and, more recently, the pervasive images of the media. Young people who are in search of role models are especially vulnerable to the variety of images confronting them today. The media may offer us images of what we desire to be, or influence what we think we should be. The following excerpts describe the kinds of role models the media and our popular culture give us and suggest how they are often constructions of reality, not a reflection of real life.

Rock 'n' Role models. Identify the celebrities of this look-alike contest. In one or two words, summarize the image presented by each.

Invented in 1959 by Mattel Inc., the Barbie doll—with her huge wardrobe and many accessories—is still a popular commodity for millions of young girls. A successful pop icon—an object or image that is held in high regard or worshipped—the Barbie doll raises questions not only about gender stereotyping but also about the happiness associated with owning consumer goods.

I Want to Be a Barbie Doll When I Grow Up:
The Cultural Significance of the Barbie Doll

by Marilyn Ferris Motz

The voluptuous plastic Barbie Doll is an object familiar to almost every American. Probably the most popular doll ever produced, Barbie, at twenty-five years of age, is already raising her second generation of children. She has appeared in countless newspaper and magazine stories and cartoons and has even entered into our everyday speech. Barbie has become an icon. Much more than a mere toy, she has come to represent much of what we, as Americans, most admire and fear about ourselves. She embodies our love/hate relationship with our consumption-oriented society. As a model for feminine behavior, Barbie is curiously outdated. Perhaps she was an anachronism even at the time she was invented in the late 1950s. Yet she functions as an icon because she represents so well the values of modern American society, devoting herself to the pursuit of happiness through leisure and material goods. Elizabeth and Stewart Ewen have defined fashion as a language of "social dialogue in which desires are expressed, and symbolically met." This is the language that Barbie speaks, and she translates it for children, teaching them the skills by which their future success will be measured: purchase of the proper high-status goods, popularity with their peers, creation of the correct personal appearance, and the visible achievement of "fun" through appropriate leisure activities. . . . Writing in the feminist magazine *Ms.* in 1979, Jane Leavy describes the Barbie doll as "a stereotype made flesh—"well, vinyl, anyway," retaining "the shape and sensibility of the year she was born, 1959," while teaching girls to be "sex objects and consumers." . . . *The Saturday Evening Post* in 1964 articulated the concern many Americans felt even then about the influence of the Barbie doll. William K. Zinsser writes sarcastically that Barbie truly "is a person of sensitivity and taste, a fit model for American girlhood, which sees projected in her—in her lavish clothes, coiffures and activities—

its dream of the ideal life.'' Zinsser goes on to discuss the extent to which the Barbie doll may reveal some unpleasant truths about our society. ''With its emphasis on possession and its worship of appearance, it is modern America in miniature—a tiny parody of our pursuit of the beautiful, the material, and the trivial.''

The Barbie doll was the first doll to have a fully developed woman's body and she outdoes her predecessors in the volume of her clothes and accessories. From the middle of the nineteenth century to the middle of the twentieth century, baby dolls were the overwhelming favorite of girls and parents. The girl playing with her baby doll reflected both the childlike innocence and the maternal nature attributed to the ideal woman. These dolls represented cultural values to adults and taught them to children, placing motherhood as the central experience in a woman's life.

By the late twentieth century, American society had shifted its focus from woman as mother to woman as sexual and social being. The baby doll has been joined, perhaps even supplanted, by the fashion doll as a favorite girls' toy. . . .

A perusal of the shelves of Barbie paraphernalia in a local Toys 'R Us store reveals not a single item of clothing suitable for an office. Mattel did produce a doctor's outfit and astronaut suit for Barbie, but the clothes failed to sell. According to Mattel's marketing manager, ''We

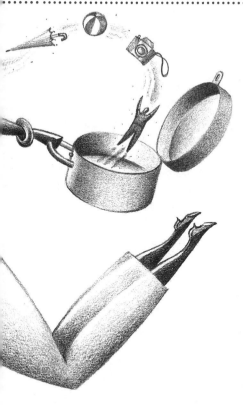

only kept the doctor's uniform in the line as long as we did because public relations begged us to give them something they could point to as progress," in avoiding stereotyped roles for women. In the 1960s, Mattel produced "all the elegant accessories" for the patio, including a telephone, television, radio, fashion magazines and a photograph of Barbie and Ken. The "Busy Barbie," created in 1972, had hands that could grasp objects and came equipped with a telephone, television, record player, "soda set" with two glasses and a tray, and a travel case. Apparently Barbie kept busy only with leisure activities; she seems unable to grasp a book or a pen. When Barbie went to college in the 1970s, her "campus" con-

sisted of a dormitory room, soda shop (with phone booth), football stadium, and a drive-in movie! Today Barbie travels in her camper, rides her horse, plays with her dog and cat, swims in her pool and lounges in her bubble bath (both with real water). . . .

Not only is Barbie a conspicuous consumer who lives a life of leisure; standing as she does, on her toes, she is as immobilized as the nineteenth-century woman that Thorstein Veblen described in *The Theory of the Leisure Class*. Indeed, Veblen writes that in societies in which women are expected to confer status on their husbands and fathers through their display of leisure activities, "the ideal requires delicate and diminutive hands and feet and a slender waist. These features, together with the other, related faults of structure that commonly go with them, go to show that the person so affected is incapable of useful effort and must therefore be supported in idleness by her owner. She is useless and expensive, and she is consequently valuable as evidence of [high status]." Consequently, Veblen continues, "women take thought to alter their persons, so as to conform more nearly to the requirements of the instructed taste of the time," while men learn to "find the resulting artificially induced pathological features attractive." With her miniscule hands, feet and waist, Barbie presents just such a model of feminine beauty. Indeed her $33 \times 18 \times 28$ figure is similar to those of women who were laced into corsets in the nineteenth century. Perhaps in modern American society, when few women are willing or able to provide such ostentatious consumption and leisure, the doll itself provides the ritual family display of female uselessness. . . .

Barbie clearly expects to achieve success on the basis of her social skills. The "Queen of the Prom," a Barbie board game produced in 1961 and 1962, had as its goal being crowned Prom Queen, a feat accomplished by getting a date with a popular boy, buying an appropriate prom dress, and being elected

> **With the creation of Barbie and her friends, Mattel enabled children to buy themselves an entire peer group . . .**

president of a school club. In the 1960s the Barbie doll could be either a cheerleader or a drum majorette. She had special outfits not only for sports activities, but also for "a lunch date, an after-five date, a Friday night date, Saturday Matinee, theater date, golden evening" and a masquerade party. Of the 64 outfits available for Barbie in 1963, seventeen were evening clothes.

Barbie's world consisted of numerous friends, many of whom are no longer produced. By joining the Barbie Fan Club a girl could, in the 1970s, receive a poster signed by all the members of Barbie's social circle with such sentiments as "Be good, Ken," "Your friend Barbie," "To my friend, Skipper,"

"With love, Francie," and "Do Your Thing, P.J." The pictures on the boxes that house Barbie's pool and other accessories show Barbie happily involved with her friends. One collector estimates that Barbie's entourage has included at one time or another 52 different friends, relatives and pets. Describing contemporary American society in 1950, David Riesman wrote that "making good becomes almost equivalent to making friends, or at any rate the right kind of friends." When popularity, or acceptance by one's peers, becomes the primary goal in life, then "people and friendships are viewed as the greatest of all consumables; the peer group is itself a main object of consumption." With the creation of Barbie and her friends, Mattel enabled children to buy themselves an entire peer group, to "collect friends" quite literally.

Despite changes in the lives and expectations of real women, Barbie remains essentially the woman described by Veblen in the 1890s, excluded from the world of work with its attendant sense of achievement, forced to live a life based on leisure activities, personal appearance, the accumulation of possessions, and the search for popularity. While large numbers of women reject this role, Barbie embraces it. The Barbie doll serves as an icon that symbolically conveys to children and adults the measures of success in modern America: be rich, be beautiful, be popular and above all, have fun.

—*POPULAR CULTURE READER*, 1983

RESPONSES

1. If you or your classmates still have any Barbie and Ken dolls and their clothes and accessories bring them to class. Or find some ads for Barbie in catalogues and flyers. Discuss the dolls in light of Marilyn Ferris Motz's article.

2. a) If you played with Barbie and Ken or other dolls as a child, discuss the games you played and situations you portrayed. How important were the dolls in influencing your behaviour?
   b) If you know children who play with dolls now, observe the situations they portray. How is their play similar to and different from yours? Discuss possible reasons for any differences. (Remember your study of children's games in the Violence chapter.)

3. Discuss how Barbie embodies the elements listed by Marilyn Ferris Motz: "high status goods, popularity with peers, creation of the correct personal appearance and the visible achievement of fun." Why do you think Barbie has lasted so long as an icon of our popular culture?

4. Is Ken the male equivalent of Barbie? Explain the kind of male image Ken projects.

5. The author writes that Barbie "represents so well the values of modern American society." Discuss whether or not Barbie also represents the values of Canadian society.

6. Discuss the following statement: "Barbie and Ken influence their owners to have false expectations about body image and unhealthy consumer habits." What examples does the author give of "false expectations about body image"? What do you think the author means by "unhealthy consumer habits"?

7. In groups, write and dramatize a short skit in which Barbie, Ken, and G.I. Joe have an evening out together. From the results, what did you learn about the image of each doll? You might want to videotape the skit and show it to the class.

8. Write an essay on the roles of Barbie and Ken as contemporary pop icons.

Barbie and Ken may embody false images of beauty and what bodies look like. Beauty, it is said, is "in the eye of the beholder." The beholder, however, is often influenced by current trends in popular culture as shown to us by the media. For example, what was thought to be attractive in the 1960s may be considered quite the opposite today. This excerpt, and the quotes that follow, describe the "cult of the thin" of the 1980s.

One Size Does Not Fit All:

Being Beautiful, Thin and Female in America

by Jane Caputi

In contemporary America, not only sex appeal, but beauty, success, intelligence, morality, health, and likeability are just some of the qualities that are put to the sales. For example, one study of college admission rates found that overweight girls have only one third the chance of being admitted to prestigious colleges as slim girls with identical records. In college, as everywhere else, only one female body type is socially valued—the trim line, slender-all, maxithin, or Virginia slim. Even our consumer products display the desired form for the cult of the thin has invaded every facet of the culture. The thin ideal is visually preached not only by commodities, but by celebrity images, fashion models, and rituals such as beauty contests. It is acted out for us by "weight saints" such as Jane Fonda and Richard Simmons. It is prescribed by best-selling diet and workout books, women's magazines and TV shows, and shamed into us by the unfunny jokes of family and friends or the unfriendly, but trendy advice of health professionals.

—*POPULAR CULTURE READER*, 1983

"I won't even lick a postage stamp—one never knows about calories."

—ESTHER, AN ANOREXIC

"The modern cult of women's beauty has nothing to do with what women naturally look like, which is why *Playboy* doesn't run pictures of pregnant women or average women, and heavily airbrushes its carefully selected beauties."

—UNA STANNARD, "THE MASK OF BEAUTY," 1971

RESPONSES

1. Survey the visual media—the models in ads, television characters, music videos, film—to confirm our culture's obsession with the image of the slim woman. What women in the media or in prominent public positions depart from this image? Discuss the problems that this idea of beauty creates for women and for society .

2. Look through some women's magazines that offer the latest diets and fitness advice and then note the number of ads for food. How many of the ads are for food that might be considered fattening? What is the connection between the cult of thinness and eating disorders such as anorexia nervosa and bulimia? Find some case studies in books and magazines and discuss them.

3. Is physical appearance as significant for men as it is for women? Do you think people are less concerned about dieting and slimness for men? Give reasons for your answers. What role do men play in perpetuating the slim woman image?

4. Find some images of male and/or female standards of beauty from the past. Depending on how far back you want to go, you could look through art books, old magazines, old movies, books about old movies, or find a book on the subject. How have these images changed through the years? Share your findings with the class.

5. How do standards of beauty vary in different cultures? If you have lived or travelled in other countries, perhaps you could give some insight. Refer to your examination of transnational advertising in the Advertising chapter, and discuss how western perceptions of beauty may affect the perceptions of people in other countries.

Musicians are often powerful role models. Think of some performers and the images you think they convey to their fans. With music videos, the performers' images — their clothes, style, movements — have become much more visible. Madonna, for example, has had a loyal following of young people, especially among those who make up the biggest audience for music videos, the 10-15 year olds. How much do you think fans are affected by the messages stars like Madonna send? Think about this as you read the following excerpt from an article about her.

Madonna Rocks the Land

My image to people, I think, is that I'm this brazen, aggressive young woman who has an O.K. voice with some pretty exciting songs, who wears what she wants to wear and says what she wants to say and who has potential as an actress. Sex symbol? That is such a weird question. I guess I would be perceived as that because I have a typically voluptuous body and because the way I dress accents my femininity, and because a lot of what I am about is just expressing sexual desire and not really caring what people think about it. Maybe that would make you a sex symbol. I don't know. There is a very modest side to me too. How far away is the

Opposite Page: How has Madonna's image shifted from the one she presents here?

image from me? It's about 20 steps away.

Phenomenon.

I'm not really sure what is going on. My fans come from a wide age range. I think it goes beyond sexuality. Maybe my fearlessness and courage give people a good feeling. I think I have a real sweetness inside and love for life and a good sense of humor. Maybe people see that. I think a lot of people are afraid to express themselves that way, so maybe they feel they can attach themselves to an innocence and joy. I believe that dreams come true: that you can do what you want to do. I don't mean that in a *Rocky III* kind of way either. I don't mean you have to go out and conquer the world and be a star. I mean, I came from a boring sort of middle-class lifestyle and a big family and I wasn't born with a perfect body.

It all has to do with an attitude and loving yourself the way you are. Think of all the anorexics and suicides. Young people seem to be obsessed with not liking themselves. I don't think that what I'm trying to say is hard to understand. I don't go overboard really in any direction. I don't shave the side of my head. My hair is not pink. I don't feel that I'm putting on a costume. It's part of my personality and the mood that I'm in. Also I think that for the last 10 or 20 years, that part of a women has been suppressed. There has been the feeling that it's not right to want to dress up and be feminine, because women think that if they indulge in that, men won't respect them or take them seriously. Maybe kids now see someone in the public eye doing what I do. Maybe that's the phenomenon and why young girls are dressing up like me—because finally someone else is showing that it's OK. . . .

—TIME, MAY 27, 1985

Letters to the editors of *Time*

As one of the many Madonna Wanna Be's, I found your article helped me understand why I admire this woman. It is fun for me, a 15-year-old, to dress up like Madonna. I get the attention I long for, yet people know I am not like the trashy outfits I wear.
Gwyneth Joy Magdalena Creitz
Rockville, Md.

If I had my life to live over again, I would do it like Madonna. Instead of forging forward into a man's world by repressing my femininity, I would start out showing all my stuff and screaming, "Take me or leave me." Thank goodness for the continuing evolution of the feminist movement. Now someone like Madonna blossoms, and someone like me, a 35-year-old "successful attorney," hunts for black push-up bras, and we both do it without guilt.
Deborah L. Arron
Seattle, Wash.

Madonna is like a marshmallow: light and sugary but without substance.
Matt Bodie
Cockeysville, Md.

RESPONSES

1. Account for the popularity of Madonna. Refer not only to her comments but also to the letters from her fans. Examine the lyrics of some of her songs and describe the various images she has portrayed. What are the messages associated with these images?

2. Some people have suggested that the way Madonna flaunts her sexuality on stage and in videos is a setback for feminists. How does Madonna, as well as some of her fans, deny this? Explain why you agree or disagree that celebrities have a responsibility to their fans about the messages they send. Discuss this in groups.

3. David Bowie, like Madonna, has had a number of different personas, or images, in his career, from Ziggy Stardust to the "thin white duke." Trace the careers of a few bands or performers and describe how their images have changed over the years. Find examples that show how their styles have been imitated by their fans.

4. How much importance do you place on a performer's style as you form your opinion of a song or an entire album? To help you measure this, imagine some of your current favourite songs being performed by another performer or band. Enact some of these scenarios by lip-synching a song by one performer while copying the style and dress of another. Discuss the importance of style to the success of a performer.

5. Write a brief biography of a woman (or women) in the music industry who you think has broken away from the traditional role of women in rock.

6. Choose some songs that you think contain some feminist values and some that you consider to be negative toward women. In groups, listen to and discuss the songs. What images or symbols are used? How does the melody and performance of the song enhance the meaning?

CHANGE AND PROGRESS

We are still experiencing the effects of the new electronic media and the sexual liberation of the 1960s. Many people think the outcome of these changes has been mostly positive, but it is difficult to predict if people will still feel that way in the future. It will also be interesting to see the effects that our responses to the media's use of sexual stereotyping and misleading messages about sexuality will have in the future. How can we respond? Even an awareness and understanding of the way the media works is a progressive step. Discuss the following quotes and your ideas about the need for change in the media's portrayals of men and women.

"The mass media have a virtual monopoly on large-scale communication, and they reinforce sexist values and pornographic conventions. We have to find ways to counteract this power and influence. We must find the ways and means to substitute a true plurality of images and meanings for the false "average" or stereotyped meanings created by the mass media."

—VARDA BURSTYN, *WOMEN AGAINST CENSORSHIP*, 1985

"I don't think law is the answer to start legislating new attitudes. I think it has to come through the imagination of people. So, we've got to change the storytelling in the media; we've got to change the storytelling that goes on in advertising, in commercials, in fashion layouts and magazines, in the pornographic magazines . . . Instead of this man over women, men dominating women, we've got to see a mutuality and equality. . . . In short, we are taking into account a need to raise up the archetypes and to make them more human."

—HELEN PORTER, IN AN INTERVIEW ON *MACLEAN HUNTER CABLE TV*, 1986

ISSUES FOR FURTHER STUDY

Where do we go from here? What are some answers to the complex social and moral issues of sexism and sexuality in the media? Can you propose some alternatives and some strategies for change? You may have found that there are films, literature, and television shows that present non-sexist views of the world. But will they prevail over the typical images that command our attention—images of dominant men and submissive women, of consumer goods that are portrayed erotically, of misleading sexual portrayals, or of violence that is associated with sexuality?

Varda Burstyn asserts that "we must find the means and ways to substitute a true plurality of images and meanings for the false 'average' or stereotypical meanings created by the mass media." Do you agree? Why?

The following questions ask you to think some more about the issues dealt with in this chapter, and to do some further research. Knowing the problems is the first step in solving them. You might want to brainstorm to develop other related questions or problems.

1. What are your solutions to the problems and issues raised by the material in this chapter? How would you initiate changes? It may be appropriate to hold a forum on this topic in your school. Invite members of your community to present their views. You might include teachers, feminists, members of the clergy, social workers (or people from a rape crisis centre, members of the police force, or staff from women's shelters), and people who work in the media.

2. Write an assessment of the social and sexual messages in one or more of the following:
a) current teen films
b) images of beauty in popular culture—a detailed study of male and female representations
c) exercise clubs—their philosophy, their advertising, the participants and their motivation
d) the world of professional modeling—the nature of their business, what models feel their role is, and how they feel about their influence on people

3. Research some of the arguments for and against censorship in the media.

4. Write reviews of two or three Hollywood films from a feminist perspective.

5. Examine a variety of male images or archetypes in the media.

6. Write a report on non-sexist representations in the media. You could consider several media and assess current examples or focus on one medium. Or, propose some ideas for scripts that deal with issues in a non-sexist way or present sexuality in a caring and consensual way.

7. Examine the textbooks you are currently studying—for example, history, marketing, family studies, literature, math, languages, and this text—for possible sexist messages. Write your findings in a report or in chart form.

8. "Rock video is generally very conservative, a '50s throwback to when men were seen as active and women passive." By referring to a good cross section of rock video, discuss the validity of this statement. View several rock videos and assess the following: the portrayal of relationships between men and women; the definition of happiness; typical heroes and villains; gender roles.

9. Prepare a study of women in film. You could report on women who are directors, actors, and/or screenwriters. Or, examine gender role portrayals in recent films.

INDEX

ACKNOWLEDGEMENTS

Chapter 1

p. 16, **Popular Culture: quote** from Introduction to *The Popular Culture Reader*, 3rd edition, edited by Christopher D. Geist and Jack Nachbar. Reprinted by permission of Bowling Green University Popular Press. p. 20, excerpts from **Pop Goes the Culture:** Copyright 1986 Time Inc. All rights reserved. Reprinted by permission from TIME. p. 23, **What's In and What's Out:** by Rosie DiManno. Reprinted with permission, The Toronto Star Syndicate. pp. 26-28, **American Fads:** excerpts from pp. 7-8, 167-172, from *American Fads* by Richard A. Johnson. Reprinted by permission of William Morrow & Co. p. 30, **Adaptation of fast food poem:** from *Ronald Revisited: The World of Ronald McDonald* by permission of The Popular Press, Bowling Green State University. p. 31, McDonald's advertising slogan: by kind permission of McDonald Restaurants of Canada Ltd. **The Image-Makers: quote** from *The Image-Makers* by William Meyers. Copyright © 1984 by William Meyers. Reprinted by permission of Times Books, a Division of Random House, Inc. **Grinding It Out: The Making of McDonald's: quote** from *Grinding It Out: The Making of McDonald's* © 1977 by Ray Kroc and Robert Anderson. Reprinted by permission of Contemporary Books, Inc. Chicago. pp. 33-35, **The Psychology of Fast Food Happiness:** by Gregory Hall, from *Ronald Revisited: The World of Ronald McDonald* by permission of The Popular Press, Bowling Green State University. pp. 38-40, **The Malling of Main Street:** excerpts from *The Malling of America* by William Severini Kowinski. Copyright © 1985 by William Severini Kowinski. By permission of William Morrow & Co. pp. 43-48, **Shop Till You Drop:** by Ian Pearson. Originally published in *Saturday Night* magazine, May 1986, in a much longer form. Copyright © 1986, Ian Pearson. Used by permission. p. 48, **The Nature of Celebrity:** adapted from *Celebrity* by James Monaco. Copyright © 1978 by James Monaco. Reprinted by permission of Virginia Barber Literary Agency. pp. 50-53, **The Meaning of Celebrity:** excerpts from *The Meaning of Celebrity* by Barbara Goldsmith. Copyright © 1983 by Barbara Goldsmith. Reprinted by permission of International Creative Management. First published in The New York Times, Dec. 4, 1983. Copyright © New York Times Company. Reprinted by permission.

Chapter 2

pp. 63-65, **Television and Our Private Lives:** by Jeanne Betancourt. Copyright (1981 or 1985), *Channels* Magazine. Reprinted by permission. p. 64. **Feiffer** (cartoon) copyright 1981, Jules Feiffer, reprinted with permission of Universal Press Syndicate. All rights reserved. p. 67, **Calvin and Hobbes** (cartoon) copyright 1986, Universal Press Syndicate, reprinted with permission. All rights reserved. pp. 67-69, **Why You Watch What You Watch When You Watch:** by Paul Klein. Reprinted with permission from *TV Guide Magazine.* Copyright © 1971 by Triangle Publications, Inc., Radnor, Pennsylvania. pp. 71-72, **A Child's Garden of Fantasy** by Bruno Bettelheim. Copyright © (1981 or 1985), *Channels* Magazine. Reprinted by permission. pp. 77-80, **Soaps' Search for Tomorrow:** by Brian D. Johnson. Reprinted by permission of *Maclean's* Magazine. pp. 89-92, **Blueberry Bicycle, Spirit Bay:** Screenplay by Amy Jo Cooper from a story by Donna Young. Copyright 1984 by Amy Jo Cooper. Reprinted by permission. p. 95-97, **Arabs – TV's Villains of Choice:** by Jack G. Shaheen. Copyright (1984 or 1985), *Channels* Magazine. Reprinted by permission. p. 97. **Networks Read Those Cards and Letters:** by Sally Steenland, deputy director of the National Commission on Working Women. From *Media and Values*, #40-41, Summer/Fall 1987. Reprinted by permission of *Media and Values*, a quarterly resource for media awareness education. Centre for Media and Values, 1962 South Shenandoah, Los Angeles, CA 90034. In Canada: 85 St. Clair Avenue E. Toronto, Ontario, M4T 1M8. pp. 99-101, **TV As a Shaper of Culture:** by Christopher Reed. Reprinted by permission of Christopher Reed and *The Globe and Mail*, Toronto. pp. 104-107, **The First Law of Commercial Television:** excerpt from *Jolts: The TV Wasteland and the Canadian Oasis* by Morris Wolfe. Copyright © 1985 by James Lorimer & Co. Ltd. Reprinted by permission. pp. 109-111, **The Age of Show Business:** by Neil Postman from *Amusing Ourselves To Death* by Neil Postman. Copyright © 1985 by Neil Postman. All rights reserved. Reprinted by permission of Viking Penguin Inc. and William Heinemann Limited. pp. 114-117, **On Top of the News in Prime Time:** by Martin Knelman. Copyright © (1984 or 1985), *Channels* Magazine. Reprinted by permission.

Chapter 3
pp. 130-133, **John Hughes: The Teen Film Director as Auteur:** by Theressa Puchta. Reprinted with permission of the author. p. 135. **Yonge Street Saturday Night:** by Raymond Souster. Reprinted from *Collected Poems of Raymond Souster* by permission of Oberon Press. pp. 141-145, **The Pure and the Impure:** by Pauline Kael. From *Taking It All In* by Pauline Kael. Copyright © 1984 by Pauline Kael. Reprinted by permission of Henry Holt and Co., Inc. and Marion Boyars Publishers Ltd., London, New York. Originally apeared in *The New Yorker*. p. 149, **This Is Where We Came In:** by Martin Knelman. Excerpt from *This Is Where We Came In: The Career and Character of Canadian Film* by Martin Knelman. Used by permission of the Canadian Publishers, McClelland and Stewart, Toronto. pp. 153-155, **Conjuring Up a Lost Age of Innocence:** by Brian Johnson. Reprinted by permission of *Maclean's* magazine. pp. 157-160, **Hollywood Since 1975: Some Fast Cuts:** adapted from "Ten Years That Shook the World" by Jim Hoberman. Published in *American Film*, June 1985. Adapted by permission of Georges Borchardt, Inc. and the author. Copyright © 1985 by Jim Hoberman.

Chapter 4
pp. 169-172 **Institutional Sound** by Gary Gumpert and pp. 174-177, **Walls of Sound:** by Gary Gumpert. Excerpts from *Talking Tombstones and Other Tales of the Media Age* by Gary Gumpert. Copyright © 1987 by Oxford University Press, Inc. Reprinted by permission. p. 176, **Nestlings** (cartoon). Reprinted with permission of Warren Clements/Sylvan Press. p. 178, **How Much Rock Groups Make** and p. 180, **Hot 100 Singles** (chart): Copyright © 1987 by Billboard Publications, Inc. Reprinted with permission. pp. 180-183, **How Hits Are Made: Radio's Rating Game:** by Rosalind Silver, Associate Editor of *Media and Values*. From *Media and Values*, Winter 1986. *Media and Values*, a quarterly resource for media awareness education. Centre for Media and Values, 1962 South Shenandoah, Los Angeles, CA 90034. In Canada: 85 St. Clair Avenue E. Toronto, Ontario, M4T 1M8. p. 183, **Hot Tracks** (chart): courtesy C100/Chum Canada. pp. 186-188, **The Bubble Has Popped for Teen-Oriented Music:** by Greg Quill. Reprinted with permission, The Toronto Star Syndicate. pp. 190-192, **What Pop Lyrics Say To Us Today:** by Robert Palmer. Copyright © 1985 by the New York Times Company. Reprinted by permission. pp. 195-197, **The Beat Goes Off: How Technology Gummed Up Rock's Grooves:** by Mark Hunter, Reprinted from *Harper's* Magazine, May 1987. p. 192, **Hartland** (cartoon): Reprinted with special permission of King Features Syndicate. p. 194, **Barron** (cartoon): Reprinted with permission, Toronto Star Syndicate. p. 200, **Blvd., Looking Ahead:** by Dave Watson, courtesy of *Rock Express*. p. 201, **INXS:** by John Robson. Copyright by Billboard Publications, Inc. Reprinted with permission. p. 201, **Idjah Hadidjah:** by J.D. Considine. Reprinted with permission of *Musician* Magazine. p. 202, **Luba, Between the Earth and Sky:** by Keith Sharp. Courtesy of *Rock Express*.

Chapter 5
p. 222, **People Who Own the News:** (map and chart) reproduced with permission of the Minister of Supply and Services Canada. pp. 228-231, **Lords of the Atlantic:** by Alexander Bruce. Reprinted with permission of *The Globe and Mail*, Toronto. p. 233, **Animal Crackers** (cartoon): Reprinted with permission, Tribune Media Services. p. 236,

Alberta Environment News Release: Reprinted with permission of Alberta Environment, Communications Branch. pp. 245-252, **As Time Goes By:** by David MacFarlane. Abridged from an article published in *Saturday Night* magazine, October 1983. Mr. MacFarlane is currently senior writer for *Toronto*. pp. 253-255, **Backstage Mozambique: A Flagrant Violant of Rights**, by Barbara Amiel. Reprinted by permission of *Maclean's* Magazine. pp. 256-257, **Amiel: Beyond the Fringe:** by Rick Salutin, copyright © 1984 by Rick Salutin. From *Marginal Notes* by Rick Salutin. Used by permission of Lester & Orpen Dennys Ltd., Toronto, Canada. pp. 259-261, **Television's Electronic Curse: Views of World Are Distorted:** by David Suzuki. Reprinted with the author's permission.

Chapter 6
pp. 267-272, **How To Produce Advertising That Sells:** by David Ogilvy. Reprinted from *Ogilvy on Advertising* by David Ogilvy. Copyright © 1983 by David Ogilvy. Used by permission of Crown Publishers, Inc. and Multimedia Publications (UK) Limited. pp. 275-278, **Psychographics:** by William Meyers. Excerpts from *The Image-Makers* by William Meyers. Copyright © 1984 by William Meyers. Reprinted by permission of Times Books, a Division of Random House, Inc. pp. 282-285, **Meet Me Tonight in TV Dreamland:** by John Fisher. pp. 287-288, **Sex and a New Hard Sell:** by Anne Steacy. Reprinted by permission of *Maclean's* Magazine. p. 288. **A Success Story:** excerpt from "Strategies for Social Change: Mediawatch (and other) Complaint Actions" by Tova Wagman, as printed in *Canadian Woman Studies*, Spring 1987. Used by permission of the author. pp. 291-294, **Battle of the Booze Ads** by Elaine Carey. Reprinted with permission, The Toronto Star Syndicate. pp. 296-298, **Cloning the Consumer Culture: How International Marketing Sells the Western Lifestyle:** by Noreene Janus. Excerpts from "Advertising and Global Culture" by Noreene Janus. Reprinted with permission of *Cultural Survival Quarterly*, Vol. 7, No. 2, p. 303. **Top Canadian Advertisers** (chart): Reprinted courtesy of Media Measurement Services, Inc. Toronto. p. 302, **Where Money Goes** (chart): Reprinted courtesy of Maclean Hunter Research Bureau taken from *Advertising Revenues in Canada*.

Chapter 7
pp. 309-310, **The Enemy Within:** by Robert S. Moyer. Reprinted with permission from *Psychology Today* Magazine. Copyright © 1985 (APA). pp. 314-319, **The Shortcake Strategy:** by Tom Englehardt. Copyright © 1986 by Tom Englehardt. Reprinted from *Watching Television*, edited by Todd Gitlin. By permission of Pantheon Books, a Division of Random House, Inc. pp. 324-326, **Do You Know What Your Children Are Watching?:** by John Hofsess. Reprinted by permission of the author. John Hofsess is the author of *Inner Views: Ten Canadian Filmmakers*. pp. 329-330, **Killing Them Loudly: TV Sports Teaches Violent Lessons:** by Robert E. Gould, M.D.. *Media and Values*, Summer 1986. *Media and Values*, a quarterly resource for media awareness education. Centre for Media and Values, 1962 South Shenandoah, Los Angeles, CA 90034. In Canada: 85 St. Clair Avenue E. Toronto, Ontario, M4T 1M8. pp. 332-334, **From Professional to Youth Hockey Violence: the Role of the Mass Media:** by Michael D. Smith. Reprinted by permission Michael D. Smith, Department of Sociology, York University. p. 336-338, **Hype is the Key to Wrestling Mania:** by Rocco Rossi. Reprinted by permission of the

author. pp. 341-342, **Sex and Violence:** by Max Allen. Excerpts from *Sex and Violence* by Max Allen. Copyright 1985, Canadian Broadcasting Corporation. p. 345, **TV Isn't Violent Enough:** by Mike Oppenheim, M.D. Reprinted by permission of the author.

Chapter 8
p. 355, **The Importance of the Archetype:** Excerpts from an interview with Helen Porter. Reprinted by permission Maclean Hunter Cable TV and Helen Porter. pp. 356-359, **Images of Women:** excerpt from CRTC report on *Sex Role Stereotyping in the Broadcast Media, A Report on Industry Self-Regulation.* Courtesy of CRTC. pp. 360-361, **Male-Watching:** by Penney Kome. From an article entitled "Woman's Place" by Penney Kome. Reprinted from *Homemaker's* Magazine Jan/Feb 1985. pp. 363-365, **TV Portrayals Praised For Realism:** Courtesy The Associated Press. pp. 367-370, **I Want To Be a Barbie Doll When I Grow Up: The Cultural Significance of the Barbie Doll:** by Marilyn Ferris Motz and p. 372, **One Size Does Not Fit All: Being Beautiful, Thin and Female in America:** by Jane Caputi. Both reprinted from *The Popular Culture Reader*, by permission of the Bowling Green University Popular Press. p. 373, **The Mask of Beauty:** by Una Stannard. Quotation from *Women in Sexist Society: Studies in Power and Powerlessness.* Edited by Vivian Gornick and B. Moran. Copyright © 1971 by Basic books, Inc. pp. 374-375, **Madonna Rocks the Land:** excerpts from "Madonna Rocks the Land". Copyright 1985 Time Inc. All rights reserved. Reprinted by permission from TIME.

PHOTOGRAPHS
Chapter 1
25, courtesy of BrainReserve; 27, 28, courtesy of Coleco Industries Inc.; 43, 44, 44-45, 45, courtesy of Triple Five Corporation Ltd./West Edmonton Mall; 48, 49, Canapress Photo Service
Chapter 2
74, top left, Museum of Modern Art/Film Stills Archive; 74, top centre, top right, bottom right, CBC Enterprises; 74, bottom left, courtesy of Merv Griffin Enterprises; 75, CBC Enterprises; 76, Museum of Modern Art/Film Stills Archive; 78, Canapress Photo Service; 80, Museum of Modern Art/Film Stills Archive; 83, Gregory Heisler/The Image Bank Canada; 107, courtesy of The National Broadcasting Company, Inc.; 114, CBC Enterprises
Chapter 3
123-163, right pages, bottom right, Edward Muybridge photos, Museum of Modern Art/Film Stills Archive; 124, Museum of Modern Art/Film Stills Archive; 126, top, Canapress Photo Service; 126, centre, Museum of Modern Art/Film Stills Archive; 126, bottom left, H. Armstrong Roberts/Miller Comstock Inc., 126-127, 127, Museum of Modern Art/Film Stills Archive; 130, 132-133, Museum of Modern Art/Film Stills Archive; 141, Canapress Photo Service; 142, 144-145, Copyright © 1982 Universal City Studios, Inc. All rights reserved. Courtesy of Amblin Entertainment; 148, photo and logo courtesy of the National Film Board of Canada; 150, top left, centre left, National Archives of Canada, Moving Image and Sound Archives, courtesy of Evdon Films Ltd.; 150-151, courtesy of Vos Productions Inc.; 150, bottom right, National Archives of Canada, Moving Image and Sound Archives, courtesy of International Cinemedia Center; 151, centre, courtesy of Mercury Pictures Inc., a Mercury Pictures/

Peter O'Brian Production; 150, bottom left, 151, bottom left, courtesy of Big Island Motion Pictures Inc., a Peter O'Brian/Independent Pictures Production; 153, 154, courtesy of Okanagan Motion Pictures Inc., a Peter O'Brian/Independent Pictures Production, in association with Borderline Productions Inc.; 155, Spectrafilm Inc., courtesy of Okanagan Motion Pictures Inc., 158, 158-159, 159, Museum of Modern Art/Film Stills Archive
Chapter 4
185, Canapress Photo Service; 187, Palmer/Kane Inc/Masterfile; 189, Canapress Photo Service; 190, courtesy of MCA Records (Canada) and Finkelstein Management Co.; 196, courtesy of Le Studio Andre Perry Inc.; 199, courtesy of *Rock Express*/Rock Express Communications Inc. and *Canadian Musician*/Norris Publications; 200, courtesy of MCA Records (Canada) and Bruce Allen Talent; 201, courtesy of Martha Troup Agency; 202, Canapress Photo Service
Chapter 5
228, 228-229, 231, Canapress Photo Service; 235, Canapress Photo Service; 245, 246, 247, 248, 249, 250, 251, Nigel Dickson; 253, Canapress Photo Service; 256-257, used by permission of Lester & Orpen Dennys Ltd.
Chapter 6
267, 268, 269, 270, 271, *Ogilvy on Advertising*; 274-275, courtesy of Young & Rubicam Ltd. and FritoLay; 276, courtesy of Young & Rubicam and Ford Motor Co.; 292, courtesy of the Ontario Ministry of Transportation and Communications, Public Safety Information Branch; 298, *Ogilvy on Advertising*; 300, top, and right, courtesy of the Canadian Egg Marketing Agency; left, courtesy of Young & Rubicam and Canada Dry; centre left and bottom, courtesy of Young & Rubicam and the Ford Motor Co.; centre, top, courtesy of Young & Rubicam and The Art Gallery of Ontario; centre, bottom, courtesy of Young & Rubicam and General Foods
Chapter 7
318, The Toronto Star; 321, Canapress Photo Service; 324-325, Bob Leafe/Star File Photo Agency Inc.; 330, 333, 334, 336-337, 344, Canapress Photo Service
Chapter 8
358, Canapress Photo Service; 360, Museum of Modern Art/Film Stills Archive; 363, Danny Chin/Star File Photo Agency Inc.; 366, Chuck Pulin/Star File Photo Agency Inc.; 375, Bob Gruen/Star File Photo Agency Inc.

Care has been taken to trace the ownership of copyright material used in this text. The publishers will welcome any information enabling them to rectify any references or credit in subsequent editions.

ILLUSTRATIONS
Michael Stokely: 8-9, 16-17, 58-59, 120-121, 164-165, 206-207, 220-221, 264-265, 304-305, 348-349, *Nadia Eve Maryniak:* 19, 374, *Tracy Johnson:* 22, *Bob Hambly:* 24, *Craig Turlson:* 30-31, 173, *John Dawson:* 34, *Jill Chen:* 38-39, *Arnold Winterhoff:* 43, 44-45, *Ian Begg:* 50, 315, *Scott Cameron:* 71, *Thom Sevalrud:* 77, 85, 354, *Nick Vitacco:* 94, 168-169, *Frank Viva:* 100, 286-287, *Blair Clark:* 104-105, 290-291, *Emmanuel Lopez:* 109, 110-111, 238, 280-281, *Martin Gould:* 135, *Chris McElcheran:* 138, *John Grafe:* 175, *John Molnar:* 219, *Janice Carbert:* 262, *Mike Custode:* 282, *Dave Groff:* 296-297, *Brian Hladin:* 308-309, 360-361, *Lori Langille:* 341, *Rick Frieze:* 346, *Joe Biafore:* 368-369